THE
SECRET
OF THE
BIBLE

E. JAMES DICKEY

ISBN: 978-1-4497-4617-9 (sc)
ISBN: 978-1-4497-4618-6 (e)
ISBN: 978-1-4497-4619-3 (hc)

Library of Congress Control Number: 2012906231

WestBow Press books may be ordered through booksellers or by contacting:

WestBow Press
A Division of Thomas Nelson
1663 Liberty Drive
Bloomington, IN 47403
www.westbowpress.com
1-(866) 928-1240

Because of the dynamic nature of the Internet, any web addresses or links contained in this book may have changed since publication and may no longer be valid. The views expressed in this work are solely those of the author and do not necessarily reflect the views of the publisher, and the publisher hereby disclaims any responsibility for them.

Any people depicted in stock imagery provided by Thinkstock are models, and such images are being used for illustrative purposes only. Certain stock imagery © Thinkstock.

Scripture quotations are from the New Revised Standard Version Bible, copyright 1989, Division of Christian Education of the National Council of the Churches of Christ in the United States of America. Used by permission. All rights reserved.

Printed in the United States of America

WestBow Press rev. date: 4/10/2012

WESTBOW
PRESS
A DIVISION OF THOMAS NELSON

Dedicated
To those who have loved the Bible
And the one, true God
Espoused therein

to Jim and Phyllis,   12/4/16
I deep appreciation for your
devotion to the Christian faith
through the years and especially
with the scripture. Hope this
is really meaningful to you.
Merry Christmas!
                    Jim

Appreciation is extended to Dr. Harrell F. Beck, Dr. Edwin Prince Booth, Dr. James L. Burke, Betsy Burke, Missy Cotrell, Sally Reiff Dickey, Dr. Donald Eyssen, Dr. Samuel Pratt, Janet Seese, Mr. Joe Simon, Springfield Literary Clubs and the Tuesday Bible Study group in southwest Florida for their formidable teaching, devoted assistance and support in making this book possible.

TABLE OF CONTENTS

Foreword   6

Chapter 1 – The Mysterious Nature of the Bible   9

Chapter 2 – The First Human Beings   13

Chapter 3 – The Surviving Family after the Flood   17

Chapter 4 – The Family of the Patriarchs   21

Chapter 5 – People of the Exodus   63

Chapter 6 – Judges and Kings in Israel   81

Chapter 7 – Prophets of Israel and Judah   119

Chapter 8 – Jesus of Nazareth   189

Chapter 9 – Disciples and Family of Jesus   213

Chapter 10 – The Apostles   259

Chapter 11 – Early Christian People   295

Chapter 12 – Epilogue   313

FOREWORD

My love for the Bible began at a very early age. Well before pre-school days, I remember sitting in Sunday school with other children of my age each week and singing: "Jesus loves me! This I know, for the Bible tells me so!" That message resounded true and deep within me.

Upon departing from those wonderful Sunday school classes during primary years as I was learning to read, we were given a leaflet describing the Biblical lesson of the day complete with drawings of the Biblical persons involved, which I greatly cherished.

When my grandmother died, my mother gave me the first copy of scripture in honor of her own mother, who was a Sunday school teacher in Dresden, Ohio, and according to my father was the best teacher he ever had. What was handed to me at that time was a pocket-sized "King James Version" of the New Testament with the Psalms added, which I loved.

Years later, I learned from the writings of Dietrich Bonhoeffer that the Psalms became Jesus' prayer book. That made a combination of the New Testament with Psalms, to which I was riveted as a child, even more meaningful.

Upon my high school graduation, my brother and sister presented to me a recently published copy of the "Revised Standard Version" of the whole Bible, which I deeply appreciated over many decades, until the "New Revised Standard Version" became a reality, which I have used to the present day.

In a required Introductory Course to the Bible at Ohio Wesleyan University during the 1950s, I encountered a critical approach to the Bible for the first time. I struggled immensely with that course, because the material was foreign to me. I had extreme difficultly discerning the manner of the teacher.

One thing would be expressed in class, and then something totally different would be on the test. Then I learned that the fashionable neo-orthodox approach to the scriptures of that time undergirded the whole course, a stance which I did not appreciate in the least.

As a result, the grade from my first test was near zero, but I did not give up. I struggled back until I finally reached a higher level in the course than ever expected. An interesting sequel to that story surprisingly evolved afterward. Not only I was commended for my effort among other persons, but more importantly, that professor ended up turning somewhat away from the Christian faith to embrace eastern religions, such as Buddhism, Hinduism and Taoism.

My second encounter with the scriptures on the collegiate level was more palatable. It involved the well-known, controversial Dr. Goldie McCue. Even though she stripped away people's preconceived notions about the Bible, which caused harm to many an uncritical mind, she clearly was understandable, and I fared much better under her tutelage.

Biblical scholarship in seminary was another matter entirely. It was awesome to say the least, especially under the leadership of Old Testament Professor, Dr. Harrell Beck. He brought the scriptures alive from a historical perspective. Beginning each session with devotions, he opened eyes daily to an encounter with the true, ever-living God from the Patriarchs though the Judges, Kings, Psalms and Prophets. It was joy beyond compare to be in his presence, which was consummated by a fabulous trip to the Holy Land with nineteen seminary students and their spouses upon graduation from seminary in 1960, and just prior to heading into forty years of appointive ministry with the church.

During the forty years of active Ordained Ministry, I attended Biblical Seminars, studied the scriptures incessantly, preached from Biblical texts without end and attempted to apply the text to people's needs and life in general. Even in retirement, I continue in that same vein.

The most rewarding aspect of this endeavor surprisingly transpired in southwest Florida beginning in the year of 2002 AD. During the spring of that year, Jerry and Mary Hooper friends of ours for well over forty years, asked me to lead a Bible Study during the Lenten Season. I said that I had no materials on hand to accomplish anything of this nature, but perhaps in the fall, it might be possible, if they so desired at that time.

Upon returning to Florida in the autumn of that year, the Hoopers did call again, and I was prepared. Beginning with the four of us, we started a Bible Study with the Psalms, which as stated already, I had appreciated since childhood. Soon, others joined in that weekly event during the winter months until as many as thirty persons gathered each week in subsequent winter months to study other portions of the Bible. It grew to become a most meaningful time for this ecumenical gathering of an outstanding group of persons.

During those same early days in retirement at the beginning of the twenty-first century, my own focus was increasingly directed toward the total message of the Bible. When I suggested the title of this book to a former Associate Minister in the church, it came as a complete shock to that person, who stated in return: "You mean, Jim, that you are going to take on the whole Bible in its entirety?"

My response to the utter amazement of that marvelous person was: "That is my hope." The following pages are the result of this intent.

CHAPTER 1

THE MYSTERIOUS NATURE OF THE BIBLE

What is the mystery of the Bible — if there is such a thing?

Of course, some think that there is no mystery to it whatsoever. In the common vernacular, the Bible is cut and dried.

Others insist that there is nothing valid about the Bible. It's just full of conjecture and distorted opinions. Apparent contradictions, as well as the report of all kinds of unnatural phenomena, further fuel such negativity.

However, most people are convinced that there is a basic, intrinsic value in the whole Bible but are not quite sure of how to go about finding it because the task is so enormous. Thus, the mystery!

If there is a strong message underlying this huge volume of words accumulated over many centuries, what is the key to unlocking this magnificent treasure? Obviously, it is found in the methodology — the first of which has been called, for want of a better word, doctrine!

Here it has been asserted that the way to really understand the content of the entire Biblical record is found through some sort of belief system. This procedure can range from simple, strong statements as: "The Bible says" to embracing prophetic utterances and high theological expressions.

There is no doubt that doctrinal content is found throughout the Bible, which can be dissected, debated and adhered. Some of the finest and most holy expressions of God are found in scripture, but they do not encompass every thought, word and action upon these written scrolls and printed pages. Thus, as important as it is, doctrine cannot embrace the totality or unlock the mystery therein.

9

Then the whole Bible can be seen from a sacramental point of view. All of Holy Writ is to be viewed with dignity and reverence as one of the most sacred things ever to have been made available to human beings in this life.

There is much to be said about this approach to the Bible. Without a sacramental view of the scriptures, the Bible simply would not have endured as long as it has. Devoted scribes, monks and ordinary spiritually minded persons carefully and methodically preserved these ancient manuscripts and reverently passed them along from generation to generation. Therefore, very few other matters of faith can be held in such high regard as the scriptures.

Nevertheless, the Bible in its totality does not fit into the category of being wholly and only sacred. The reader cannot proceed into its pages very far before all kinds of evil thoughts and deeds spring forth from the sentences contained therein. In some instances, the attempt even is made to justify what clearly is harmful, wicked and wrong in the name and for the sake of the one, true God. Thus, the sacramental view of the scriptures cannot be sustained throughout the entire Bible.

Another attempt to uncover the true meaning of the Bible has been located in the ancient manuscripts themselves and the culture surrounding these ancient gems. Recent archeology, the discovery of previously unknown manuscripts, marked stones and primitive works of art, as well as exceptional scholastic work with all kinds of artifacts have unleashed tremendous knowledge about the scriptures.

Also, the content of the Bible has been verified or disputed and illuminated in ways not accomplished until now. Fascination, joy, sincere questions and factual answers have resulted from these findings and painstaking ways, but again this scientific procedure falls far short of encompassing the whole content of the Bible.

Closely related to these findings in ancient cultures but separate from it is the historical approach to the Bible. In fact, according to some scholars such as Mircea Eliade in his book, *The Myth of the Eternal Return*,[1] history was invented, for want of a better word, by the literary Prophets of ancient Israel whose writings are recorded in the Holy Bible.

Prior to that time and for many years thereafter, human existence on earth was viewed in cyclical fashion as repeated over and over again in the revolving change of seasons. All gods were seen in terms of animals, inanimate objects and super conceived human beings.

In radical contrast, the literary prophets looked upon human existence as a straight line of unique events with a beginning and an end. Furthermore, the one true God, author and sustainer of the whole universe, was asserted as over, above and underneath all things.

This overall viewpoint is evidenced throughout the Bible, but it is far from the meaning of the whole script. Rather, the true significance of the Bible is contained in a very specific kind of history known as biography.

Therefore, the true key to unlocking the secret of the Bible is found in biography. No other spiritual or religious documents in the world have this element. Instead, dictums, commandments, sayings, maxims and axioms dominate such writings. Valid as they are, the truly human element is missing.

Moreover, the relationship with the one, true God and one another is dictated by those words — be they inspired, revealed or fashioned. So, any relationship tends to become subservient to the statements themselves. Thus, freedom is thwarted and throttled at its very roots.

Granted, biography often is somewhat sketchy throughout the scriptures, but enough elements are there to portray a real picture of the people involved. To look at the Bible from the primary relationship with the one, true God and live human beings is the key to the scriptures and when sincere — will produce fruits beyond compare.

It is to this end that we now deal with the pages of this Holy Writ titled the Bible — from the beginning to the very last person.

———————

1. Mircea Eliade, *The Myth of the Eternal Return* (Princeton, New Jersey: Princeton University Press, 1965).

CHAPTER 2

THE FIRST HUMAN BEINGS

Adam and Eve were the first human beings — according to the Bible. In fact, the name Adam means first man.

Moreover, at the time that this portion of scripture was scrolled, the words Adam and Eve were plural in nature to let people know that all of them were brothers and sisters who were descended from the same set of divinely created parents. By the first century AD, however, it was acknowledged that Adam and Eve were created as a single male and a single female.[1]

Who were these first human beings? The answer is: They were the crown of all creation. According to every available source, they were the peak of all that lived throughout the earth (Genesis 1:1-2:4a, 2:4b-22; Psalm 8). Everything else was subject to them, and human capability made that possible.

Technically speaking, this ability is centered in the human mind, which is far superior to all else in creation and produces what no other creature or object can accomplish including the establishment of priority in the act of thinking and reasoning. Every other creature lives by instinct, and all other objects exist by energy that is either hidden from view or overt in its expression.

Furthermore, there is one more ingredient, which Adam and Eve possessed according to the Bible that was even more important to existence — their relationship with the one, true God who is the creator, sustainer and ever present reality. This differential, be it a sudden burst in creation, a gradual process, or both is the key factor here. A relationship with God, then, is the overall distinguishing mark among human beings — according to the Bible.

13

As a result, those first human beings who were made in the image of God were like a newborn child in all innocence before God. They lived in a lush paradise on earth, a Garden of Eden in harmony with God and one another, but that did not last long.

Living in harmony with God and one another quickly went awry and deteriorated — according to the Bible. Those first human beings, Adam and Eve, soon thought of themselves as God. They chose to turn their backs on the one, true God and assert themselves as the king and queen of the whole universe. It was a stolen identity, which led to the demise and downfall of themselves and everyone to follow them.

This deteriorating process of falling into sin, where the letter "I" is at the center of human existence, began with giving into temptation. That resulted in the knowledge of good and evil, which was unknown throughout the animal kingdom at that time as well as now. This knowledge of good and evil was meant for the one and only purpose of acting as if we were THE GOD of the whole universe. By pride, arrogance and conceit, human beings rebelled from the one, true God and subtly or overtly elevated self in perverted fashion as the only judge and jury throughout existence.

From this knowledge of good and evil arose a sense of shame and guilt with the intense desire to hide. Of course that was and still is impossible with an all-seeing, all-knowing God. When confronted with what had been done, those first true human beings, Adam and Eve, began to make excuses and blame one another.

In the process, more than innocence was lost. Paradise and perfect fulfillment in this life were removed forever. Separation from God, separation from one another and separation from the free and perfect enjoyment of life prevailed.

One tragic act led to another — which included murder, lying, cheating, torture, stealing, idolatry and so forth —

14

until the whole earth seemed to be filled with wrongdoing and apparently has not subsided since that time. Suffering, misery and futility were felt everywhere and still hangs like a pall over life upon the face of the earth.

Adam and Eve's degradation followed immediately afterward among their children and continued with their descendants listed in chapter 5 of the Book of Genesis in the Bible. A biography of the sons of Adam and Eve is recorded in chapter 4 of the Bible.

The first two brothers mentioned were Cain and Abel. The older one named Cain was an agriculturalist, who later turned nomad and then became a city-dweller. The second one, Abel, was a sheep-herder whose life and livelihood was rated by people of that time as superior to the settled agricultural community.

According to verses 2-7 in chapter 4 with the Book of Genesis, both boys sought divine favor by means of sacrifice, but only Abel received a favorable omen from God. At that, Cain grew sullen and angry before God, who apparently admonished Cain to do better the next time by mastering the sin when it came knocking at the door of his heart.

However, Cain did not heed the warning for whatever reason and murdered his brother, Abel. As a result, Cain was driven from the soil, but he was protected from being further harmed himself by God's supposed decree that anyone who killed Cain would be punished seven times more than Cain was.

Afterward, another son named Seth was born to Adam and Eve, who was meant to replace Abel.

Thus, two distinct groups are said to be arising on the face of the earth at this point: 1) The ones who show indifference to sinfulness and evil, and 2) Those who call upon the name of God. They are the descendants of Seth who took the place of Abel as leader.

Thus, the underlying issue of the Bible from the outset features sin as turning away from God. Sin before the very existence of God from the time of Adam and Eve is the chief characteristic of human beings. To deny this fact is folly and adds to a nightmare everywhere. Recognition of this basic premise is the only realistic appraisal of human beings and alone holds the potential of pointing toward a new day.

---

1. Philip Culbertson, "The Pharisaic Jesus and His Gospel Parables" in *Christian Century* magazine, January 23, 1985 (Chicago: The Christian Century Foundation, 1985), p. 75.

CHAPTER 3

THE SURVIVING FAMILY
AFTER THE FLOOD

Noah and his family are featured persons during the time of the Great Flood. According to the Bible, they were the only people who survived this mega disaster. Furthermore, there truly was a flood that covered the civilized landscape around 5,000 BC, which is recorded in other documents as well.

According to chapter 6 in the Book of Genesis of the Bible, there was a rebellion against God among the people that brought a return to chaos. This sin is said to have grieved God's heart. The meaning here is not that God regretted creating humanity, but that God was expressing sorrow for what they had done to themselves, as a parent might express sorrow over a rebellious child. Thus, God decided to begin again with human beings by not obliterating the past, but by God's grace to produce a new beginning for humankind.

In the midst of the human degradation at that time, Noah accordingly pleased God. In fact, Noah was reported as "blameless in his generation" (Genesis 6:9-10). It did not mean that Noah never sinned. Rather, the suggestion here was that he wholeheartedly loved God and walked with God at each step along the way.

As a result, God established a new covenant with Noah by which Noah would become the new father of humanity. In the process, Noah was instructed to build an ark on dry ground. As recorded, this ark was to be a length of one and half football fields in today's terms and as high as a four-story building.

The ark was exactly six times longer than it was wide in the same ratio used by modern shipbuilders today. Supposedly, pairs of every animal joined Noah in the ark along with his family. An estimate of 4,500 animals could have fit into the ark, but of the some 30 million animals on earth, only about 260 animals are listed in the Bible.

The flood, which either covered the earth or destroyed the inhabitants, reportedly was followed by the promise from God that destruction never again would occur to such an extent. An apparent sign to prove the validity of this promise became known as a "rainbow" that followed the flood.

From the scriptural point of view, this sign of the rainbow is evidence of God's mercy toward creation on earth and that God has laid aside the "bow" of war. Furthermore, this covenant or promise of God involves three parts: 1) Never again will a flood cause total destruction on the face of the earth; 2) As long as the earth remains, the seasons always will come as expected; 3) The rainbow will be visible when it rains as a sign to everyone that God's promises will be kept.

Upon arriving on dry ground after the waters of the flood subsided, Noah becomes the first tiller of the soil and the first one to plant a vineyard, of which the consequences of the latter did not fare well at all. With the three unmarried sons, who apparently lived with Noah, the grapes of the vine were harvested and pressed into new wine. Then, Noah, the great hero of the Hebrews, got drunk, which became a very poor example of godliness before his own sons.

According to some analysts, the inclusion of this event in the Bible is meant to show that even godly people can go astray, and their bad influence does affect their families negatively as well. Therefore, it is true that the possibility of evil did exist in the heart of Noah as well as with the family thereafter.

In chapter 9, Noah's curse was directed toward the Canaanite nation, which accordingly would become wicked. In no way was this curse meant to support racial prejudice or even slavery, as it sometimes wrongfully was used later. Nevertheless, this curse seemingly did become fulfilled when the Israelites entered the Promised Land and drove out the Canaanites, as is recorded in the Book of Joshua of the Bible.

In chapter 10 of the Book of Genesis, a genealogy of the sons of Noah, namely: Shem, Ham and Japheth, is listed. There is an attempt here to classify the peoples of the earth into three groups. This listing is put together territorially and politically, not racially or linguistically.

Not always is it certain whether these names refer to land or people, but the geography definitely is that of the seventh century BC in the Near East. Japheth represents the peoples of the west and north. Shem includes people of the east, and Ham those of the south. This also signifies that all peoples in the Middle East are related to one another.

Finally, the genealogical table that is placed at this point in the Book of Genesis shows the political background from whom the nation of Israel, who is the people of the one, true God, is to emerge.

CHAPTER 4

THE FAMILY
OF THE PATRIARCHS

The Patriarchs and their families span the years of approximately 2000 BC to 1600 BC from the time of Abraham through the life of Joseph. According to the Biblical record, most of this period is characterized by sin-filled relationships among human beings in the presence of the one, true God.

Nevertheless, brilliant shafts of light among those same people before God do pierce through the darkness to enlighten human beings at critical points along the way and illumine countless lives even to this very day. All is uncovered in the details of the script now before us, in which the genealogical field of vision in Genesis 11:10-31 abruptly narrows from "the face of all the earth" to "Shem's descendants" concentrated here on Abraham, or "Abram," as he is called at this point.

Abraham, Sarah, Hagar and Keturah

The word "Abram" or "Abiram" means "the father is exalted." The change in name from "Abram" to "Abraham" or "Abhamon" occurred after God's covenant with him. It suggests that the covenant extends to the "nations" of Palestine and is not meant for Israel alone. Likewise, the name "Sarai," meaning "princess," is changed during God's covenant with Abraham to "Sarah," which means that she, who is barren at an advanced age, bears a son according to God's promise.

According to the Biblical record (Genesis 11:31-32), Abraham originally came from "Ur of the Chaldeans" and settled for a time in Haran on the way to Canaan. Archeology has revealed that "Ur" was a center of probably the first great civilization on earth, the Sumerian culture. In Abraham's time, Ur yet was a city of wealth and culture. This city carried on extensive trade with its neighbors and had a vast library. Thus, growing up in Ur probably meant that Abraham was educated.

In verses 1-3 in chapter 12 of the Book of Genesis — powerful, unique words are recorded, which were unheard prior to Abraham. At the call of the one, true God, who is the Creator of the whole universe and Lord of all history, Abraham launched out in faith toward places unknown, which was for the one and only purpose of establishing a nation by the promise of God.

Not only did Abraham not know where this calling would take him, but also he was without any children by his wife, Sarah, as his successor. Therefore, he could only continue in the faith that this inner call of God was true, and that God's promise to him would be just as it was communicated to him.

As a result, and contrary to every other person and people of that era, Abraham never went back or questioned his forward movement in time. Thus, Abraham became the father of faith throughout history. In fact, this is why he is called Father Abraham throughout the Bible and forcefully is asserted in the New Testament (Luke 16:22-31; John 8:39-43; Galatians 3:29; Hebrews 11:8-10).

Therefore, Abraham, who is the founder of faith in the one, true God, is the bedrock upon which all else stands for human beings and the primary force that moves people forward in scripture and throughout this life.

Between 2,000 and 1,900 BC, Abram migrated from the reputed godless, self-centered, Babylonian city, Ur of the Chaldeans. He moved along the banks of the Euphrates River, northwest to Haran where he stayed for a period of time. Then he proceeded southwest to Shechem, Bethel and Salem known today as Jerusalem. From that point, Abram migrated into the fertile land of Canaan where a God-centered, moral nation could be established via the promise of

God. This well-traveled route was indirect, but it followed along the rivers rather than making an attempt to cross the vast desert.

Upon arriving in Canaan, Abram built an altar to the Lord. Altars were used in many religions as a place of sacrifice, but for God's people, altars symbolized communion with God and commemorated notable encounters with God. Built of rough stones and earth, these altars in honor of the one, true God often remained for years as a reminder of God's protection and promises.

Abram built altars to God for two reasons: 1) for prayer and worship, and 2) as reminders of God's promise to bless him. Abram could not survive spiritually without regularly renewing his loyalty to God, who was at the center of his life. Moreover, neither can anyone else!

When famine struck, Abram traveled through what is known today as the Gulf of Agaba and the southern tip of the Dead Sea, to Egypt where there was plenty of food and good land for his flocks. Again, Abram did not question God's leading at this point. He just went.

There, Abram supposedly encountered a struggle between the Pharaoh of Egypt and Abram's wife, Sarai. Evidently, Sarai was a very beautiful woman, and the Pharaoh wanted to have her as a part of his harem.

According to the "Hurrian" laws of that time, sistership was a transferable relationship. Thus, a woman given in marriage by her brother that had transpired in Sarai's marriage to Abram — legally became her husband's sister. As a result, prestige was assured for the wife as well as purity for her husband.

However, Abram in acting out of fear asked Sarai to tell a half-truth by saying to Pharoah that she was his sister. She was his sister, but even more so — she was his wife. Abram's intent was to deceive the Egyptians. He feared that if the Egyptians knew the whole truth, they would kill him.

Sarai would have been a desirable addition to Pharaoh's harem because of her wealth, beauty and tremendous potential for political alliance. Also, as Sarai's brother, Abram would have been given a place of honor. As her husband, however, Abram's life would be in danger, because Sarai could not enter Pharaoh's harem unless Abram was dead.

At this point, Abram lost faith in God's protection, and he told a half-truth. Furthermore, this shows how lying compounds the effects of sin. When Abram lied, Abram's problems multiplied. Because Abram was a person of faith, it did not exempt him from the ability to sin.

According to scripture, God did not appreciate Sarai being in the harem of Pharaoh — even more than Abram's telling a half-truth. So plagues afflicted the Pharaoh not as a punishment but as a warning of continuing evil upon Egypt unless Sarai was returned to her husband.

When Pharaoh heard, by whatever means, that Sarai was Abram's wife, he confronted Abram by asking: "Why didn't you tell me that Sarai was your wife?" Then, without further word, Pharaoh apparently gave his men orders to escort Abram and all with him out of Egypt.

When Abram returned to the land of Canaan between Bethel and Ai with his nephew, Lot, whose father had died, he recognized that the land would not sustain both of them and their livestock because each of them had become quite wealthy. So, Abram looked over the land and generously gave Lot the first choice, even though Abram by being older had the right to choose first.

At that, Lot chose the best territory, the plain of Jordan, which was well-watered everywhere like the land of Egypt. However, the land was near Sodom and Gomorrah and the supposed wicked people who lived there. On the other hand, Abram settled near Hebron in the land of Canaan, where the bones of Abraham and his descendents are presumed to be today.

In chapter 14 of the Book of Genesis, Abram's victory over the eastern kings and the rescue of Lot highlights the text. Wars and rivalries among kings were common during this time. A conquered city paid tribute to the victorious king.

Nothing historically is known about the person Chedorlaomer other than what is in the Bible, but apparently he was quite powerful. Five cities, including Sodom, paid tribute to Chedorlaomer for twelve years. As a result, these five cities formed an alliance and rebelled by not paying the tribute.

Cherdorlaomer reacted swiftly and conquered all five of these cities again. Upon defeating Sodom, he captured Lot, his family and his possessions. With only 318 men, Abram chased Chedorlaomer's army and attacked him at night near Damascus. According to the Bible, Abram defeated them and recovered Lot, his family and his possessions.

Analyzing the situation, Lot's greedy attitude led him into sinful surroundings. His burning desire for possessions and personal gain cost him his freedom, and as a captive, Lot faced torture, slavery or death. With Abram, these incidents portray two solid characteristics: 1) He had the courage that came from God to attack a terrible foe; 2) He was prepared by taking the time to train his men for potential conflict. When Abram learned that Lot was a prisoner, he immediately proceeded to help his nephew.

Abram and a man by the name of Melchizedek are featured in verses 18-24 in Genesis 14. The name Melchizedek meant "king of righteousness" and "king of peace," as mentioned also in Hebrews 7:2. He apparently lived in Salem, the ancient name for Jerusalem.

Interestingly, the reoccurrence of the name Melchizedek in Psalm 110 evidently was based on this passage from Genesis. It suggests that Melchizedek, as both priest and king of Jerusalem, was to be the true prototype of the ideal Davidic ruler, which also is mentioned in Hebrews 7.

Melchizedek may have played a role in the defeat of the eastern kings by being a leader of the Palestinian coalition. In any event, when Abram returned from the defeat of Chedorlaomer, he apparently was received by Melchizedek and accepted the blessing of a Canaanite priest who was acceptant of Yahweh, the God of Abram, the God of the universe, the God of the most high and now the God of Melchizedek too.

As a result, Abram gave one tenth of the booty to Melchizedek. Even in some pagan religions it was traditional to give one tenth of the booty to the gods. Abram followed this tradition. Nonetheless, Abram refused to take any booty from the king of Sodom.

Even though this huge amount of booty would have significantly increased what Abram could have given to God, he chose to reject it for much more important reasons to him. Abram did not want the ungodly king of Sodom to say, "I have made Abram rich." In Abram's eyes, accepting these gifts would have focused everyone's attention on Abram or the king of Sodom rather than on the one, true God, who alone was the giver of victory.

In chapter 15 of the Book of Genesis, deep sleep was caused to fall upon Abram, which meant in Biblical terms — a God-given trance that opens the mind to revelation and ecstasy. In this instance, God apparently revealed the plan to Abram and to Israel that the chosen people would inherit the land.

Here it is affirmed that everything accomplished by God is true to God's character: God is merciful, knows all things, acts justly and always at the perfect time, which in most every instance is different from human timing and activity.

In chapter 16 of the Book of Genesis, Sarai is despairing of not having a child and gives her personal maid, Hagar, to Abram. Her hope is that through her slave, she may become a "mother." According to both Hurrian and Babylonian law, this procedure was both legally and morally acceptable.

When Hagar becomes pregnant, however, Sarai turns against her maid. Furthermore, by Sarai's initiative, Abram gains ownership of Hagar. So, Sarai strongly complains that Abram alone is to deal with Hagar, because she is his. Justice is his total responsibility.

The unhappy and pathetic reply of Abram simply is to restore the arrogant slave, Hagar, to his wife, Sarai. Life thereby becomes so miserable for the pregnant girl Hagar that she flees to Egypt. In the process, the question of an heir for Abram fervently is reopened.

When Hagar almost reaches the Egyptian frontier, she reportedly is confronted by an angel, a messenger of Yahweh. At that moment she is told that she will bear a son to be called "Ishmael," which means "God hears," because God has paid heed to Hagar's distress.

In running away from her mistress, the messenger of Yahweh gave this strong advice: 1) Return and face Sarai, who is the cause of her problem, and 2) work on her own attitude no matter how justified she may feel and get rid of all arrogance.

This Biblical story of Hagar does emphasize Abram's apparent vain expectation of God's promise and casts light on how Israel viewed the history of neighboring kinsmen, the Ishmaelites or Arabs, who worshiped Yahweh too and were blessed by Yahweh equally as well as they were. Moreover, Moslems today, who are direct descendants of Ishmael, claim through the Prophet Mohammed that they are the true descendants of Abraham of the first and highest order.

From the point of view of the Israelites, they were acknowledging their kinship with the Ishmaelites, which is the name for all Arabs to later Jews, and whose presence in Palestine preceded their own. On the other hand, Israelites looked down upon them condescendingly as descendants of an Egyptian mother, because Ishmael married an Egyptian wife (Genesis 21:21).

In chapter 17 of the Book of Genesis, Abram receives the divine command to conduct himself in complete obedience to God's covenant, which meant: 1) Sabbath observance, 2) abstinence from eating blood, and 3) circumcision. At this point, the name "Abram" is changed to "Abraham," which means "the ancestor of nations," and Sarai's name changed to "Sarah," as already has been stated.

The sign of this covenant is to be circumcision. Circumcision is quite ancient and not just to the Jews. It is known to have been practiced at Egypt in 3000 BC, or a thousand years before the time of Abraham. It also was practiced by a number of Israelite neighbors, but not at all in Mesopotamia or among the Philistines. The statistic that Ishmael was thirteen when he was circumcised reflects the customary time for circumcision among Israel's nomadic neighbors and an age more in tune with the original significance of the rite.

Three men are reported as suddenly appearing before Abraham by the oaks of Mamre, but they are unrecognizable to him. When the promise of a son via Sarah is given, Abraham suspects who they are, but the relationship of these three men is cloudy at best. In one account, Abraham talks with Yahweh who may be the one behind the others and who go on to Sodom. A later interpretation considers Yahweh to be one of the three men.

Nevertheless, the unmistakable object of this visit is to predict the birth of a son to Sarah in nine month's time. His name is to be called "Isaac," a name associated with laughter, which both Abraham and Sarah expressed when they heard that Sarah at such an advanced age of ninety years would bear a son. This incident, however, does incorporate the remarkable affirmation of God's omnipotence in the ability to do the seemingly impossible.

28

It does appear that Sarah overheard the three men say to Abraham outside their tent that they would return in due time when Sarah gave birth to a son, and apparently Sarah did laugh heartily at such a thought in her advanced age. When Sarah was asked "why" she laughed, however, Sarah denied it because she was afraid of being discovered as one who actually did laugh.

As Abraham contemplates the sordid situation in the city of Sodom from the hills east of Hebron some forty miles away, he grows troubled over the destruction of people's lives in the sight of God. Abraham ruminates over the hard question: To what extent can God's mercy be increased in human existence?

The problem cannot be resolved. However, according to the encounter of Abraham in questioning Yahweh at this point, the response apparently was: "For the sake of a handful of righteous people, God would spare a wicked city."

Afterward, the pitiful sequel of the destruction of Sodom unfolds, and the life of the people during Abraham's time proceeds from bad to worse. Through it all Abraham's undying faith remains true even amidst massive human frailty and sinfulness. Abraham never lost faith in the one, true God — Yahweh.

In Sodom, Lot reportedly greeted two angelic men, whom he hospitably invited to stay at his house overnight. He fed them a feast in kosher style, but before they lay down to sleep, men of the city of Sodom reportedly broke into the house with abusive, sexually perverse, evil intent to molest and degrade the whole household.

At that point, angelic messengers pleaded with Lot and his family to escape from the city of Sodom to the mountains and never look back. Apparently, Lot's wife did turn back and lost her life in the process. Lot was alone in a mountain cave with his two daughters and feared that they would never marry. The daughters then supposedly made their father drunk with wine and committed incest.

The result of this sexual act with their father produced two sons named Moab and Ammon. They became the source of the Moabites and the Ammonites, according to this portion of the Bible, who obviously were not in any way liked by the Israelites. Moreover, since Lot could have sought husbands for his girls long before this time, the Biblical reference points at the moral bankruptcy of Lot.

In the next chapter of Genesis, Lot's uncle Abraham also exemplified sinful behavior when he moved south to dwell in Gerar. While there, King Abimelech was told that Sarah was Abraham's sister. Abimelech sent for and took Sarah into his household. Almost immediately he was told in a dream that Sarah was Abraham's wife, and she should be returned to Abraham, which the king did. Abraham's deception to protect himself a second time risked turning a sinful act into a pattern of lying whenever he thought that his life would be in danger.

In chapter 21 of the Book of Genesis, the motif of laughter and skepticism, which dominated the conception of Isaac, changes dramatically as Sarah finally cries out with "joy" and "surprise" at the birth of her son. Sarah soon discovers both children of Abraham playing together, and the sight of this equality in status ferociously angers the jealous Sarah.

In Sarah's eyes, Ishmael threatens her son Isaac's position of honor. Thus, Ishmael must go. Abraham is indignant over Sarah's demand, but it seems to be removed by God's apparent approval of Sarah, as well as God's promise of a future for the "son of the slave woman." In spite of this incredulity, outrage, joy and hope as human values constantly seem to be turned upside down, Abraham remained faithful and believed God in spite of everything.

Then, in verses 1-19 of chapter 22 in the Book of Genesis, the most excruciatingly brutal trial of Abraham's faith is recorded. In fact, this written discourse is acclaimed as a literary masterpiece that is unparalleled in human history. The nineteenth-century Danish philosophical/theologian Soren Kierkegaard coined the phrase "leap of faith" concerning this event where Abraham utterly and unflinchingly obeyed God's call.[1]

This trial of faith involved God's command that Abraham sacrifice "your son, Isaac, whom you love" (Genesis 22:2). This testing goes to the heart of Abraham's life. Previously, he had been asked to cut himself off from his entire past. Now Abraham is told to give up his whole future. He must give up the child of his old age on whose life the fulfillment of God's promise depends.

Why did God ask Abraham to perform human sacrifice? Heathen nations and pagan cultures always practiced it. Even Hebrew people were known to have accomplished it at points along the way, but it was contrary to the law as contained in Leviticus 20:1-5. Thus, it was condemned as a terrible sin.

The answer to this exceedingly hard question is not that God wanted Isaac to die. The one, true God clearly is not a sadist. God wanted Abraham to sacrifice Isaac purely in his "heart," in order that it would be absolutely clear that Abraham loved God more than he loved his promised and long-awaited son.

God was testing Abraham solely for the purpose of strengthening his character and deepening his commitment to God in God's "own" perfect timing. As a result of Abraham's total obedience to God in this ultimate test of faith, Abraham's hand was stopped prior to the knife striking Isaac. Abraham was provided a lamb in the thicket for sacrifice in place of his son. Furthermore, Abraham received abundant blessings afterward that never seemed to end.

First, God gave Abraham's descendants, small in might and number as these people were, the ability to conquer

31

their enemies. Second, God promised Abraham — children and grandchildren who would in turn bless the whole earth. Perhaps most importantly, people's lives would be changed forever as a result of knowing the faith of Abraham and his descendants. Furthermore, these blessings would overflow to other people everywhere and throughout all time among those who know the faith of Abraham.

Chapter 23 in the Book of Genesis has to do with Abraham's purchase of a grave for his wife, Sarah, near Hebron. Four hundred shekel was a very high asking price for the property. In fact, it was exorbitant, but the people who lived there were not in any way thrilled about foreigners such as Abraham buying up lots from their property.

Thus, a man named Ephron asked an outrageous price. The custom of the day was to ask double the fair market value of the land, fully expecting the buyer to ask half of the stated price in return, but Abraham did not bargain. He simply paid the initial price, because he did not want to take anything that he did not deserve.

Abraham's final act of faith in God's promise was in obtaining a wife for his son, Isaac. Although Abraham knew that Isaac's destiny was in the land of Canaan, the normal pattern of intermarriage with heathen neighbors was not an option to him. Isaac needed to marry the right woman from among his relatives in the land from which Abraham came. Abraham was fully convinced that God would choose Isaac's wife and that was ultimately confirmed by Abraham's steward or servant, who was sent on this journey in Abraham's behalf.

Following the death of Sarah, Abraham took another wife, Keturah, and reportedly had another half a dozen more sons, which ultimately were sent away from Isaac — eastward. Abraham gave many gifts to these offspring, but all authority went to Isaac: the apparent principle heir. At a good ripe old age, Abraham died and was buried in the cave of Machpelah in the field of Ephron with Sarah, his wife.

The successors of Abraham do not reach the high level of faith, obedience and devotion to God, which was exemplified with Abraham. A solid attempt to continue his legacy is held high throughout the years to follow. Most importantly, the one, true God continues to keep the promises made in spite of any and all attempt by later generations to abuse God's intent and fully mess up the entire situation. That is the true miracle throughout the whole Biblical narrative.

Isaac and Rebekah

When Eliezer, Abraham's steward or servant, was instructed to go to the land from which Abraham came and find a wife for Isaac, he went without hesitation. As Eliezer approached the city of Haran, he stopped at a well, the chief source of water for the entire area. At that spot, farmers and shepherds would come from nearby fields to draw water for their animals. The well was also a good place to meet new friends or chat with old ones.

Prior to arriving at this place, however, Eliezer asked God to show him a woman who would go beyond the expected pattern of behavior and display a "servant's heart." Eliezer did not ask for a woman of wealth or good looks. He knew that the most important matter was "having a right heart," and Eliezer simply asked God to help him with the task. Isn't this remarkable and utterly extraordinary that such high quality intent would be recorded for us some 4,000 years later?

The hospitality of that time required women to offer water for weary travelers at the well but not to their animals. It is at this crucial point that a woman by the name of Rebekah entered the scene. She would have visited this well twice daily to draw water for her family. Moreover, she was a person of stunning external beauty, but that was not what Eliezer sought for Isaac. He wanted inner beauty that comes from such things as joy, patience and kindness, which he miraculously would witness before his own eyes upon very short notice.

When Eliezer and his camels approached the well, Rebekah quickly and willingly drew water for Eliezer as well as for his camels. It took a lot of water to satisfy a thirsty camel. In fact, 25 gallons of water per camel were needed after a week's travel. Moreover, the pots used for carrying the water were large and heavy. Nevertheless, Rebekah went right to work with a glad and generous heart and gloriously did much more than was necessary by exemplifying a servant's heart of gold.

Witnessing such a radiant display of extraordinary helpfulness, Eliezer knew that this was the woman of his prayerful petition before God. As a result, he returned to Abraham and Isaac with a wife greater than all dreams and in keeping with the magnanimous promise of God. When Rebekah saw her husband-to-be coming toward her in the southern part of the land of Canaan, she followed the customs of the time. She dismounted her camel to show respect and then she placed a veil over her face as the bride.

Upon being married to Rebekah, Isaac loved her and was comforted by her at the death of his parents. Because Rebekah was barren, however, Isaac prayed to the Lord, and his prayer was answered. Rebekah conceived, and she held twin boys in her womb, who apparently fought from this time forth. The first boy was Esau. He grew up to be a skillful hunter, a rough and ready man of the field. The second one named Jacob, meaning one who supplants and of whom God protects, became a quiet man living in tents as a civilized herdsman.

Isaac was fond of Esau because he loved game, but Rebekah loved Jacob. The stage was set for a battle between the two boys and their parents, which made a huge difference among Isaac's legacy for generations to come — even to this very day.

According to the Bible, the essence of this struggle centered on two events. First, there was the supposed selling of the birthright from Esau to Jacob. The second, and probably most significant one, was the trickery involved in the stolen blessing during the latter years of Isaac — from the rightful heir and favored firstborn son to the reprehensible, less likely, second son.

The Book of Genesis almost seems to suggest here that the righteous Abraham never found a worthy successor; that Israel's history moved between the poles of faithful obedience to the divine summons and of the crassest self-seeking and irresponsibility. No one in this recording could escape condemnation. But in God's providence, the more reprehensible, less likely brother, Jacob, became the bearer of promise to Abraham, while the victimized, legitimate heir, Esau was passed over without recognition or recourse.

In Genesis 25:29-34, the issue surrounding the birthright is brought to the forefront. At that time, a birthright was a special honor given to the firstborn son. It involved a claim to a double share of his father's property, which is known from Assyrian law. It also involves being the leader of a family or tribe. However, the oldest son could sell his birthright or give it away if he chose, but obviously he would lose both material goods and his leadership position in so doing.

According to the Biblical record, when Esau was coming back one day from a hard day's work in the field, tired and very hungry, he confronted Jacob, who was having a bowl of what was presumed to be a prized dish of stew. Esau immediately demanded to have that food.

Jacob quickly shot back: "Not until you sell me your birthright." Esau just as quickly responded: "I am famished and feel like I am about to die. So of what use is a birthright to me?"

"Swear to me first," Jacob insisted, and Esau swore to him and sold his birthright to Jacob. At that, Jacob gave Esau bread and lentil soup, which seemed a far cry from what may have been expected. At any rate, it appears that Esau acted purely upon the impulse of satisfying his immediate desire for food. He traded away the lasting benefits of his birthright without pausing to consider the long-range consequences of what he was doing, which he later came to regret.

For the Israelites, they no doubt grew more and more delighted over the fact that their ancestor, Jacob, outwitted their Edomite ancestor, Esau, whose descendants lived in the mountain range southeast of the Dead Sea.

Pertaining to the person Isaac, traditions about him are quite scant. If there ever were more said about Isaac, it has been forever put aside in favor of Abraham. In fact, it appears that Isaac is blessed by Yahweh solely for Abraham's sake.

The only recording about Isaac himself surrounded wells that were dug in the desolate Gerar area. Water definitely was as precious as gold in that region. If a person dug a well during that era, a claim to the land had to be made. Some wells had locks to keep thieves from stealing the water. To stop or plug up someone's well became an act of war. To do such a thing was one of the most serious crimes in the area.

During the three times that Isaac and his men dug new wells, disputes over the first two that were dug reportedly arose. Isaac simply moved elsewhere each time. Finally on the third try, there was not room for everyone, and when his wells were ruined, Isaac had every reason to strike back. However, he chose the way of peace. In the end, Isaac was respected. When Isaac's enemies decided to make peace, Isaac was quick to respond, and the occasion was turned into a celebration.

As Isaac grew older and his eyesight began to fail, Rebekah learned that Isaac was preparing to bless Esau. She quickly devised a plan to trick Isaac into blessing Jacob instead. When that deceitful plan was communicated to Jacob, he hesitated at first. Sadly, Jacob was not concerned in the least about the evil intent of the idea or the wrongness of the act. His only reason for pause involved the fear of being caught in that devious process.

Jacob asked his mother to reconsider her plan, but Rebekah had become so wrapped up in her clandestine thought that she no longer could see clearly about what she was doing. Rebekah did not change her mind, and Jacob being as close to his mother as he was, acquiesced to her way of thinking.

According to Genesis 27:1-29, Esau went out into the field to bring game back for savory food, which Isaac requested of him. In turn Isaac would bless Esau with the rite and privilege to carry on the legacy of Abraham. Rebekah gathered together items that would make Jacob appear as Esau before the dimming eyes of Isaac.

For Isaac, she prepared savory food from two choice kids, which Rebekah asked Jacob to bring to her from their flock. She took the best garments of her elder son, Esau, and put them upon Jacob. Rebekah also secured skins from the two animals and put them on the smooth skin of the neck and hands of Jacob in order that he would appear like the hairy man that Esau apparently was.

Afterward, Jacob went to his father, and Isaac bought into the whole scheme "hook, line and sinker," as the saying goes, and Isaac blessed Jacob as the heir to the promise of Abraham. When Esau returned from the field and discovered what had transpired, he was furious, as can be imagined. Thereafter, Esau grew increasingly determined to stalk his brother, Jacob, and kill him.

In those days, a ceremony of blessing before the death of the father was crucial to the furtherance of the family's lineage and livelihood. Even though the firstborn son was entitled to the birthright, it was not actually his until the blessing was pronounced by the father. Before the blessing was given, the father could take the birthright away from the eldest son and give it to what appeared to be a more deserving son. However, after the blessing had been given, the birthright could no longer be taken away. That is why fathers usually waited until late in life to pronounce the blessing.

When the birthright was stolen from Esau, there literally was no other recourse. Nonetheless, Esau became so angry at Jacob that he failed in the process to see his own wrong of giving away the birthright in the first place. Reacting in jealous rage and deciding to murder Jacob became worse than being internally upset.

From the perspective of both Isaac and Rebekah, according to the Bible, they were deeply distressed about Esau's marriage to a Hittite woman. So, they sent Jacob away — not specifically to escape Esau's anger — but rather to find a suitable wife among his mother's relatives.

In an attempt to please his father after all of the damage that had been done, Esau married another woman from his father's family. The Biblical reference to Ishmael at this point may mean the tribal kinship between the Edomites and Esau's heritage and the Ishmaelites of Isaac's half-brother, Ishmael.

Upon leaving Isaac and Rebekah, Jacob came to lodge overnight at a place then called "Lutz." There a vision appeared to him in a dream — a "ladder" to heaven, which more accurately could be stated as a "stairway" or a "ramp" suggesting a Mesopotamian temple tower or "ziggurat." At the summit, which only was accessible by a ramp, their god was supposed to dwell.

This event described in Genesis 28:11-22, therefore, expresses how Jacob unintentionally uncovers the place where God's angelic messengers set out upon the earth for their divinely appointed missions. In this discovery, God seemingly stood right beside Jacob. Here, God personally renewed to Jacob — his promise to Abraham.

When Jacob awoke, he breathlessly proclaimed: "Surely the Lord is in this place. How awesome! This is none other than the house of God and the gate of heaven."

At that point in eighteenth century BC, Jacob set up a pillar, which he called "Bethel," meaning "house of God," or "house of Yahweh," which exists today among the excavated ruins.

Thus, Jacob received the blessing that he wanted from Isaac and a later blessing directly from God at the place called "Bethel," but it cost him dearly. Some of the consequences of his actions and deceit were: 1) He never saw his mother again; 2) His brother, Esau, wanted to murder him; 3) He was deceived himself by his Uncle Laban; 4) His family became torn by strife; 5) His brother, Esau, became the founder of an enemy nation, Edom; and 6) Jacob was exiled from the rest of the family for many years.

Ultimately, Isaac and Rebekah died and were buried with Abraham and Sarah.

Jacob and the Twelve Tribes of Israel

On his way to find a wife among his mother's kin, Jacob ran directly into Rachel, and it was love at first sight. Rachel was the keeper of her father Laban's sheep. Laban was Rebekah's brother. Of course, Rebekah was Jacob's mother. Upon seeing Jacob at a distance, Laban ran to greet Jacob and embraced him, but sadly it was all "downhill" after that, so to speak.

Jacob wanted to marry Rachel outright, but since Jacob had no dowry, substantial gift, or material possessions to give for his marriage, he offered to work seven years for Laban, to which Laban was non-committal. The reason that Laban became non-committal was because Laban had another custom in mind. The older daughter had to be married first, but Laban did not reveal that fact to Jacob.

At the end of seven years, Laban tricked Jacob by slipping the older daughter, Leah, into Jacob's place after the wedding feast, which Jacob did not discover until morning. When Jacob learned that Laban had tricked him, he flew into a rage. The deceiver of Esau now was deceived himself.

Therefore, the cunning Jacob is outwitted by his scheming uncle. Becoming enraged at an injustice to him, Jacob becomes blind to the injustice that he had caused himself. So, Jacob had to work another seven years for Rachel, which to his everlasting credit, he did and at last was married to Rachel.

As a result of Jacob's perseverance, his name was changed from Jacob, or one who supplants, to Israel, or "a prince who prevails with God." Jacob's character also changed. From this point onward, Jacob no longer was a deceiver but a God-honoring man.

In the meantime, conflicts emerge among other family members — especially the women in Jacob's life. Leah feels unwanted and unloved. So she has more children in the hope that Jacob will love her, which does not seem to happen.

Rachel becomes envious of her sister, because Rachel is without any children. Both women send their maid-servants to have children by Jacob. None of these women seem content or happy. In fact, all of them including Laban and his children grow jealous of one another and become a dysfunctional family of the highest order.

In spite of Rachel's preferential status before Jacob, she does not become pregnant even with the aid of "mandrakes," a Eurasian plant with a branched root looking like the human body, which was thought at the time to be a stimulant for conception.

According to Genesis 30:22-23, "God remembered Rachel," and ultimately she bore a son named Joseph. To some people, it may have been that Joseph's birth was related to the eating of mandrakes after all, while Laban thought that the divination from his idols had made him to be blessed by Jacob, which only added to a further conflict on the horizon.

After fourteen years of service for his wives, Jacob definitely was ready to return to the land of Canaan where he was born. However, Laban strongly wanted Jacob to stay. Thus, the two clever and mistrusting men strike an overall bargain.

Jacob at once is to receive all of the speckled sheep and goats as well as a small number of black lambs among the many white sheep and black goats from Laban's flocks for his wage with a further term of service. Nevertheless, Laban does not give these animals to Jacob, but he entrusts them to his own sons, whom he sends away at a distance of some three days travel time. All of the abnormally colored animals in Jacob's care alone will belong to him.

What appears as a bargain favorable to Laban is turned to Jacob's advantage by his own skillful, ingenious breeding technique. Ignorant of Jacob's strategy at Laban's distance from his son-in-law, Jacob becomes very wealthy to the envy of Laban's own sons.

In Genesis 31:4-16, Jacob mandates that his wives, Leah and Rachel, accompany him to Canaan. To avoid legal difficulties, Jacob requires their consent because they still are considered members of Laban's household. At the same time, leaving home was not difficult in the least for the women because their father, Laban, had treated them as poorly as he had dealt with Jacob.

According to the custom of the day, Leah and Rachel were to receive the benefits of the dowry that Jacob had paid for them with fourteen years of hard work. When Laban would not give them what rightfully was theirs, they knew that they never would inherit anything from their father. So they wholeheartedly approved of Jacob's plan to take the wealth that he personally had gained and leave. Even though

Laban had treated Jacob most unfairly, the Bible clearly states that Jacob's prosperity increased by the gracious and generous hand of God.

Jacob chooses the busy shearing season culminating in a feast as the opportune time for his flight, according to Genesis 3:17-20. In the process, Rachel stole her father's idols. She was afraid that Laban would either consult them and learn where she and Jacob had gone, or she just simply wanted to claim the family inheritance.

Many people kept these small wooden or metal idols in their homes. They were believed to protect the home and offer advice in time of need. Also of legal significance, these idols were passed on to an heir, who thereby could claim the greater part of the family inheritance.

When Laban learned that his idols were missing, it is understandable that he was deeply agitated. When Jacob said that the offender ought to be killed, Rachel's safety was in serious jeopardy. In fast pursuit, Laban overtakes Jacob in three days.

In the process, Rachel spares herself from being caught by rendering the idols unclean. Then, Jacob delivers the speech of a lifetime in the presence of Laban expressing everything that he had accomplished as a good, faithful and generous servant without any benefits or thanks. Jacob stated that he took losses upon himself when flocks were attacked and did not split the difference with Laban in any way whatsoever.

He continued to work hard even after several pay cuts, but his diligence ultimately paid off as his flocks began to multiply. Jacob demonstrated that making a habit of doing more than was expected of him actually produced benefits in the presence of the one, true God.

As a result of this remarkable speech, Laban was totally subdued. He unprecedentedly acquiesced before everyone, which led to a remarkable covenant between Jacob and Laban that produced an unforgettable Mizpah benediction frequently used since that time: "May the Lord watch between you and me while we are absent one from the other" (Genesis 31:49). Laban bid farewell complete with hugs and kisses among his daughters and grandchildren.

The next gigantic hurdle before Jacob was an anticipated encounter with his brother, Esau, upon approaching the land of Canaan. First, Jacob sent messengers ahead to his brother in the country of Edom. This message contained what had transpired in his life along with a present of some 550 animals.

For fear of what might happen, Jacob wrestled all night with God and supposed divinely sent human beings. Moreover, Jacob prevailed. Again, Jacob was pronounced Israel, because he had struggled with God face-to-face, and his life was preserved. In the meantime he reportedly was struck on the hip socket at the thigh muscle causing him to limp ever after that encounter (Genesis 32:24-32).

When Jacob finally was confronted by his brother, Esau's attitude was surprisingly magnanimous in contrast to his previous murderous intent. Jacob's response was totally different as well. Jacob commented that seeing the face of Esau was like seeing the face of God.

Thus at the meeting of the two brothers, only the way of reconciliation and peace prevailed thereafter. No doubt, intense prayer helped immensely in this situation. Most importantly, this event gives people hope that the later pronouncement in the New Testament: "Love your enemies; pray for those who persecute you; do good to those who hate you" (Matthew 5:44; Luke 6:27-35; Romans 12:20) will take root and become true in fact, even if those enemies be among one's own family and friends, or within oneself.

From that time forward, Esau proceeds to Edomite territory, while Jacob moves only a few miles to "Succoth," a lovely site on the eastern side of the River Jordan. Upon departure, Jacob bows low seven times, which is the sign of

43

respect for a king. Jacob evidently takes every possible avenue to prevent any residual thoughts of revenge.

The bitterness of Esau over losing his birthright and blessing of Isaac vanishes from the scene. Esau is content now with what he has, and Jacob exclaims how great it is to see his brother. Jacob in reality is pleased with Esau. Truly, each brother is able to see that their relationship is more important than their real estate, which as stated at the outset is what the Bible is all about. So, Jacob and Esau went forth in peace.

Most importantly in the relationship exhibited among human beings, the one, true God of the universe and Lord of history always is faithful, just and kind toward God's people. God is doing what is promised, while human beings continue to choose unwisely. Again, the Bible is the only known religious writing in the world to have all of this material in it!

Chapter 34 in the Book of Genesis speaks about the molestation of Jacob's only daughter, Dinah, by his wife named Leah. Apparently, Shechem rapes Dinah. He offers to marry her, but Dinah's brothers, Simeon and Levi, take vengeance by murdering Shechem and his family. Afterward, all of the sons of Jacob employ circumcision to disable the Shechemites so that they can sack the entire city.

What strongly is noted here is emphasis upon the value of female chastity, as well as the danger of adopting Canaanitic ways of life, which would lead to compromising Israel's principles. However, in taking revenge against Shechem, Simeon and Levi lied, stole and murdered. Their desire for justice may have been understandable, but their ways of achieving it were wrong. As a result of this great sin, their father Jacob ended up cursing both of them with his dying breath. Generations later, their descendants lost the part of the Promised Land allotted to them.

Why did Simeon and Levi take such harsh action in the first place? It is true that the family of Jacob saw themselves as set apart from others. God had set them apart from their heathen neighbors, but the sin-filled mistake of the brothers was that they thought being set apart automatically made them better than others. It was this arrogant attitude that led them to a terrible slaughter of innocent people. Even today this type of thinking produces similar problems among people.

In chapter 35 with the Book of Genesis, Jacob returns to Bethel to fulfill his vow of renouncing everything unholy to him and to dispose of all idols. Idols at that time were more like good luck charms than actual gods. Even though Israelites worshiped Yahweh, some of them had idols in their homes. Jacob believed that idols should have no place in his household. He wanted nothing to divert spiritual focus from Yahweh, or the one, true God of all creation.

Why did the people give even their earrings to Jacob? At that time, people often wore earrings to ward off evil. Jacob wanted his family to cleanse themselves of all pagan and heathen influences that included any reminders of foreign gods. Even though Jacob's whole life was laden with difficulties and trials, his new name, Israel, meant to stay close to God and persevere. He would prove it again by cleansing and purifying himself and his people in every way possible.

In verses 16-20, Rachel died in childbirth, fulfilling her hope for another son, Benjamin. He was the only son of Jacob who was born in the land of Canaan. According to verse 22, Reuben then committed the sin of having sex with his father's concubine. Not only did Reuben usurp his father's authority at this point, but he also gave further reason to disqualify himself as the firstborn son of Jacob and therefore as leader of Israel. Thus, Reuben's sin ultimately is very costly.

Reuben may have thought he got away with his sin at that moment. No more is mentioned of it until Jacob on his deathbed assembled his family for the final blessing. Suddenly he took away the double portion of the family inheritance from Reuben as well as the place of leadership among his people.

Instead, Jacob gave the blessing to Judah, which became the origin of the name "Jew." Among Judah's descendants are King David and Jesus, who was claimed by his followers as being the Messiah. The reason that Reuben lost out in Jacob's eyes clearly is stated: "You went up onto your father's bed; then you defiled it."

Joseph and His Family

Joseph, the older of two sons born to Rachel and Jacob, was given a coat similar to that of royalty. It was a symbol of Jacob's favoritism toward Joseph. This as well as two other reasons angered his other ten brothers fathered by Jacob. First in the common vernacular, Joseph apparently was a "tattle tale." In other words, Joseph's brothers discovered that he was conveying "an ill report" of them to his father (Genesis 37:2). In addition, Joseph let it be known publicly that he was having dreams about his preeminence among his siblings (Genesis 37:5-11). All three of these reasons produced an intense dislike of Joseph among his brothers.

As far as the regal robe was concerned, everyone in that era around 1700 BC had a robe or cloak similar to what people in the mid-East wear today. Most cloaks were knee length, short-sleeved and plain. Joseph's cloak was long-sleeved, ankle length and colorful. The gift of this special cloak from Jacob to Joseph not only was a symbol of his privileged status, but most likely indicated that he stood above manual labor, because laborers wore the shorter garments to free their arms and legs.

In that time, Joseph's dreams were not seen as divine revelations but as God's providence made known in human terms, which must be interpreted and could be misunderstood. How Joseph interpreted the dreams that were providentially given to him as the favored one is what infuriated

46

his brothers. That they would be ruled by little brother coupled with Joseph's immature attitude and boastful manner is what fueled the angry brothers into an ugly rage that blinded them completely to what is right.

Jacob apparently is unaware of his sons' hostility toward Joseph and naively delivers him into their devious power. Joseph heads toward Shechem to find his brothers, as was requested by Jacob, but they have advanced to Dothan about fifteen miles north of Shechem, which is the spot on the map of an ancient trade route over the plain toward Egypt. Joseph unsuspectingly is intercepted by his angry brothers at that point.

The brother named Judah persuades the other brothers not to kill Joseph but to "sell him" to the passing Ishmaelites, his second cousins, which leave them guiltless of murder. However, the brother named Reuben prevails on the others and throws Joseph alive into a pit, which was an empty cistern.

While the brothers were eating lunch, the Midianites kidnap Joseph. After selling him, they send him to Egypt. When Reuben returned to the pit, Joseph was gone. Because of the hostility in Reuben's heart, his immediate response was not: "What has happened to Joseph, but what is going to happen to me and where can I now turn for help out of this mess?"

The brothers together slaughtered a goat and dipped Joseph's robe in the blood. They returned to Jacob and covered their actions by deceiving their father into thinking that Joseph was dead. At that, Jacob embarked upon a "lifelong mourning" and pattern of grief. He began that trek by tearing his clothes and wearing sackcloth, which is like wearing black today.

In Genesis 38, the focus of attention shifts to Judah, who is separated from his brothers and is living in South Palestine with the Canaanites, among whom he has found a wife and had sons. One son named Er was married to a woman by the

47

name of Tamar. When Er died, the son Onan was required by customary law to take on Tamar on behalf of Er, but he refused to take the responsibility.

After Onan died, Judah is required to give his third son, Shelah, to Tamar, which Shelah refused to accomplish. So, the determined Tamar decided to take matters into her own hands and preserve the name of her dead husband. She abandoned her widow's garments and disguised herself as a harlot with the sole purpose in mind of seducing Judah.

More than willingly, Judah succumbs to Tamar's seduction, but then he takes great pains to avoid publicity. When Tamar produces evidence of Judah's "signet," or the seal to authenticate legal documents as payment for the sexual services, he was compelled to admit that he was the father of those, who became his own twin boys. Generations later they would become heir to the Davidic line. At that moment, however, the immoral activity of Judah stood in vast contrast to the impeccable godliness and increasing ethical intrepidness of Joseph.

Those who kidnapped Joseph and took him to Egypt sold him to "Potiphar," a high official of Pharaoh and captain of the guard. The date of Joseph's arrival in Egypt is debatable. Many believe he arrived during the period of the "Hyksos," the chariot warriors who were foreigners and came to the region of Canaan. They invaded Egypt and controlled the land for almost 150 years.

If Joseph arrived during their rule, it is easy to see why he was rapidly promoted up the social ladder. Since the Hyksos were foreigners themselves, they would not hold this brilliant young foreigner's ancestry against him.

Potiphar apparently was an extremely rich officer in Pharaoh's service. Rich families like Potiphar had elaborate homes two or three stories tall with beautiful gardens and balconies. They enjoyed live entertainment at home, as they chose delicious fruit from very expensive bowls. They surrounded themselves with alabaster vases, paintings, beautiful rugs and hand-carved chairs. Dinner was served on golden tableware, and the rooms were lighted with gold candlesticks. Servants, like Joseph, worked on the first floor, while the family occupied the second level.

In Genesis 39:6-10, the harmonious state of affairs comes unraveled when the mistress of the house solicits Joseph's affection, but he refuses outright. Joseph's rebuff of her advances, according to the scriptural record, is based upon an honest regard for his divine master and a morality, which Joseph considers to be God-given.

In fact, Potiphar's wife utterly failed to seduce Joseph. He totally resisted the temptation by proclaiming that it would be "a sin against God." Joseph did not say to Potiphar's wife, "I'd be hurting you," or "I'd be sinning against Potiphar," or "I'd be sinning against myself." Under pressure, these excuses could be rationalized away. More importantly, people who use excuses usually get away with them — even now. That makes the rare kind of integrity like that of Joseph all the more important in a sinful society.

When the thwarted persistence of Potiphar's wife finds opportunity, she cunningly procures damaging evidence against Joseph by forcing him to flee from her and leaving his outer garment in her possession. As a result, Joseph was put in prison.

Prisons were grim places with vile conditions. They were used to hold forced laborers or, like Joseph, the accused awaiting trial. In those days, prisoners were guilty until proven innocent. There was no such thing as a right to speedy trial. Many prisoners never made it to court because trials were held only at the whim of the ruler. Moreover, the word "Hebrew" denotes not an ethnic group but a social group of an extremely low status. Only gradually and much later did this word come to designate the people of Israel as a unified nation.

As a prisoner and slave, Joseph could have seen this situation as hopeless, but he did not. He performed each small task before him in the best way possible. Therefore, his diligence and positive attitude were noticed by the jail warden, who promoted him to prison administrator. In Genesis 40, Joseph interprets two dreams for the cupbearer and the baker to whom Joseph was in charge as prison administrator.

The cupbearer and the baker of the Pharaoh were the two most trusted men in Pharaoh's kingdom. The baker was in charge of making the king's food. The cupbearer tasted all of the king's food and drink before giving it to him in event that any of it was contaminated or poisoned. These trusted men must have been suspected of serious wrongdoing — perhaps even conspiring against Pharaoh. Later, the cupbearer was released, but the baker was executed.

Evidently, the cupbearer and the chief baker had separate dreams one evening and had no one to interpret them. At that point, Joseph focused upon God. Rather than using the situation to make himself look good, Joseph turned the conversation with them into a powerful witness of the one, true God.

Dreams were different in pagan cultures from those of the Hebrews. For pagans, dreams were considered a science of divination. Joseph was not trained in these techniques. Instead, he thoroughly believed that God-given dreams must be interpreted through God-given inspiration, of which he was a recipient.

For the dreams of the cupbearer and the baker, then, Joseph presents opposing interpretations and thereby demonstrates his gift. The only request that he made to them for his service was to be remembered to Pharaoh, but when the cupbearer was freed from prison, he forgot about Joseph. It was a full two more years before Joseph had another opportunity to be freed. Nevertheless, Joseph's faith was deep, and he would be ready for the next opportunity.

In Genesis 41, when the cupbearer at last does remember Joseph's skills in interpreting dreams, Joseph's second opportunity becomes a reality. Joseph is called before Pharaoh to interpret his strange dream, which none of Pharaoh's wizards, who believed in many gods, could accomplish. According to Joseph, this dream meant that seven good years of crops would be followed by seven years of scarcity via extreme drought-ridden conditions.

Then, following the interpretation of this dream, Joseph presented a survival plan for the next fourteen years. By saving up grain during the seven years of plenty, the country could make it through the seven years of scarcity without starvation. In this manner, Joseph was able to save an entire nation not only by interpreting the dream rightly, but also by translating it into practical action. Therefore, planning is never just an option. It is an absolute necessity in bringing dreams into reality by the gracious, all-knowing, omnipotent hand of God.

The public storing of grain definitely was common practice in Egypt from earliest times, but the narrative in Genesis 41:33-36 seems to represent Joseph as the originator of this policy. Moreover, Joseph's sudden elevation from slave to virtual ruler in Egypt is a referendum on this proclaimed truth that the real wisdom comes from God.

According to the Bible, such wisdom is self-authenticating. The possessor of this gift carries its own responsibility, which Joseph fully recognizes and assumes. Furthermore, Joseph ultimately is rewarded.

To verify this so-called truth at that time, Pharaoh has no other need for interpretation of his dreams, nor does he seek further advice for official policy. He officially recognizes in Joseph "one in whom is the spirit of God" (Genesis 41:37). He entrusts to him the responsibility of procuring grain for the entire country. However, it is not to be overlooked that the quick rise of Joseph from prison walls to Pharaoh's palace involved important training — first as a slave and then as a prisoner. In each situation, Joseph learned the importance of serving God and other people.

Joseph was thirty years old when he became "vizier," or governor, of Egypt. He was seventeen when he was sold into slavery via his brothers. He spent eleven years as an Egyptian slave and two years in prison.

The "signet ring" that was given to Joseph by Pharaoh was shaped in such a way as to be worn on a finger. More importantly, its possession literally was a "blank check" to issue orders in the Pharaoh's name. Other insignia of Joseph's official position, which authentically are Egyptian, include the splendid garments of fine linen, the gold chain of honor, the chariot and the criers who precede Joseph when he goes forth.

Joseph also is given a new Egyptian name, Zapenath-paneah, to make him more acceptable among the people and an Egyptian wife named "Asenath." The new name for Joseph and marriage into the ranking priestly family in Egypt are reported Biblically without even a hint of a change in religion or wavering in his father's faith.

In Genesis 42, the need for grain becomes acute for Jacob and his family. Jacob sends ten of his sons to buy grain in Egypt, but he did not send Benjamin, because he was Joseph's only full brother. As far as Jacob knew, Benjamin was the only surviving son of his beloved wife, Rachel.

When the ten brothers arrived on the scene, Joseph's treatment of them can only be sustained emotionally, not rationally. They are now in Joseph's power not he in theirs, and Joseph's last memory of them was looking upon their faces in horror as slave traders carried him away.

The question before Joseph now had to be: Were these brothers still evil and treacherous or had they changed?

Since Joseph did not know the answer and apparently was unrecognizable to them, he decided to put them through some tests in order to find out their true feelings. So, Joseph was rough on his ten brothers, but not vengeful.

Then, there were the internal questions lodged deeply within him. Joseph remembered his dreams about his brothers bowing down to him, and those dreams were coming true before his very eyes. As a young boy, Joseph was boastful and arrogant about those dreams, but now, as a man, he no longer would flaunt his superior status.

Joseph definitely did not feel the need to say: "I told you so." Joseph did not even need to satisfy himself about the attitudes and motives of his brothers. He just kept quiet. He truly had grown up and matured to the full extent of strength in the Lord, and the methods that he employed psychologically, which were most credible, proved it.

As the ten brothers of Joseph stand before him unsuspectingly, he accuses them of being spies, and he intimidates them with a three-day prison sentence. In defense of themselves, the ten brothers insist that they are not spies. They are ten of twelve brothers — one of whom is with their father and the other is "no more."

To verify the truth of what they had said, Joseph demands that they must bring the younger brother to Egypt. In response, the brothers muttered among themselves that they now were paying God's penalty for what they had done to their brother, Joseph, and Reuben could not resist in saying: "I told you so."

In overhearing the fact that Reuben had meant to rescue him, Joseph keeps the second older brother, Simeon, as a hostage to guarantee the return of the others with Benjamin. On the way out of Egypt, the nine brothers found money in the grain sacks, which Joseph secretly had planted there as a gift, but the money only baffled the whole family as some sort of ominous sign.

Upon hearing the Egyptian governor's demand of seeing Benjamin, Jacob accuses his nine sons of sacrificing his children one by one. Ultimately, Judah accepts full responsibility for Benjamin's safe return, and Jacob finally yields to Judah's plea.

Nonetheless, Jacob spares no pains in seeking to assure the Egyptian "vizier," or governor. He sends some precious products from Palestine and double the money for the grain, which is what Joseph returned, plus an equal amount for the impending purchase. Here, Jacob again demonstrated, as he did with Laban, that he was a man of integrity. He paid for what he bought whether or not he needed to do it.

When the eleven brothers present themselves to Joseph at his office, he directs that they be received at his house. The frightened brothers speak anxiously with the steward and offer to return the money that they found in the sacks. The steward, who knows Joseph's purpose, congratulates them on their good fortune and informs them of Joseph's invitation to dine at noon.

Upon greeting his family, and they bowing before him in honor and respect, Joseph inquired about the welfare of their father. Then, he asked if their brother, Benjamin was with them. They replied: "Our father is well and alive," and it was obvious to Joseph at the sight of Benjamin that it was he.

At that, Joseph, who was overcome with emotion, immediately removed himself from the scene. He went into a private room to weep. He washed his face, came out and controlling himself said: "Let's eat." At the meal, the guests were seated by themselves apart from Joseph and separated from the other Egyptians, because it was the law of the Egyptian caste system.

Egyptians considered themselves highly sophisticated and intelligent. They looked upon shepherds and nomads as being uncultured and even vulgar. As a Hebrew, Joseph could not eat with Egyptians, even though he outranked them. As foreigners and shepherds, his brothers were lower in rank than any Egyptian citizens. Thus, they had to eat separately too.

However, much to their astonishment, the brothers not only were seated according to their age at the table, but more importantly, they were honored by marvelous portions of food from Joseph's own special table. In addition, Benjamin received five times the honor in relation to the other brothers.

On the evening before the departure of the eleven brothers for the land of Canaan, Joseph presented one more test before his brothers by instructing the steward to place his silver cup in Benjamin's sack of grain. After the brothers left, Joseph's instruction was to overtake them and make accusation, specifically to Benjamin, for stealing it.

Joseph's silver cup was a symbol of his authority. Furthermore, the Egyptians thought that it had supernatural powers. These goblets were used for predicting the future. A person poured water into the cup and interpreted the reflections, ripples and bubbles. Conclusions were drawn from the figures dropped into the liquid.

Thus, theft of such an object was a very serious crime in Egypt at the time — even if Joseph did not use it for such a purpose, which accordingly he did not. As a result, Joseph's brothers had to know that Joseph was just another Egyptian. When Joseph stated to them the Egyptian purpose of the cup, it further reinforced to them that Joseph was an Egyptian.

When Joseph insisted that the guilty one would suffer for the crime, it was more pressure than Judah could take, and he makes a speech, which becomes one of the finest ever recorded in human history. In Genesis 43:18-34, Judah recounts the events that led up to the present dilemma omitting, of course, the circumstances with the loss of Benjamin's brother, Joseph.

Then Judah describes his father's fear of losing Benjamin, of which the confirmation of that loss no doubt would cause his death. Finally and most powerfully, Judah offers to take Benjamin's place as a slave in Joseph's household, if only Benjamin would be spared.

The effect of this speech on Joseph is overwhelming, and what has transpired in the person of Judah over all of these years is phenomenal by anyone's analysis. When Judah was younger, he showed absolutely no regard for his brother, Joseph, or his father, Jacob.

First, he convinced his brothers to sell Joseph as a slave. Then he joined his brothers in lying to his father about Joseph's demise. After that, he became known for trying to defraud his daughter-in-law, but now Judah totally is different. He is a transformed person.

Judah, who sold one favored little brother into slavery, offered to become a slave himself to save another favored little brother. At this point, he was so concerned for his father and younger brother that he was willing to die for them.

> As a result of his willingness to give up his own life, Judah ultimately was chosen to be the ancestor of Israel's line of kings, even the king of kings who, according to the New Testament, was willing to lay down his own life not only for the accumulated sins of his own people but also for the sins of the whole human race. Therefore, as later reported: "The [kingly] scepter shall not depart from Judah." — Genesis 49:11-12

In Genesis 45, one of the most dramatic turnarounds among a family of people in the Bible, as well as throughout the entire history of humanity, is witnessed. Joseph immediately breaks down in the presence of his brothers and reveals who he really is — their long lost brother, Joseph.

Through great tears, Joseph asks his brothers not to be upset with what they once did to him or even to be angry with themselves, because "God sent me before you to preserve life, to sustain a remnant on earth of the one, true God and to keep alive many survivors for you." Again Joseph insists that it was not their evil intent that was responsible for his transference to Egypt, but God's will to provide for him and the whole family.

The brothers are not absolved of their guilt here. That would be granted in the New Testament, but they can be delivered from the fear of revenge (Genesis 45:3) and from mutual recrimination (Genesis 45:24) by God's overarching, all inclusive providence.

On his own authority, Joseph invites his entire family to move to Egypt and settle "in the land of Goshen." When Pharaoh hears of the brothers, he is delighted at the opportunity to show his gratitude to Joseph by inviting the whole family to come and "enjoy the best land of Egypt."

In Genesis 45:21-27, Joseph provided wagons, provisions, garments and silver for the journey back to Canaan and to Jacob their father. When Jacob receives word that Joseph was alive, he needed evidence. The relayed words of Joseph and seeing the wagons became the proof that Jacob needed. As a result, Jacob was revived and decided to go with them to see Joseph before he, the aged Jacob, died.

In Genesis 46, Jacob was told by the one, true God, named Yahweh, not to fear going to Egypt, because God would be with him and take care of him. Jacob would not return to Canaan, but he was promised that his descendants would. Also, Joseph would attend to him as he faces death, and Jacob would never know the bitterness of being lonely again.

As Jacob approached the end of his days in Egypt, he blessed Joseph's two Egyptian boys, Ephraim and Manasseh, and orders that they be counted as clans in the land of Canaan. That became a reality when the tribes of Ephraim and Manasseh occupied the east and west side of the River

Jordan as stated in the Book of Joshua 16. Jacob speaks of God as the one who was his shepherd throughout his whole life. In his old age, Jacob could see clearly his dependence upon God, which is a total change in attitude from that of his scheming, dishonest youth.

In Genesis 49, Jacob blessed each one of his sons and then made a prediction of each one's future. Reuben came first because he was Jacob's firstborn son, but as already mentioned, his untrustworthy character, especially in his younger days, led him out of the birthright blessing and produced eventual political obscurity in nomadic life east of the River Jordan for his tribe. Nevertheless, it is interesting to note that both Moses and Aaron came from the tribe of Reuben.

Simeon and Levi being responsible for the massacre at Shechem were denied the birthright blessing. Ultimately they lost whatever land they had by being cruel, dangerous men and tribes, even though the tribe of Simeon became absorbed by the tribe of Judah. After the elimination of the three oldest sons, Judah assumes leadership among the tribes of Israel. The Bible indicates here that Judah will exercise tribal authority until the monarchy is established with a Judahite on the throne.

Zebulon is stated simply as located on the Phoenician coast. Apparently, the tribe at one time was forced to move. Then, with a promise of ease and comfort, Issachar gave up the original territory of the tribe by exchanging freedom for servitude.

Dan supposedly was one of the weakest tribes but used its strength effectively. The Danites were among the last of the Israelites to secure a permanent territory and had to change their area of settlement several times. In the middle of his prophecy to Dan, Jacob exclaimed: "I wait for your salvation, O Lord." He was emphasizing to Dan that he would become a strong leader only if his trust was in God and not in his natural strength and ability.

Evidently, Dan effectively repulsed marauding bands of nomads on the east side of the River Jordan for sometime, but eventually succumbed to them. Asher held a rich land that produced "royal dainties," and they became a very happy people. Naphtali was situated in a fertile area on the western shore of Lake Gennesaret, or the Sea of Galilee, which is all that can be discerned from this portion of scripture.

It is difficult to translate the meaning of the text relating to Joseph and his tribe, but these verses do stress Joseph's importance in economic and military prosperity because of God's help. Again, it is true that God rescued Joseph when his enemies attacked him, and he was able to draw closer to God as adversity mounted. Among Joseph's heroic descendants were Joshua, who would lead the Israelites into the Promised Land, Deborah, Gideon and Jephthah. All were great leaders of Israel.

The last, but not the least, was Benjamin, whose warriors in his tribe included some 700 left-handed shooters, who were renowned for their predatory abilities.

With the last chapter in the Book of Genesis, the beginning of chapter 50 deals with the death and burial of Jacob. Although Jacob died in Egypt under the benevolent care of Joseph, embalmed according to Egyptian practice and mourned for several months there, he was buried in the cave of Machpelah near Hebron with Sarah and Abraham and the rest of the family.

Following the death of Jacob, severe anxiety began to mount among Joseph's brothers. They feared revenge from Joseph for selling him into slavery now that Jacob was gone. It could have been that Joseph was waiting for this moment to get back at his brothers, because Joseph's only genuine interest until this point was being reunited with Benjamin and his father Jacob.

What actually happened involved a singular focus on the one, true God. That total focus translated into a miraculous transformation of those persons, which could not have happened in any other way. Moreover, it is at the very heart and soul of Israel, as well as people throughout all time who are grounded in that same relationship with God.

In Genesis 50:19-20, the final verdict reportedly is pronounced by Joseph to his brothers: "You meant evil. God meant good! How can I add or detract from what God has done?"

In other words, the mystery of human freedom amidst the necessity of God's providential care is a paradox that humbles both Joseph and his brothers before one another and before God. Joseph's forgiveness is his acceptance of God's providential care, which includes the evil deed of his brothers. There is no possibility of accepting one without the other. Only God's providential care produces forgiveness of others, according to the Bible. Never anything else, such as human will alone, makes forgiveness of others transpire. The truth is that human will seeks revenge. The will of God produces forgiveness.

Jumping vastly ahead: That is what Jesus of Nazareth meant when he reportedly concluded in prayer at the Garden of Gethsemane: "Not my will, but Thine be done" — Forgiveness! This is reinforced when Jesus proclaimed before Pilate: "My kingdom is not of this world, because my followers do not fight to protect me."

As a result of God's graciousness, Joseph not only forgave his brothers but also generously offered to care for them and their families. Therefore, Joseph's forgiveness was complete. He literally demonstrated how God graciously accepts us, even when we do not deserve it. Because God graciously accepts us, even when we have ignored or rejected God, we must graciously forgive others. No one can forego the forgiveness of others when the focus is upon how much God really and truly cares for us.

Throughout Joseph's own life, God in fact brought good from evil in many ways: 1) the brothers' evil deed; 2) the false accusations of Potiphar's wife; 3) the cupbearer's neglect, and 4) seven years of famine. Joseph recognized that out of these horrific experiences in his life — God brings good from evil for those who put their trust in God. As a result of the recognition of this fundamental truth, Joseph became "the" leader in all of Israel at this critical juncture in the life of Israel.

Finally, Joseph lives to see his great-grandchildren in Egypt. Then he is ready to die. He literally had no doubt that God would keep the promise of one day bringing the Israelites back to their homeland. Thus, the stage is set for what would begin to happen in the Exodus and come to completion in Joshua, a descendant of Joseph.

God truly was going to make Jacob's family into a great nation, lead them out of Egypt and bring them into the land promised to them. The nation would rely heavily upon this promise, and it would come true in the realization that God was with them, would care for them and lead them in spite of their huge deficiencies and sinfulness. Later, Joseph's mummy in its sarcophagus was carried out of Egypt by Moses and buried at Shechem.

---

1. Soren Kierkegaard, *The Sickness Unto Death* (Princeton, New Jersey: Princeton University Press, 1941).

CHAPTER 5

PEOPLE OF THE EXODUS

Some 400 years had passed since Joseph moved his family to Egypt, but by this time the descendants of Abraham, Isaac and Jacob had grown to be over two million people. These numbers were frightening to the new, traditional Pharaoh long after the Hyksos lost control and left the scene. These Hebrews were now simply foreigners to Pharaoh and had become a dreaded group of people in Egypt's midst.

These Hebrews noticeably were quite different from the Egyptians in many respects: 1) The Hebrews worshiped one God, the Egyptians worshiped many gods; 2) The Hebrews were wanderers, the Egyptians had a deeply rooted culture; 3) The Hebrews were shepherds, the Egyptians were builders; and 4) The Hebrews were separated from the Egyptians by living in the land of Goshen, which lay north of Egyptian cultural centers.

Pharaoh decided to make slaves of the Hebrews in order that they would not upset the balance of power in the Egyptian community. The decision may have been Pharaoh's biggest mistake, because the one, true God of the Hebrews reportedly intervened by coming to their aid and ultimately to their rescue, as recorded in the Bible.

Of course, a man named Moses was the chief one in responding to the call of God, but many others were involved including Moses' sister, Miriam; his brother, Aaron; his nephews, Nadab and Abihu; priests, Levites, Caleb, Korah, Eleazer, Balaam, and then Joshua, who led the people into the Promised Land where the Canaanites were occupants.

There were levels of slavery in Egypt. There were some slaves, who worked long hours in mud pits, while others were skilled carpenters, jewelers and craftsmen. Regardless of their skill or level, all slaves were watched closely by ruthless taskmasters or supervisors, whose assignment was to make slaves work as fast as possible. Thus, slavery in Egypt was utterly miserable for the Hebrews, but strangely enough — the more that they were oppressed, the more they seemed to multiply.

Ancient records indicate that the cities of Pitham and Raamses were built by the Hebrews in 1290 BC, which is why some scholars believe that the Hebrews departed Egypt at that time during the reign of Ramses II, who was Pharaoh in 1290 BC. Other scholars believe that the Hebrews left Egypt in 1446 BC.

How could the Hebrews build two cities 150 years after they had left? These scholars suggest that Ramses II did not build these two cities. Instead, he renamed two cities that actually had been built 150 years previously. It was common practice for an Egyptian ruler to make improvements on a city and then take credit for building it. Thus, all records of previous founders were wiped out.

With this background in mind, the drama of the exodus through years in the barren wilderness and into the land of Canaan transpires.

Moses and the Hebrews Exiting Egypt

According to the Biblical record in the Book of Exodus, Moses was born at a time when Pharaoh was attempting to rid the nation of all male children among the Hebrews. Through an apparently God-given, ingenious means, however, Miriam, the older sister of Moses, was able to put the baby Moses into the adoptive hands of Pharaoh's wife and then to have Moses nursed and nurtured by his own mother. Thus, Moses was raised in Pharaoh's household as his own son and as an Egyptian.

When Moses became of age and was confronted with the sullied oppression of the Hebrew people, he was appalled. In fact, he became so infuriated at an Egyptian overseer in the beating of a Hebrew that he murdered the Egyptian on the spot. Supposedly, when Pharaoh heard about it, he sought to kill Moses, and Moses had to escape for his life.

Finally, Moses made it to the land of Midian, became a sheep-herder and married a woman named Zipporah, who gave birth to their two sons, Gersham and Eliezer. Years later, the king and Pharaoh died, and the desperate cries of the Hebrews for help in their bitter state of slavery "rose up to God" (Exodus 2:23).

At that point, God heard their cry and remembered the covenant made to Abraham, Isaac and Jacob. While Moses was keeping the flock of his father-in-law, Jethro, the angelic messenger of the Lord appeared to Moses in a fiery bush on Mount Horeb, which was blazing but not consumed.

Then God called to Moses out of the bush to go unto Pharaoh back in Egypt and lead the Hebrews out of Egypt. Conversation ensued back and forth between the two of them, in which Moses felt quite inadequate. At the end of a lengthy period, Moses expressed his total frustration with the prospect of such a daunting task by responding thusly before the awesome presence of God: "O my Lord, please send someone else" (Exodus 4:13).

Nevertheless, with the absolute assurance that the one and only God would be with Moses every step along the way, Moses finally accepted the seemingly impossible task and overshadowing burden. Moses proceeded to his father-in-law, Jethro, and asked for permission to go back to Egypt and see if his kindred were even alive. Jethro forthrightly and affirmatively responded without any hesitation: "Go in peace" (Exodus 4:18).

Moses took his wife and sons back to Egypt with the reassuring word from God that all who sought to kill Moses now were dead. In Egypt, Moses confronted the new Pharaoh with the statement reportedly from the Lord: "Let my people go!" (Exodus 8:1), but the Pharaoh would not allow it at all because his heart was hardened. Pharaoh would not even let the Hebrews go into the wilderness for just three days and sacrifice to the Lord their God. He called the Hebrews lazy and crybabies, who just wanted an excuse for not working.

The Egyptian overseers and taskmasters were instructed to impose even stricter measures of work upon the Hebrews, which produced even more hardship and suffering for them. Instead of providing straw to make their mud bricks, the Hebrews had to provide straw themselves and do their job twice as fast.

The process of making bricks in Egypt was not pleasant in the least. The black mud of the Delta was molded into bricks in a puddle, which then were dried in the sun. The straw, chopped small, preserved the consistency of mud and produced bricks that became stronger. Labor was under tyrannical supervision, and meticulous scribes completed the tallying of the numbers. It was a terrible time.

When the Hebrews heard that Pharaoh would not listen to Moses and Aaron's plea by letting them go even for a few days into the wilderness to sacrifice before the Lord, they grew even more discouraged and did not want to listen to their leaders anymore. The people told Moses and Aaron that they did not want to hear anything else about God and deliverance, because the last time that they listened, all they received was more work and greater suffering. Therefore, when Moses and Aaron were asked by the Lord to return again unto Pharaoh, it was stated: The people have not listened; how then will Pharaoh listen to what is said?" (Exodus 6:12).

At that, Moses and Aaron were told by Yahweh that when Pharaoh does not listen to you, I the Lord will stretch out my hand against Egypt and bring all of you out from among them. At that point Moses and Aaron did trust those words from the one, true God and proceeded with what needed to be performed from that time onward.

A series of plagues and promises — made and broken — ensued, which included: The appearance of what seemed to be blood on the River Nile producing death to fish, an odious smell and people without water; frogs coming up from the water and covering the land; death to Egyptian livestock; boils that broke out on all Egyptians. Hailstorms killed and destroyed almost every plant. Locusts covered Egypt and ate everything left by the hail. Total darkness covered Egypt for three days so that no one even could move, and finally, death occurred to the firstborn of Egypt, while Israel was spared.

At every point along this disastrous path, Moses was instructed to demand complete liberation, rather than just to leave for the purpose only of performing religious rites in the wilderness for a few days. Finally, at the stroke of midnight after the last plague, Pharaoh evidently capitulated unconditionally by seeking the favor of Yahweh, whom he so arrogantly ignored until this point in time.

Pharaoh told the Hebrews through Moses and Aaron: "Go away from us. Hasten your departure. Take your flocks, your herds, and be gone: (Exodus 12:31-32). That pronouncement was short lived as well, because as soon as the people had fled, Pharaoh and his officials regretted having lost the service of the Hebrews and pursued them with an army numbering into the hundreds.

Nevertheless, the Hebrews did proceed out of Egypt with a pillar of cloud by day and a pillar of fire by night — to lead them, to sustain them and to assist them in knowing that God was with them. According to the scripture, God did protect the Hebrews by helping them cross the Red Sea, or Sea of Reeds, on dry ground. In the process the Pharaoh's army and chariots apparently were destroyed. The Hebrews were free from the Egyptians at last. Soon thereafter new problems arose.

Complaints from those who became known as Israelites commenced against God and Moses. They complained about their misfortunes, about the lack of meat, then water and intensely desired things that they did not have. They were upset about being stuck in the wilderness, facing those who appeared to be giants in the Promised Land and desperately wanting a return to Egypt. They fiercely rebelled against the authority of both Moses and Aaron. They grew greedy themselves for more power and authority. They blamed others for their own troubles and complained that God and Moses had brought them into this wilderness in the first place.

Despite God's power and love, Israelites began to yearn more and more for their days back in Egypt. Even slavery seemed more attractive than the uncertainty and perils of life in a barren wilderness. The slave mentality never had left them, and it took at least another generation to begin thinking otherwise.

Most importantly, the disobedience and unbelief of the Israelites reached a seeming "critical mass," even though their physical and spiritual needs continuously were provided with food and a place to worship by Yahweh, and they were judged for that. God's relationship to the people always was loving, yet firm, for the one and only purpose of redeeming the whole world, and the Israelites were to be the ones in bearing that message to all people.

The Israelites had no army, school, governors, mayors or police when they left Egypt. They had to be instructed in their constitutional laws and daily practices. Their leaders were moved by God in showing people how to worship and how to have national holidays.

This process began when Jethro, the father-in-law, came to visit Moses in the wilderness and heard about what God had done for Moses and the people of Israel in bringing them out of Egypt. Like Melchizedek, Jethro was a priest of another tradition, but through the testimony of Moses, he came to recognize the one, true God as greater than all gods. Even though God chose one nation through whom to work, Jethro realized that God's love and concern was meant for all nations. What wisdom and support that meant to Moses at a most critical juncture in time!

In a dramatic meeting with Moses on Mount Sinai, God gave the people laws for right living. This system of divine law contained three parts: 1) The Ten Commandments for spiritual and moral living before God and one another, as recorded in Exodus 20:1-17 and Deuteronomy 5:6-21; 2) Civil law with rules for people to manage their lives; and 3) Ceremonial law showing the people patterns for building the tabernacle and for regular worship. The Civil law and the Ceremonial law are recorded in the Book of Exodus, the Book of Leviticus, the Book of Numbers and the Book of Deuteronomy in the Bible.

The first census was taken in the wilderness of Sinai and recorded in the first chapter in the Book of Numbers. A grand total of 603,550 people among the twelve tribes of Israel were counted. The anointed priests of Aaron, his sons and descendants are featured with the ceremonial worship of God in the Book of Leviticus. In addition, the Levites, who were to assist the priests of Aaron, are found in the census listed with the Book of Numbers. Of the tribes named after the three sons of Levi, there were 7,500 listed under the one called Gershon; 8,600 under the one called Kohath; and 6,200 under the one called Merari.

As the Israelites approached the land of Canaan, Moses sent twelve spies to search out the territory. Only two of the twelve men came back with a positive attitude about the situation. The negative ones returned to incite the people against taking any more steps forward. They thought the task was too overwhelming even to make an attempt in overcoming the Canaanites. In their own words, they said: "We are not able to go up against this people, for they are stronger than we. We appeared like grasshoppers before them" (Numbers 13:31-33).

Joshua and Caleb were the only two people who responded affirmatively. Caleb, the minority spokesman, insisted: "We are well able to overcome them. So, let us go at once and occupy the territory" (Numbers 13:30).

Obviously, the negative minds prevailed, which resulted in a rebellion against Moses and Aaron. It is true that the fortified cities, which they saw, were surrounded by high walls 20 feet thick and 25 feet tall. Guards often were stationed on top where there was a commanding view of the countryside, and some of the inhabitants stood some seven to nine feet tall.

Nonetheless, Caleb championed the unpopular stance that with God's help and promise before them, they could prevail over the Canaanites. As a result of his faith along with Joshua, the two of them were the only ones to experience the Promised Land approximately three decades later.

They retreated into the wilderness, and the rest of the people never even saw the land that divinely was promised to them. It was not until they died and a new generation of believers came into being that the Israelites were able to move into Canaanite territory, which was described as a "land flowing with milk and honey." Although that land was relatively small measuring 150 miles long and 60 miles wide, its lush hillsides were covered with fig, date and nut trees. It was the land that God had promised to Abraham, Isaac and Jacob.

It is even of greater significance at this point that God had led the Israelites out of slavery, through the desolate wilderness and up to the edge of the Promised Land. God had protected them, fed them and fulfilled every promise, but when they were encouraged to take the last step of faith and enter the land, the people refused. Naturally as a result, Caleb and Joshua went into deep sorrow, mourning and despair over the people's refusal to enter the land.

Moses pleaded for them in prayer before the Lord, even though the people did not deserve it. Moses reportedly was concerned about God's reputation among unbelievers. For example, if Pharaoh would hear about their action, it would be a disgrace among the nations. So, Moses pleaded with God. He asked God to forgive the people, which revealed several characteristics of God, namely: 1) God is immensely patient; 2) God's love is one promise that always can be trusted; 3) God forgives again and again; and 4) God is merciful by listening to and answering human requests in God's own perfect timing.

Most importantly, the voice of the minority is not often given a human hearing, but truth cannot be measured by numbers of people. Truth often stands against majority opinion. Truth remains unchanged, because truth is guaranteed by the character of God. God is truth and is the last word, as proven in the lives of Caleb, Joshua, and the eventual overtaking of the pagan land of Canaan by the Israelites. Truth always is for genuine people of the one, true God.

After this big disappointment, Moses was asked by God to provide water for the complaining, rebellious people, but Moses and Aaron took matters into their own hands instead, which cost them their ability to enter the Promised Land. Aaron reportedly died on Mount Hor, and his son, Eleazer, became the new high priest. Moses died somewhere on the east bank of the River Jordan, after delivering several speeches to the Israelites on Mount Nebo, which are recorded in the Book of Deuteronomy.

Prior to that, a person by the name of Korah organized over 200 Levites to join with him in a rebellion against Moses. Korah confronted Moses and Aaron with a list of complaints, which included accusations such as: You are no better than anyone else. Everyone in Israel has been chosen of the Lord. Therefore, we do not need to obey you.

Korah and his associates had seen the advantages of the priesthood in Egypt. Egyptian priests had great wealth and strong political influence, which Korah seemingly desired himself. Korah did not understand that Moses' main ambition was to serve God rather than to control others. Thus, Moses supposedly saw through the motivation of Korah and the others. Korah's hidden agenda was: "I have as much right to lead as Moses does." Moses might have agreed with his words, but the application of his thoughts via his hidden agenda was wrong. That error not only cost Korah his job but also his life (Numbers 16:32).

A message was then sent to Edom requesting passage for the Israelites through their land on the main highway of a well-traveled trade route, but Edom, the descendants of Esau, brother to Jacob and their Israelite ancestor, said no. They did not trust the Israelites. The Edomites were afraid that this great horde of people would either attack them or devour their crops. So, the Israelites turned back and traveled a different route to the Promised Land.

Following that, a sorcerer by the name of Balaam was called to curse the Israelites. According to pagans, sorcerers were thought to have great hidden power. Thus, the king of Moab paid a fee for Balaam to use his magical powers of divination in anticipation that the God of Israel would turn against God's own people. By a strange twist of circumstances, Balaam ends up blessing the Israelites instead. The scripture implies that God's purposes are accomplished even by people and nations who do not serve the Lord, which occurred in Egypt as well.

When the old generation died in the wilderness, another census was needed to record the Israelites who were readied to enter the Promised Land. The census revealed that even though 600,000 men, not counting any women and children, had died in the wilderness, the male population of Israel now numbered 601,730. Again, Caleb and Joshua were the only ones remaining from that old generation some 38 years later.

This quiet but powerful miracle often overlooks the fact that a whole nation moved from one land to another, lost its entire adult population and yet managed to maintain their spiritual direction. Sometimes it does not seem like God is working miracles, but as in this instance, God works in quiet ways to bring about long-range purposes even beyond short-lived human existence.

As Moses approached the end of his time, he did not want to leave his work without making sure that a new leader was ready to replace him. Moses asked God to help him in finding a replacement. When Joshua was selected, Moses entrusted to him a variety of tasks to ease the transition into a new position, laid his hands upon him and commissioned him.

Moses clearly informed the people that Joshua had the authority and ability to lead the nation. His confidence in Joshua was good for both Joshua and the people of Israel and helped immensely to minimize the leadership gap. No less should ever be accomplished in any similar situation.

At that, a song from the lips of Moses was voiced. Moses blessed all of the tribes and died full of all kinds of praise for the mighty deeds that God had wrought through him.

Joshua and the Conquest of Canaan

Commissioned by God through the strong hand of Moses, Joshua was the right leader at the right time to lead the Israelites in overtaking the land of Canaan according to the promise of God given to Abraham, Isaac and Jacob and as recorded in the first five books of the Bible. Why? Because Joshua was intensely obedient to God's leading, according to the Bible, and it became a compelling spiritual influence upon other people, which prevailed for many years afterward.

Furthermore, as a gift from God and being responsive to the dynamics of the situation at hand, Joshua proved to be a brilliant military leader. It was evidenced from the start of his invasion into the land of Canaan and throughout his remaining days. In addition to his natural gifts and positive attitude for the task ahead of him, Joshua was well prepared for the job. He knew what was required of him and followed through admirably with each and every responsibility in a way that greatly is needed and exceedingly rare among leaders throughout all time.

In summation, Joshua was an excellent leader. He was confident in God's strength, courageous in the face of opposition, willing to seek God's word in all things and responded faithfully to what was asked of him and his people in the presence of the one, true God.

When the Israelites at long last were ready to move into the Promised Land, the dominant people in the area were the Canaanites. They were a Semitic people who lived mainly in the valleys and coastal regions where water was relatively plentiful and farming fairly easy. The lives of the Canaanites revolved around sturdy walled cities scattered throughout the lowlands. There was no central government. Each city virtually existed as a little kingdom with its own ruler, aristocrats, military establishment, commercial enterprises, religious institutions and serfs.

The feudal culture had been in existence for more than six centuries. At their height of power, the Canaanites had been technologically advanced and artistically refined, but by the time Joshua and the Israelites had arrived upon the scene, the Canaanites had lost much of their vigor and creativeness.

The hill country, which runs like a backbone down the middle of Palestine, was only sparsely settled because water was scarce, and farming became more difficult on the stony hillsides. The Canaanites could not exercise strong military control there. Merchants did not wish to take their caravans into the hills if they could not go by way of the coast and valleys.

As a result, the mountains became a refuge for dispossessed people like the Jebusites, Hivites and Perizzites. Little is known about them but their names. These people lived a more rural life than their neighbors on the plains. In Transjordan, for example, semi-nomad existence was a long-established way of life.

The most vivid contrast between the Canaanites and the Israelites, who were poised to invade Canaanite territory, involved whom they worshiped. The Canaanites were pagans who worshiped idols and many gods. The most favorite was Baal, the god of fertility. The cult animal was the bull.

At the opposite end of the spectrum were the Israelites who worshiped the one, true God. God had been the distinguishing characteristic in the community of Israel throughout the centuries. Moreover, the most common name for the one, true God at that time was Yahweh. This uniqueness among the Israelites and the apparent promise of the one and only God became the number one reason, motivation and driving force behind the movement of Joshua and the Israelites, who sought to overtake the so-called land of the Canaanites.

One other matter needs to be taken into consideration here. Historically speaking, not all of the Israelites were involved with the descent into Egypt and the subsequent exodus from Egypt. In fact, it appears that the great majority of those who called themselves Israelites did not participate in this sojourn. Instead, they wandered off into the sparsely settled hill country to build villages and to till the soil.

Why? The answer centers upon the Canaanites. By settling down in the area of the Canaanites, these more stationary Israelites learned the ways of the Canaanites and adopted their language, which became the parent of the Hebrew language. However, the Canaanites never seemed to allow these landless people to forget that they were outsiders.

The Canaanites called them, Habiru or Hebrews, which became a term of scorn synonymous with "serf" or "slave," in the same manner that they were named in Egypt by the Egyptians. Being aware of the seeming hopelessness of their situation within the closed society of the Canaanites, these Habiru or Hebrews began to settle in the hill country, where they mostly were free of Canaanite oppression.

The two groups of Hebrews at the time of Joshua were remarkably similar: both originally had come from the same background as traders and free people. Both had settled in foreign lands and had become serfs. At last both had broken free in seeking land and freedom. Sharing in common their belief in Yahweh and having a great distrust in oppressive rule of all sorts, these dissidents ultimately bonded together at the time of Joshua and thereafter in the cause of overcoming the Canaanites. They formed a confederation and happily welcomed those who wished to join their ranks.

Currently, what is before this band of Israelites of more than two million strong under the leadership of Joshua is a surge into the land of Canaan from the east bank of the River Jordan to the west bank and onward. That surge began with Jericho.

Jericho lay at the intersection of important trade routes in the Jordan Valley and had been a commercial center for thousands of years before Joshua even approached the scene. The city itself was not more than a few acres in size and contained a few thousand inhabitants. Houses were crowded right up to the city wall. The roofs were flat and used for such practical purposes as drying and storing produce. There were two walls about twelve to fifteen feet apart. Houses were built on wooden logs across the tops of those two walls.

Joshua's procedure was clear and solid with this initial surge. First, he sent two spies secretly to Jericho, because Joshua did not want the possibility of another negative report to stir up the people in revolt. The spies left the Israelite camp and slipped into Jericho with the help of a Canaanite prostitute named Rahab. She willingly risked everything, according to the Bible, for a God that she barely even knew. Rahab probably lived in a house atop those two walls with a window that looked out over the outside wall.

Then, just before crossing over into the Promised Land, Joshua gathered the people to hear words of the Lord. They were to focus solely on God and remember who truly was guiding them. Last but not least, the celebration of the Passover was presented as marking the end of one era in Israelite history and the beginning of another along with the cessation of manna. Then, it was onward to Jericho.

According to the first verse of chapter 6 in the Book of Joshua, the Israelites enforced an embargo upon Jericho. The final stage of the siege began as Joshua's army marched around the city each day for an entire week.

Many of the details about Joshua's siege seem to be based on good, reasonable military strategy. That included devices for insuring complete blockage of supplies to the city, ways of unnerving the enemy while keeping up the morale and physical condition of Israel's army as well as signals to indicate the maneuvers to be executed. The marching, the ark carrying, the horn blowing and the shouting seemed to have overtones of religious ritual that was reflective of life together among Israelites.

The city of Jericho became theirs. Everything in this captured place was destroyed, which was usual practice of the time and as an act of high devotion to Yahweh. Supposedly only Rahab's household and perhaps precious metals were spared.

Next the Israelites went after the city of "Ai," which today is extremely difficult in discerning where it actually was located at the time of Joshua. According to the Bible, the Israelites were defeated there initially. Reportedly it was because they thought they could succeed purely by their own skill. After it was realized what had happened, Joshua prayed. He sought God's forgiveness and refocused upon God before moving forward anew. As a result, the second attempt at battle seemingly fared much better.

During the night, Joshua sent one detachment of soldiers west of Ai to lie in wait. He led a second group north of Ai the next morning. A third group was positioned northwest to cut off any possibility of reinforcements from Bethel or of any opposition soldiers attempting to flee from Ai. When the army of Ai attacked, the Israelites to the north pretended to scatter, only to turn on the opposition as the men lying in ambush moved in and burned the city. Afterward, the Israelites celebrated in sacrificial worship before Yahweh with an altar built of natural stones. This was to prevent the people from worshiping altars full of idols or of worshiping the craftsmanship of the workers.

From that point, it was on to Gibeon with the hope of working with them against many pagan kings in the area who had united their forces against the Israelites. However, trickery reportedly was involved on the part of the Gibeonites in an alliance with the Israelites, but Joshua upheld his part of the bargain. Again, with the presence of the one, true God, five armies apparently were defeated in the long standing noonday sun.

Then, there was the battle of Hazor, the largest Canaanite center in the region of Galilee. By a surprise attack, the chariots of the enemies were rendered useless in the dense forests. All in all, some 31 kings and their cities had been defeated. As reported in the Book of Joshua, the Israelites had overpowered the Hittites, the Amorites, the Canaanites, the Perizzites, the Hivites and the Jabusites.

Most all of these conquests transpired in the middle part of Palestine, which left other peoples living in Canaan yet to be conquered. Moreover, the Israeli conquest seems to have taken place for at least two centuries, 1400-1200 BC, which does not in any way lessen the marvelous accomplishments of Joshua and the people under the continuing leadership of Yahweh.

Beginning with the Book of Joshua 12 and forward, the distribution of the land, which was promised for a long time, is reiterated. The necessity of sharing the wealth is proclaimed. As Joshua seemed to be dying, he reportedly called all of the leaders in what now is described as a nation — to give them his final words of encouragement and instruction.

The heart of his message involved the proclamation that the people had to decide whether they would obey the Lord, who had proven to be trustworthy again and again, or obey the local gods, which were man-made idols. In Joshua's own words recorded in the Book of Joshua: "Be careful, therefore, to love the Lord your God" (Joshua 23:11). Choose this day whom you will serve, whether the gods that your ancestors served in the region beyond the river or the gods of the Amorites in whose land you now dwell; but as for me, all of my household [and followers] we will serve the Lord" (Joshua 24:15).

Joshua then succumbed and was buried in the hill country of Ephraim at Timnathserah.

CHAPTER 6

JUDGES AND KINGS IN ISRAEL

Leaders, a vacuum of leadership and response among people are the issue in Israel from 1100 BC to 800 BC generally speaking. Leadership means not only human leadership, but more importantly, divine leadership, according to the Bible.

There is no activity in scripture without consideration of God's involvement in the affairs of human beings. Most of the time people are found on the wrong side of the equation. In fact, the Deuteronomic Philosophy of History so pervades the Book of Judges and other portions of holy writ that it is difficult, if not impossible, to find anything else of value here. Nonetheless, the Book of Judges does seem to contain a highly accurate evaluation of human beings in the sight of God, without which all other considerations seem vain and lead nowhere.

The Deuteronomic Philosophy of History clearly is summarized in Judges 2:17-23, which simply involves the trajectory that righteousness leads to prosperity, and wickedness leads to ruin. In theocratic terms the people of Israel obey God and God's righteousness, which brings on prosperity. People turn away from God with rebellious and sinful behavior, which causes their downfall. When they repent and turn toward God again, they are lifted out of their wrongdoing and misery. That puts them on the right track again until the next time they turn away.

Sin is not primarily transgression, as in later times, but rebellion. Righteousness at this point is ethical in nature, but even more importantly, it means concern for the helpless. Furthermore, there is a tendency in the history of Israel to judge all people in light of the doctrine of divine-earthly retribution, which means that justice falls in line with the cursing and blessing of God. This motif especially is evident in the Book of Judges. Judges definitely is a book that imposes a doctrine of divine judgment, punishment and then restoration on the history of Israel — from the invasion into the land of Canaan to the first king of the nation.

The so-called "judges" in Israel were known simply as "heroes," and they were in evidence for a total of about 410 years, which coincided with each period of oppression for the Israelites. They did not in any way render a courtroom verdict, which often is true upon the contemporary scene. The judge in ancient Canaanite and Israelite usage was not so much a legal expert as one who upheld and defended the customs of the people.

Therefore, a judge in Israel became a deliverer of wronged people who were not strong enough to obtain justice for themselves — widows, orphans and victims of military aggression. In fact, the Bible often refers to their heroes as "deliverers." Clearly, tribal leaders did not conform to one narrow role: one was a military commander (Judges 11:6, 11); another was a prophetess (Judges 4:4). Some judges even had ties with certain sanctuaries (I Samuel 1-12).

Most learned people agree that the time of the judges was approximately from 1200 BC to 1050 BC. During this period of time in Palestine, Mesopotamian, Egyptian and Hittite powers faded into insignificance. This left the small nations in the region, such as the Israelites, to pursue their own policies of expansion.

The Israelite tribes already were established in the hill country and perhaps in parts of North Transjordan by this time. They needed to fend off the hostile forces of the Midianites, the Ammonites, the Moabites and others who wished to press westward across the River Jordan. The Canaanites continued to occupy many of their lowland city-states as well as a few isolated cities such as Shechem and Jerusalem in the hill country.

During this period of time, Israel's history mainly became one of consolidating the settlements previously made and defending tribal territories from adjoining peoples. Each tribe largely pursued an independent course, even though all of them shared a common heritage and were bound by treaties and covenants with one another. Life mostly centered around these tribal relationships rather than with the cities.

The religious outlook and practice of the Israelites was diverse and sometimes involved linkage with Canaanite belief and practice. There has been strong evidence of reverence for trees, wooden pillars and idols among the Israelites during this time, but without question, it was a relatively minor aspect of life among the Israelites. That was a tremendous tribute to Israel's faith in the one, true God called Yahweh.

In summation, the contemporary value with the Book of Judges does not lie in the moral example the judges set. These heroes do display such vices as lying, cruelty, murder, hatred and sexual immorality. On occasion they do try to justify these vices in the name and for the sake of God, as even is attempted among people today. What the Book of Judges powerfully does show is the Israelites at an early stage of their self-identity under the one, true God named Yahweh.

The period of the kings in Israel dates primarily from 1020 BC to 935 BC during the reigns of Kings Saul, David and Solomon. Then, as recorded also in the Bible, there are the lesser kings from 935 BC to the end of the divided kingdom – Israel to the north and Judah to the south. Israel is defeated by the Assyrians in 721 BC, and Judah falls to the Babylonians in 598 BC. All of these captured people are carried off into exile.

Again, with all of this data in mind, the focus now is turned toward significant people among the Israelites during this period of the judges and kings.

Major Judges

Othniel was Israel's first judge or hero who had a rich spiritual heritage. His uncle was Caleb, a man of unwavering faith in God, and Othniel followed right along in his relative's footsteps. Being in the Caleb clan, Othniel belonged to a group loosely associated with the clan of Judah.

Under Othniel's leadership, he led the people in freedom from the oppression of Cushanrishathaim, king of Mesopotamia, which more than likely was located in the southeast. These people had foraged their way into South Palestine. Following Othniel's death, it did not seem to take long for the Israelites to fall back into their rebellious, sinful ways, according to the Bible.

The second hero or judge of the Israelites was Ehud — called a "deliverer" from the left-handed tribe of Benjamin. According to the Bible, King Eglon of Moab conquered part of Israel and set up his throne in the city of Jericho. Ehud was chosen to take Israel's tribute there, but in the process, he killed King Eglon and escaped into the hill country of Ephraim.

From that point, Ehud gathered together an army to cut off any Moabites who tried to escape across the River Jordan. This was the first time that nations attacked the Israelites from outside the land of Canaan, which in part now belonged to the Israelites. Ehud's courageous faith apparently resulted in peace for the nation of Israel many years thereafter. The key verse in the Bible at this point is: "When the Israelites cried out to the Lord, God raised up for them a deliverer, Ehud, son of Gera, the Benjaminite" (Judges 3:15).

The mention of Shamgar as hero or judge in Israel is tantalizingly brief with just one verse, but like Ehud, Shamgar is remembered for his unusual method of exterminating Israel's enemies. According to Judges 3:31, Shamgar killed 600 Philistines with an oxgoad.

An oxgoad was a long stick with a small flat piece of iron on one side and a sharp point on the other. The sharp side was used to drive the oxen during the times of plowing, and the flat end was used to clean the mud off of the plow. The oxgoad is used in the Middle East to drive oxen yet today. Eight-foot-long oxgoads have been found in excavations. So, in times of crisis such as briefly reported here, oxgoads easily could have been used as spears, which Shamgar apparently did.

The fourth and fifth heroes or judges in Israel comes next, of whom the fourth named <u>Deborah</u> could be regarded as the most famous. It is certain that she was the only female judge as well as one of the most formidable women in Biblical history. She and Barak are often placed together in the Bible, but Deborah clearly is the exceptional person here.

The reason is straightforward and simple as recorded in Judges 4:8-9. Deborah told Barak that God would be with him in battle, but that was not enough for Barak. He only would go into battle if Deborah would go with him. Without hesitation, she did lead the way in taking people into battle against the Canaanites.

More than that, Deborah exemplified the character of a great leader by looking to God and taking charge as God directed. Furthermore, she influenced the people as a prophetess — to live for God even after the battle was completed. Her strong personality drew people together and commanded the respect even of Barak, a military general.

As recorded in Judges 4:2-3, the Israelites had been sold into the hand of King Jabin. The Israelites cried out to the Lord for help after many years of cruel oppression by the Canaanites. Nothing is known about King Jabin of Canaan, who supposedly reigned in Hazor and whose commander of the army was Sisera. What is known is that this is the only time during the period of the judges when the enemies of the Israelites came from within their own land, and the Israelites had failed to expel all of the Canaanites. Therefore, these Canaanites had regrouped and were attempting to restore their lost power.

Chariots made of iron or wood were the tanks of the ancient world. They were pulled by one or two horses and were the most feared, powerful weapons of the day. Some chariots even had razor sharp knives extending from the wheels, which were designed to mutilate helpless foot soldiers. The Canaanite army had some 900 iron chariots, and Israel seemingly was not powerful enough to defeat such an invincible army. Therefore, Jabin and Sisera had no trouble oppressing the people until the faithful woman by the name of Deborah reportedly called upon God.

Thus, Deborah traveled from her home between Ramah and Bethel to go with Barak and the Israelite army against Hazor. Sisera, the commander of Hazor's army, assembled his men at Harosheth to defend his territory against Israelite attack. Barak gathered his army on Mount Tabor, perhaps for pre-battle religious rites. Barak then marched into the valley where the Israelites were at complete disadvantage, because Sisera's chariots operated most effectively on the plain.

The description of the battle almost is devoid of any detail, but the implication is that Barak's soldiers astoundingly won their victory by combat. Sisera fled to Harosheth-hagoiim where there had been peace between King Jabin of Hazor and the clan of Heber the Kenite, a longtime ally of Israel. Strangely, however, Heber decided to throw his whole lot with Jabin and his forces, while his wife, Jael, did not.

Sisera could not have been more pleased upon arrival at their place, being welcomed by Jael, who offered her a tent as a hiding place. Since Jael was the wife of Heber, who was a man loyal to Sisera's forces and who may have told Sisera that the Israelites were camped near Mount Tabor, Sisera thought that Jael could be trusted. How wrong that judgment turned out to be.

Also, since men never were allowed to enter a woman's tent, no one ever would think to look for Sisera there. Women of that day, however, were in charge of pitching the tents. So, while Sisera rested and lay fast asleep from weariness, Jael had no problem with driving a tent peg into Sisera's head while he slept.

When Barak arrived in pursuit of Sisera, Jael went out to meet him saying: "Come and I will show you the man whom you are seeking" (Judges 4:22). So, Barak went into the tent and found Sisera dead with a tent peg in his head. Then, the hand of the Israelites apparently bore harder and harder upon King Jabin of Canaan until they completely destroyed him and his forces.

Afterward, there was a great celebration among the Israelites. The Song of Deborah, which is recorded in the Book of Judges 5, grew to become one of the greatest expressions ever composed and sung. Most importantly, God's greatness was given full credit for this massive victory.

In the midst of this joyous celebration with the singing of praises to God, Deborah fulfilled all of her leadership skills as a mediator, advisor and counselor. Then when called to lead, Deborah was able to plan, direct and delegate the whole event. Most importantly, she sustained a remarkable relationship with God. Would that there were more like her!

Gideon is the last of the major judges or heroes of the Israelites as recorded in the Book of Judges. His life unfolds during the oppression of the Midianites, a nomadic or semi-nomadic people from the desert region southeast of Palestine and who do not appear elsewhere in the Book of Judges. The encroachment of the Midianites into the hill country of Palestine is described in Judges 6:1-10.

The Midianites were a desert people who were descended from Abraham's second wife, Keturah. From this relationship, they always seemed to be a nation that was in conflict with Israel. Years earlier when the Israelites still were wandering in the wilderness, Israelites battled the Midianites and almost totally destroyed them. Because the Israelites were unable to wipe out the Midianites completely, however, the tribe repopulated. Now, Israel was facing them again.

At this time in their history, the Israelites again hit rock bottom in their common life and reportedly turned to God once more as a last resort. Supposedly, an angel, or quite simply — a messenger of God, sat under the oak at Ophrah while Gideon was beating out the wheat. This was a process of separating the grains of wheat from the useless outer shell called chaff.

That process, also called threshing, normally was effectuated in a large area. It often occurred upon a hill where the wind could blow away the lighter chaff when the farmer tossed the beaten wheat in the air. If this fellow by the name of Gideon had worked in an open area, however, he would have been an easy target for the bands of raiders who were overrunning the land. The dust cloud from threshing the wheat would draw them to his property.

So, Gideon was forced to beat his wheat by hand in the narrow confines of a rock-cut wine press hidden in the floor of his father's house. The pit was hidden from view in order that it would not be a suspect place to find farmers' crops. Personally, Gideon was with the tribe of Manasseh, and like other Israelites, he was an agriculturist by occupation and a soldier upon occasion.

Gideon had heard about the great miracles that God had accomplished with Moses in and out of the land of Egypt as well as through Joshua upon entering the land of Canaan, but he had not seen any lately. Because of the lack of personal experience at this point, Gideon assumed that God had given up on the people of Israel, but it was actually the people who seemed to have given up on God. They knew what was expected of them but chose instead not to obey God's laws.

In the midst of this rumination by Gideon, an angel — or messenger of the Lord — said to Gideon: "The Lord is with you, you mighty warrior." Gideon quickly questioned God about the problems that he and the nation faced as well as the apparent lack of help from the Lord.

Gideon immediately was told by the Lord: "I will be with you" (Judges 6:16) and give you the strength to overcome the Midianites. Nonetheless, in spite of this clear promise of strength from God, Gideon still felt totally inadequate and began to make excuses. He wanted a sign from God. When that sign was given to him, Gideon seemingly was at peace with God and was asked to pull down the altar of the pagan god, Baal, at the center of the community.

When Gideon accomplished that mission in the midst of many other persons, the townspeople wanted to kill him. Many were Israelites, but Gideon's father, Joash, intervened with words that evidently sufficed at that moment in time. Then, the Midianites, Amelekites and people of the East crossed the River Jordan and encamped in the Valley of Jezreel, the agricultural center of the entire area.

Because of the valley's resources, many major trade routes converged at the pass that led into the area and made it the site of many great battles. The only escape route was through that pass toward the River Jordan. This seemingly was why Gideon was asked to have some of his troops take control of the river's crossing points before proceeding with an all-out battle.

Then, the spirit of the Lord reportedly took such control of Gideon that it was as though the spirit was clothed with Gideon. However, before making any further move, Gideon wanted to know for sure that he had divine approval for the coming battle. Therefore, he put out a fleece a couple of times to find out whether or not God would indeed deliver the Midianites into his hand.

The use of fleece to obtain oracles before battles may have been an accepted practice of the time. For Gideon, apparently the first oracle was inconclusive, since fleece might collect dew even if the ground appeared dry. The second oracle, in which the fleece was dry while the ground was still wet, seemed to be conclusive proof that the outcome of the battle would be favorable to Gideon.

The Lord then said to Gideon that there were too many troops for the battle against the Midianites. With so many troops, people would tend to say that any success belonged to them rather than by the hand of God. So 2,000 soldiers were sent home and 10,000 remained. That again was too many for the Lord to do battle. So, the number ended up being a shabby 300 soldiers, who had collected jars and rams' horns among the larger group of the 32,000 men from the original fighting force.

At nighttime, Gideon collected his men and gave them their unusual implements of trumpets and torches in jars. Creeping up toward the tents of the Midianites an hour or two before midnight, Gideon's soldiers on signal created sudden panic among the sleeping soldiers by blowing their rams' horns, breaking their jars, exposing their lighted torches, shouting and charging all about with swords drawn. That quickly dispersed and routed the Midianites.

Other men from Naphtali, Asher, Manasseh and the hill country then joined in the chase to complete the capture, final execution and collection of booty. When the Israelites wished to make Gideon king, however, he refused on the ground that Yahweh should rule. In later life, Gideon surrendered his leadership of the army, which disbanded, and he settled down at home.

The sons attributed to Gideon amounted to some seventy in number, which in reality may allude to Gideon's whole family. Sadly, Gideon did father a son named Abimelech through a concubine, who would bring immense grief and tragedy to both Gideon's family and the nation of Israel. Moreover, this event illustrates the fact that Gideon might have been able to lead a nation, but he was unable to lead his own family.

After Gideon's rise to power, he seemed to become carried away with an accumulation of wealth, which eventually led the Israelites into idolatry. Gideon did die at a good age and was buried in the tomb of his father, Joash, at Ophrah.

Minor Judges

According to the Biblical account in Judges 9, <u>Abimelech</u> was Gideon's son by a concubine, who wanted to take his father's place as a self-proclaimed hero and judge of Israel. Even more than that, it is implied that Abimelech would elevate himself to become the first self-declared king of Israel, because he simply was power hungry and ruthless. Furthermore, it is assumed that by asserting himself as king, Abimelech even wanted to usurp the position of Lord, which belonged to God alone.

Abimelech later went to the city of Shechem, which was his mother's hometown to drum up support, set his plan in motion and dispose of anyone who would oppose him. From this point forward there are two radically different interpretations of this text.

On the one hand, Abimelech proceeded to murder all but one of his seventy half-brothers in Ophrah, while one by the name of Jotham hid from the massacre. Later Jotham stood at the top of Mount Gerizim after Abimelech became the self-asserted ruler of Shechem and spoke to the lords of Shechem in stating what actually happened to the other brothers. Then, Jotham gave the lords of Shechem a choice between rejoicing in Abimelech or firing him. Immediately afterward, Jotham ran away for fear of Abimelech.

On the other hand, those who analyze this text from a historical perspective offer quite a different slant on these events. Abimelech's most audacious plan was to take over the Canaanite city of Shechem, which had been ruled for centuries by the dynasty of Hamor. He then maintained his headquarters in the insignificant town of Arumah. Shechem was an important city at a crossroads of important trade routes. It was a natural link between the coastal plain and the Jordan valley. Whoever controlled Shechem would dominate the countryside.

The ruling house of Hamor in Shechem was by this time so decadent that Abimelech seemed able to threaten, drive away and kill so many males that none of them dared to occupy the throne. From a historical perspective only, the seventy sons appear to be more appropriate as a description of what happened to the ruling dynasty among the sons of Hamor at Shechem.

A revolt against Abimelech in Judges 9:22-49 seems to reveal how the men of Shechem act treacherously toward Abimelech without any apparent provocation on his part. Moreover, Abimelech ambushes the insurgents, slays them and razes the city. Then, the mention of Gaal, who apparently instigated the rebellion and whose appeal to the memory of the old ruling dynasty of Hamor, suggests that he may have been the one who initially fled from Abimelech.

In any event, Abimelech did continue on his rampage by leading supposedly "worthless and reckless fellows" (Judges 9:4), defeating and killing a large number of people who had fled for refuge. When Abimelech captured Thebez and the people fled to the tower there, a woman reportedly threw a millstone on Abemelech's head, which eventually crushed him to death.

Nothing is recorded about <u>Tola</u>, the next hero, except his ancestry, home and supposed length of judgeship. He was the son of Puah, a man of Issachar, who lived in the hill country of Ephraim and was buried in Shamir.

After him came the same amount of words about <u>Jair</u>. He supposedly had thirty sons, rode on thirty donkeys and was overlord of thirty villages in the land of Gilead.

Then the Israelites were sold into the hand of the Philistines and Ammonites, and they were crushed and oppressed for a period of time. According to this portion of scripture, it all happened because the anger of the Lord was kindled. The Israelites did not worship the Lord. When the people expressed sorrow for their sinful ways and rid all that would keep them from worshiping the Lord, Yahweh apparently could not bear to see the Israelites suffer any longer.

That produced a hero and judge named <u>Jephthah</u>, a Gileadite and son of a prostitute, who was chased out of the country by his half-brothers. Not only was Jephtah a mighty warrior, but more importantly, he made a horrible mistake. In a rash moment, Jephthah committed himself to make a terrible bargain with the Lord. If God would grant him victory against the Ammonites on the east side of the River Jordan, who were at the height of their power, he would sacrifice his only child, who was a virgin daughter.

Of course, the impossible did happen. The powerful Ammonites were defeated, and the first person who came to meet upon arrival at home in triumph was his daughter. Thus, Jephthah's attempt to cheat God led to a final, sad and tragic fulfilling of his own vow, which brought him unspeakable grief. The message here is that making a deal with the Lord can bring disappointment, because God does not want future promises but obedience today. Recovering alcoholics know this measure to be true, and any human being is required to do no less.

Thereafter, things tended only to grow worse. Israel had just won a great battle, but instead of joy, there was pettiness and quarreling among them. The tribe of Ephraim grew angry and jealous that they were not invited to join in the fighting, even though Jephthah insisted that he had invited them.

Nonetheless, the insults of the Ephraimites enraged Jephthah so much that he called out the troops and killed thousands of men from Ephraim. Jephthah then died and was buried in his town of Gilead.

That led to three more rather obscure heroes or judges in Israel: Ibzon of Bethlehem, Elon the Zebulite and Abdon the Pirathonite, who were known only for what they supposedly possessed and where they were buried.

Then, there was Samson, one of the most tragic figures in Israelite and recorded history. He had so much potential. Being dedicated for life as a Nazirite, he was totally set apart for God's service. He could not cut his hair, touch a dead body or drink anything containing alcohol, but he "blew it all" in the common vernacular. Samson failed to live up to his Nazarite vow when he contacted dead bodies, ate unclean food, drank wine, allowed his hair to be cut — not to mention the times when he consorted with the enemies of Israel, the Philistines.

Gifted with almost superhuman physical strength and the first one to begin the enormous task of trying to free Israel from the oppression of the gigantic Philistines, he wasted all of his strength in retaliation, in confiding with the wrong people and in being unable to control his lust of sensuality.

Samson grew up in Zorah in the tribe of Dan and married a Philistine girl from Timnah against the wishes of his parents, who ultimately gave in to Samson's demand. Tricked at his wedding feast, Samson went to Ashkelon, killed some Philistine men and stole their coats to pay off a debt.

His anger finally having been abated, Samson took a gift and proceeded onto Timnah to visit his wife during the time of the wheat harvest. There, he discovered that her father had given his wife to another man. Samson took revenge by tying lighted torches to the tails of foxes and allowed the distraught animals to run through the fields setting fire to the grain. Samson's deed sets off a fast moving feud, in which the Philistines retaliate by killing Samson's former wife and her father. Samson returns the attack and then goes to the hills.

When the Philistines sought Samson at Lehi in the territory of Judah, the men of Lehi found Samson first and persuaded him to let them hand him over to the Philistines. When that did transpire, Samson apparently is seized by divine power, breaks the bonds and slaughters the Philistines with the jawbone of an ass, which may have been a curved sickle or scimitar resembling a jawbone. Sometimes weapons at that time were likened to objects in daily life.

After sleeping with a prostitute in Gaza and skirting the Philistines, who lay in wait for him at the city gate, Samson fell in love with a woman in the valley of Sorek — whose name was Delilah. She played a minor role in Samson's life, but her effect was devastating, because she conned him into betraying his calling from God.

Motivated by greed, Delilah used her persistence to wear down Samson. His infatuation for her made him a vulnerable target. For all of his physical strength, he was no match for her, and he paid a tremendous price in submitting to her.

Delilah was a deceitful woman with honey on her lips and poison in her heart. Cold and calculating, she merely toyed with Samson by pretending to love him while only looking for personal gain. She valued money from the Philistines rather than any real, genuine relationship. In her persistence, Samson ultimately gave away the secret of his strength to her, and Delilah sold that secret to the Philistines. Then, Samson — the mighty warrior — became a slave.

Rather than kill him, the Philistines preferred to humiliate Samson by gouging out his eyes, putting him to the tough, repetitive task of grinding grain and making a spectacle of him. More importantly, Samson's relationship with God had deteriorated to such an extent that he no longer realized that God did not fill his life anymore. At a festival for the grain and harvest god of the Philistines named Dagon, they called for blind Samson to entertain them before the pillars of their temple, symbolizing how great their pagan god, Dagon, was.

Samson in that moment reportedly turned to the one, true God, whom had been left behind for so long. He sought God's help and strength anew. As a result of Samson's prayer, he was rehabilitated to such an extent that when his hands were placed between the supporting pillars of the temple, the house fell upon all who were in it. Samson's people then carried his body away and buried him in his father's tomb between the places of Zorah and Eshtaol.

People in a Dark Period of Israel

According to the Book of Judges, Israel experienced a darkened era in their existence. Originally, this nation was created to set the example for spiritual living, but now Israel slipped into a disastrous state of moral decline. They sunk more and more into idolatry, and petty infighting emerged. Instead of serving God with love and reverence in their heart, as had occurred more often than not in their culture, selfish obedience began to take a strangle hold upon their existence. According to words recorded in Judges 17:6, "People did what was right in their own eyes," which meant that the people merely followed their own desires.

A fellow by the name of Micah, who in no way resembled a later prophet by the same name, was the first exhibit here in the Bible. Micah was a man living in the hill country of Ephraim. He gave pieces of silver to an artisan, who sculptured it into an idol for his house. This Micah displayed a pagan shrine in his own dwelling.

The fact that a young Levite left his home in Bethlehem probably meant that the money received from the people there was not enough on which to live. As a result, this Levite became a pagan priest in the house of Micah, which would illustrate the religious decline on the part of priests and Levites as well as among the people.

When five men of many hundred armed people in the Danite clan passed through the hill country of Ephraim, they took from Micah all of his pagan valuables and persuaded the Levite to come with the Danite clan to be their pagan priest instead. The Danites captured a city by the name of Laish, renamed it Dan and set up the idol for themselves. Micah pursued these Danites, who had stolen from him, but it was in vain because their forces outnumbered his.

In the Book of Judges 19, a Levite of Ephraim went to Bethlehem for his concubine. On his way home, he stayed overnight at the Benjaminite town of Gibeah where he suffered a gross indignity, which aroused his anger and supposedly the wrath in all of Israel. Sexually perverse men of the city surrounded the house, took the concubine, raped her and abused her all night long. When morning came, the concubine lay dead on the doorstep. At that point, the deceased concubine was cut into twelve pieces representing the twelve tribes of Israel and sent throughout the territory of Israel.

To be noted here is that the Levite's hostility did not in any way arise out of compassion for the abused concubine, but only from the feeling that his own dignity and property rights had been violated (Judges 19:27-29). That the body of the concubine was cut into twelve pieces and spread throughout Israel only implies that the tribes of Israel must come to help the Levite in taking revenge, all of which seems to be another strong sign of the moral degeneration in Israel.

In the Book of Judges 20, the Benjaminites stand solidly behind the sexual offenders of Gibeah in defense against the incoming tide of soldiers throughout Israel. According to the scripture, the men of Israel are defeated twice, but when they perform acts of penitence (Judges 20:23-26), they are promised victory in the next battle, which accordingly does take place. Lured from the city in a clever maneuver, the Benjaminites and more plausibly — the Gibeahites — see their city go up in smoke. They are cut off and mostly slain.

In chapter 21 of the Book of Judges, an account is produced for rehabilitation and regeneration among the tribe of Benjamin. After the loss of so many Benjaminites, the surviving males either gain virgin brides among the Gadites in the Transjordan territory or choose partners from among the girls dancing at the annual vintage festival at Shiloh. Shiloh at that time is the center of all religious and social activity in Israel — not Jerusalem.

During this same period, the Biblical account of an entirely different encounter among people is highlighted. It primarily involves two remarkable women who display an incredible relationship and become an outstanding model for people throughout all time. In a degenerate era, this example resoundingly illustrates how people can make it through seemingly impossible situations with love in their heart for one another and the one, true God whom they serve.

The two featured names here are Ruth and Naomi, a loyal and lovely wife from a different country and a beloved mother-in-law respectively. It is a song for sore hearts among two wonderful people who live beautifully together for a lifetime and produce an outstanding legacy of people who are revered for generations upon generations to come.

The event begins and concludes in Bethlehem of Judea, as a fascinating journey unfolds before those who are glued to the Biblical record. Evidently, there was a famine in Israel at the time when Judges ruled the land. A man named Elimelech, his wife Naomi and two sons Mahlon and Chilion migrated into the country of Moab, which was Gentile territory.

Elimelech died leaving Naomi with two sons, who were married to girls of Moab named Orpah and Ruth. When Naomi's two sons died, she was left as a poor widow, who was bereft of money, resources, her own family, descendants and a future, according to the law and customs of the time. However, her Canaanite daughters-in-law, Orpah and Ruth, loved Naomi deeply.

Amidst this terrible situation in foreign and hostile territory, Naomi decided upon returning to Bethlehem. She lovingly entreats her daughters-in-law to find a good home in their own land with other husbands. Moreover, Naomi magnanimously prayed to the one, true God — Yahweh — to deal kindly with Orpah and Ruth and to bless them immensely in a wonderful life among their own people with their own gods.

Orpah most graciously accepted Naomi's good will and reached out to her mother-in-law and sister-in-law with tears in her eyes and unfathomed love in her heart. Then, she sadly, but gratefully, parted from them along the way.

Ruth, however, took an unprecedented course of action and leap of faith, which most inspiringly is revealed in scripture and revered forever among people everywhere. In words later put to music, Ruth poetically and magnificently proclaimed to Naomi:

> Entreat me not to leave you or turn back from following you! Where you go, I will go; where you lodge, I will lodge. Your people shall be my people and your God my God. Where you die, I will also, and I will be buried beside you. May the Lord grant this to do thusly with me — and more as well.
> — Ruth 1:16-17

So, the two of them, now poor, childless and destitute widows, of which there was nothing worse in the ancient world, journeyed together to Bethlehem and settled there. Ruth, however, did not in any way sit motionless upon arrival. She immediately went to work in the fields of Boaz during that spring barley harvest season.

Boaz was a distant relative of Naomi's late husband, Elimelech, who was a descendant of Rahab the harlot in

Jericho during the time of Joshua. Most importantly, Boaz showed himself to be an honest man of integrity and high moral standards, who followed through on all of his commitments. Then, quite unusually and most admirably, Boaz greeted reapers in the field each day with the words: "The Lord be with you" (Ruth 2:4).

Ruth prodigiously proceeded to glean the field behind the reapers, which was not an easy task or at all rewarding. Boaz took notice. He asked the reapers to welcome her directly behind the reapers, in order that she could pick up the choicest dropped grain.

Reapers were hired to cut down the stalks and tie them into bundles. Israelite law then demanded that any grain, which was dropped, should be left for poor people. They were allowed to pick it up, meaning to glean it, and to be used by them. The purpose of this law was to feed the poor and prevent the owners from hoarding it. Boaz went far beyond the intent of the gleaners' law in demonstrating kindness and generosity by not only letting Ruth glean in his field, but also by telling his workers to let some of the grain purposely fall upon her path.

After a full day of hard work, Boaz invited Ruth to sit beside the reapers at mealtime — to eat well and was welcomed to take home that which was left over. Afterward, Boaz further instructed the reapers to let Ruth glean even among the standing sheaves and to pull out handfuls from the bundles for her to glean.

When Ruth arrived at home with more than enough barley, she explained all that had happened and cited the name of Boaz, who was so kind and helpful to her. At that, Naomi eventually asked Ruth to stay close to kinsman, Boaz, especially at the threshing floor during the harvest festival. Ruth did, and Boaz apparently appreciated it. In fact, Boaz protected Ruth from the drunken men in the midnight revelry. At the suggestion of Naomi, Ruth ultimately shared the fact that she would be willing to marry Boaz and fulfill the ongoing legacy of her deceased husband and Naomi's son, Mahlon, which the next of kin needed to fulfill, according to the customary law.

Willing as Boaz was to accept this responsibility, he could not accomplish it until the immediate next of kin would relinquish his willingness to be the person. That soon transpired in the presence of ten elders at the gate of the city of Bethlehem, and the so-named legal "right of redemption" was transferred to Boaz.

Thereafter, Boaz acquired the land belonging to Elimelech, Naomi's deceased husband, as an inheritance for them. Ruth and Boaz were married, and they had a son named Obed, which meant that the names of Elimelech and Mahlon, Naomi's husband and son — and Ruth's husband, literally had been "redeemed," according to the law of Israel. Most important of all to the Israelites and to the whole world, Obed became the father of Jesse, and Jesse was the father of David, who proved to be the ancestor of Jesus of Nazareth.

King Saul

Following the judges and the dark period in Israel, the people at first wanted and then demanded a king. They pleaded with Samuel, the last judge and very early foreshadowing of the prophets, to give them a king (1 Samuel 8:1-20).

A shaky dialogue ensued between the people, Samuel and the Lord. Samuel did not wish to have a king. The people of Israel insisted all the more for one. God apparently mediated the situation by allowing a king to exist in their midst.

The reason that the people desired a king was simply because everyone else had one, which sounds even today like a teenager in the midst of growing pains. Also, they could see that the judges, who brought on a darkened period in their history, were not working out at all. Why not try what others already were doing? Who knows, the Israelites thought, it might be better for us too!

Samuel immediately surmised that a king would make subjects out of the people in Israel, which really could not be beneficial to them, but those words fell upon deaf ears among the people. Samuel expressed all of these thoughts before the one, true God, and the Lord stated to Samuel: "Listen to the voice of the people of Israel and set a king over them" (1 Samuel 8:21-22).

A person by the name of Saul was found and ultimately was anointed king in Israel. Apparently, Saul was an extremely handsome young man who stood head and shoulders above everyone else. He was the son of Kish, who was a Benjaminite and a very wealthy man. Abner, the brother of Kish and uncle to Saul, commanded Saul's army. Saul grew up as a farmer and married Abinoam. They had sons: Jonathan, Ishui, Malachishua and Methibosheth, and two daughters: Merab and Michal.

When Saul learned that he was being anointed king over all of Israel, he became humbled. Saul responded: "I am only a Benjaminite from the least of the tribes in Israel, and my family is the least in the tribe of Benjamin" (1 Samuel 9:21). After Saul was elevated ruler and king over God's people, Israel (1 Samuel 10:1), he proceeded to lead the people toward the spirit of the Lord who possessed him totally.

God definitely embraced Saul for a while. Strong leadership, bravery and generosity marked his early reign over the Philistines and Amelekites in battle. Then, Saul reportedly turned away from God, and Saul became jealous and paranoid. He tended to overstep his bounds. His kingship was removed from him (1 Samuel 16), and Saul's life moved steadily downward.

Obsessed with killing his successor (1 Samuel 20), Saul consulted a medium (1 Samuel 28) and finally committed suicide (1 Samuel 31). In the process of Saul's rule, Israel did move from a theocracy to a monarchy but not in a secular or pagan sense. Yahweh still was at the heart and soul of Israel and the one in charge above all else.

King David

During the period of the first three kings in Israel, David probably emerged as the greatest one, and as such, his legacy continues in this same vein among many people to this very day. Born in the tribe of Judah at Bethlehem around 1040 BC, David was the youngest of eight sons in the family of his father, Jesse.

While Saul still was the anointed king of Israel, but reportedly had faded from favor of both Samuel and the Lord, Samuel was invited by Yahweh to go to the house of Jesse in Bethlehem and anoint one of the chosen ones by God as the next king. Seven of Jesse's sons passed by Samuel, each of which Samuel thought would be the chosen one, but they were not acceptable in the eyes of the Lord.

Why? According to the Bible, "The Lord does not see as mortals see. People look on the outward appearance, but the Lord looks on the heart" (1 Samuel 16:5). So, Samuel said to Jesse: "The Lord has not chosen any of these seven sons. Are all of your sons here?" Jesse responded: "The youngest one remains, but he is keeping the sheep." Samuel insisted: "Bring him in!"

David was escorted in. The Lord stated: "This is the one," and David was anointed as the next king. Thereafter, David was sent into Saul's court to play the lyre and make King Saul, who now had become a tormented soul, feel better. Evidently, Saul loved David, and Saul persuaded Jesse to have David remain in the king's service.

When Saul went up against the Philistines, their giant of a leader, Goliath, was dressed in armor so weighty and strong that he called out for anyone to challenge him to a fight. Whoever was victorious would prove that their deity would be superior.

The young boy, David, accepted the challenge on behalf of the Israelites' one, true God, while by his many gods — Goliath disdained such a young, unarmed boy in front of him. Goliath cursed the one, true God named Yahweh, whom David worshiped. Nonetheless, the ruddy, handsome, youthful David slew Goliath with a smooth stone in his sling shot that sunk deep into the middle of the forehead. Goliath fell upon the ground — face down. Following that, David killed Goliath with Goliath's own sword, and all of the Philistines fled. The Israelites pursued and destroyed them.

When David returned to Saul and spoke to the king about what had transpired in the presence of Saul's son, Jonathan, two things happened. First, Jonathan became so closely knit to David that henceforth David and Jonathan grew to be inseparable in mind, heart and spirit with each other. Also, David was elevated to the position over the whole army of Israel, and he was successful wherever he went.

From that point forward, however, Saul grew more and more angry. He became extremely jealous of David and plotted to destroy him — even while he gave his daughter, Michal, who loved David at that point, in marriage. Furthermore, Saul only spoke ill of David to Jonathan, who defended David to the hilt. Saul even tried to pin David to the wall but missed in throwing his weapon. With the help of others, David managed to escape with his life.

Saul continued his rampage against David and killed anyone who stood in the way of his purpose. On one occasion in Saul's pursuit of David with his men, Saul stopped to rest at a cave. Those who were with David said that this was the opportunity of a lifetime to dispose of Saul, but David would have nothing to do with that thought, because Saul was anointed of the Lord.

Saul went on his way untouched. However, David followed after Saul, bowed before him, explained what could have transpired, but did not, because he was the Lord's anointed. At that, Saul reportedly wept and exclaimed: "Who has ever found an enemy and sent the enemy safely away? Now I know that you surely shall be king" (1 Samuel 24:19-20). Afterward, each went their separate ways.

David was confronted with a most mean-spirited man of Carmel named Nebal, but his wife, Abigail, interceded in that horrible situation with food and appeasement to all of David's people. This reversed David's whole state of mind and averted warfare, which seemingly was most appreciated.

On the morning after her husband's drunken party, Abigail told Nabal what she had done and how the Lord's spirit was involved in her meeting with David's people. "Nabal's heart died within him. He became like stone," and "about ten days later, Nabal was dead" (1 Samuel 24:37-38).

Looking upon this whole incident as a sign of God's favor, David wooed Abigail and made her his wife. In addition, David married Ahinoam of Jezreel. In the meantime, Saul's daughter, Michal, was retrieved by Saul and given to another man. Thus, Saul's warfare against David was resumed.

Saul pursued David into the wilderness of Ziph. When David found Saul asleep with his army at their encampment, David's men envisioned it as another opportunity to thrust the spear into Saul and take life from him. Again, David would have nothing to do with this sort of thing because Saul was the Lord's anointed.

Once more, conversation ensued between David and Saul, which resulted in reconciliation. Saul promised never to harm David, but by now, David did not trust Saul's words at all. Instead, David escaped to the land of the Philistines where Saul could not reach him. Then, David and his 600 men served King Achish of Gath. They made raids upon the

Geshurites, Girzites and Amalekites and were successful each time.

King Achish made David his bodyguard when the Philistines proceeded against the Israelites. Saul saw the army of the Philistines, and he was afraid. He called upon the Lord, but the Lord neither answered Saul in dreams, nor by prophets. So, Saul disguised himself and went to a medium.

At the request of Saul, the Spirit of the dead Samuel was called up. Samuel told Saul that the Lord had done just what was reported to him previously. This apparition of Samuel seemingly reiterated: "The Lord has torn the kingdom out of your hand and given it to David" (1 Samuel 28:17).

> Moreover, the Lord will give Israel along with you into the hands of the Philistines, and tomorrow you and your sons will be with me. The Lord also will give the army of Israel into the hands of the Philistines. — 1 Samuel 23:19

At that, Saul fell to the ground. There was no strength left in him. He ate nothing all day and night. Finally, a woman killed the fatted calf for a feast. She took flour, kneaded it and baked unleavened cakes. She put them before Saul and his servants. They ate and went on their way.

The Philistines gathered all of their forces against the Israelites, who were encamped at Jezreel. This included David and his men passing in the rear with King Achish. Commanders of the Philistine army questioned David's presence with them and were angry. King Achish, however, defended David as having found no fault with him, but the leaders of the Philistine militia prevailed.

Therefore, David returned home to Ziglag, but the Amalekites had burned it to the ground. Everyone and everything had been taken captive including David's two wives. The men with David were bitter and ready to stone David. So, David inquired of the Lord, who told him to go after the

Amalekites. The raid was successful. All of the people and possessions, which the Amalekites had taken, were recovered.

The Philistines fought the Israelites and overcame them, which included Saul and his sons. Having been badly wounded by them, Saul asked his armor-bearer to finish him off, rather than to have the uncircumcised Philistines do it. The armor-bearer refused. So, Saul fell upon his own sword and killed himself.

Upon Saul's death, Abner, the commander of Saul's army, made Ishbaal, son of Saul, king over five tribes for two years. The house of Judah followed David. He was king over them for more than seven years. David defeated Abner's men with the tribe of Benjamin and was made king over them.

Realizing that Saul's family was doomed to defeat and David would be the next king, Abner eventually told David that he would deliver Saul's army into his hands if he could become the Chief Commander of the army.

David accepted the offer and became king over all of the twelve tribes in Israel. They were united under King David, but the way was not easy. Jealousy continued among many factions of the people. For example, Joab murdered Abner and took the position of Chief Commander of the army. Others killed Ishbaal. Because of this slaying, David had the men, who were responsible for Ishbaal's slaughter, put to death.

Nonetheless, through strength and negotiation, people finally came together under King David. They reportedly numbered some 30,000 people. Thereafter, heads of the twelve tribes journeyed to Hebron and anointed David as King over Israel. He reigned for a total of 40 years — 7 years over Judah, and 33 years over Judah and Israel.

In the process, Michal, the daughter of Saul, was given back to David. He had many wives by this time, some six in number. He had children by all of them except Michal. Saul had one remaining son, Mephibosheth, who was lame at a young age from a terrible fall. David accepted him into his own house and cared for him throughout the rest of his life.

David's first act as king of the Israelites involved marching to Jerusalem against the Jebusites. He and the army took the stronghold of Zion, which thereafter was labeled the city of David. From that moment onward, David became greater and greater. It was perceived that the Lord, the God of hosts, was with him. Not only was David victorious in all of his efforts, but also he was known to have administered justice and equity to all of the people.

King Hiram of Tyre sent messengers along with cedar trees to David at Jerusalem. His carpenters and masons erected a house for David. It was at this point that David realized the Lord actually had established him as king and his kingdom for the sake of God's people.

In addition, when David moved from Hebron to Jerusalem, he took more concubines and wives. Thus, he had more sons and daughters. Then, David brought the ark of God to Jerusalem. He led the procession. Everyone danced before the Lord with all of their might — with songs, lyres, harps, tambourines, castanets and cymbals.

As the ark of the Lord came into Jerusalem, Michal, the daughter of Saul, looked out her window. She saw King David leaping and dancing before the Lord and despised him in her heart. After the ark had been set aside — the tent, which had been pitched for it, was placed over it. Then, David returned to bless his household, but Michal greeted him in disgust. She confronted David with how vulgar he appeared before everyone, but David insisted that it was appropriate to honor the Lord in this way, an argument which still exists among God's people today.

During this period of relative peace, King David talked to the prophet Nathan about a better place, other than a tent, for the ark of the Lord. The answer was that this would take place later from an offspring who would be his successor as king. Then, Nathan expressed what has been claimed as direct words of God's eternal promise to King David: "Your house and your kingdom shall be made sure forever before me; your throne shall be established forever" (2 Samuel 7:16).

After winning on the battlefield against every enemy, David ultimately was confronted with the greatest conflict of his life. It was the formidable enemy within himself, as recorded in 2 Samuel 11-12. It becomes one of the most powerful descriptions in the life of any person throughout all time.

In the spring of the year at the time reportedly when kings usually go out to battle, David sent Joab and his officers as well as all of Israel with him. They ravaged the Ammonites and besieged Rabbah, but David remained in Jerusalem.

Late one afternoon, when David rose from his couch and was walking about on the roof of the king's house, he saw a woman bathing, and the woman was very beautiful. David sent someone to inquire about the woman. It was reported: "This is Bathsheba, daughter of Eliam, the wife of Uriah the Hittite." So, David sent messengers to get her. She came to him, and he lay with her. Then she returned to her house.

The woman conceived and told David that she was pregnant. David sent word to Joab, "Send me Uriah the Hittite." When Uriah came to him, David asked how the soldiers fared and how the war was going. David told Uriah to go to his house, clean up and refresh himself. Uriah left the king's house but did not go to his house. Instead, he slept at the entrance way with the servants of Joab.

When David was told what happened, David spoke to Uriah saying, "You just have come from a strong journey. Why did you not go down to your house?" Uriah said to David: "The ark, Israel and Judah remain in booths. Joab and his servants are camping in the open field. Should I, then, go

109

to my house to eat, drink and lie with my wife? As you live, I will not do such a thing." David told Uriah to remain at his place for another day, and he would send him back the next day, which did transpire.

In the morning, however, David wrote a letter to Joab and sent it by the hand of Uriah. In the letter, he wrote: "Set Uriah in the forefront of the hardest fighting, and then draw back from him, so that he may be struck down and die." As Joab was besieging the city, he assigned Uriah to the place where he knew there were valiant warriors. The men of the city came out and fought with Joab as well, and some of the servants of David among the people fell. Uriah the Hittite was killed also.

Joab sent news to David about it all. When the messenger finished telling David about the fighting, he concluded with the words: "Your servant Uriah the Hittite is dead too." When Bathsheba, the wife of Uriah, heard that her husband was dead, she made lamentation for him, but when the mourning was over, David sent for Bathsheba and brought her into his house. Then, Bathsheba became his wife.

However, the thing that David had done, according to the scripture, displeased the Lord, and the Lord sent Nathan to David. Upon arriving before David, Nathan brilliantly related the following speech to David, as recorded in 2 Samuel 12:1-13.

There were two men in a certain city, the one rich and the other poor. The rich man had very many flocks and herds; but the poor man had nothing but one little ewe lamb, which he had bought. He brought it up, and it grew up with him and with his children. It used to eat of his meager fare, drink from his cup and lie in his bosom. It was like a daughter to him. Now, there came a traveler to the rich man, and he was loath to take one from his own flock or herd to prepare for the wayfarer. Instead, he took the poor man's lamb and prepared that for the guest.

David's anger was greatly kindled against the man. He exclaimed to Nathan: "As the Lord lives, the man who has done this deserves to die. He shall restore the lamb fourfold, because he did this thing and had no pity." Nathan exclaimed to David: "You are the man!"

Thus says the Lord, the God of Israel:

I appointed you king over Israel, and I rescued you from the hand of Saul. I gave you your master's house and your master's wives. I gave you the house of Israel and Judah, and if that had been too little, I would have added much more. Why have you despised the work of the Lord to do what is evil in his sight? You have struck down Uriah the Hittite with the sword, have taken his wife to be your wife and have killed him with the sword of the Ammonites.

Now, the sword shall never depart from your house, for you have despised me and have taken the wife of Uriah the Hittite to be your wife. Therefore, I will raise trouble against you from within your own house. I will take your wives before your eyes and give them to your neighbor, and he shall lie with your wives in the sight of the noonday sun. For you did it secretly, but I will do this thing before all Israel in broad daylight.

David sincerely, sorrowfully and most movingly said to Nathan: "I have sinned against the Lord." Nathan profoundly stated: "Now, the Lord has put away your sin; you shall not die!"

Afterward, the child of David and Bathsheba became very ill. David pleaded with God for the child and fasted, but the child died. David arose, washed, changed his clothes and went into the house of the Lord and worshiped. Then, David had food set before him, and he ate.

When confronted by his servants about this sudden change in behavior, David replied:

While the child was still alive, I fasted and wept, for I said "Who knows? The Lord may be gracious to me, and the child

may live. Now he is dead: Why should I fast? Can I bring him
back?"   — Samuel 12:20-23

David consoled his wife, Bathsheba. Eventually, she bore another son, who was named Solomon, but from that point onward, the turmoil within David's family began to escalate as had been predicted. David's first son, Amnon, committed incest with his half-sister, Tamar, via the assistance of David's brother. When David heard of it, he grew very angry but refused to take any disciplinary action with his son.

Then, David's son, Absalom, after two years of hiding from his father, three years being near him without being able to see him and finally receiving loving acceptance from him — plotted to overthrow King David. By glad-handing people at the gate of Jerusalem, saying that he could do a better job than David and conspiring to make himself king of Hebron, he was able to gather enough forces to come against his father in Jerusalem.

When David learned of it, he decided to leave Jerusalem. The manner in which he did it must have been very sad and at the same time marvelous to behold. King David led the exodus. He stopped at the last house in Jerusalem, set down the ark of God and all the people passed by him.

As the Levites picked up the ark to carry it forward, King David said to Zadok, the priest: "Carry the ark of God back into the city. If I find favor in the eyes of the Lord, he will bring me back" (2 Samuel 15:25-36). David went up the ascent of the Mount of Olives, weeping as he went. All the people who were with him did the same. Then, they proceeded downward to the Jordan Valley and crossed the River Jordan.

When Absalom reached unoccupied Jerusalem, he decided to pursue David with his troops. A battle between the forces of Absalom and those of David ensued in the forest

112

of Ephraim. However, David's men thought that at his age it would be better not to let David accompany them.

Absalom rode into the forest on a mule, and the mule went under the thick branches of a great oak. Absalom's head was caught fast in the oak, and he was left hanging there while the mule went on. When Joab, commander of David's army, heard it, he procured three spears and killed the injured Absalom. When David received the news, he wept, and the troops joined him in grief.

David's problems with his family and the nation of Israel began with covetousness, adultery, murder, lying and an attempted cover up. His sin was forgiven before God and the people. The guilt was removed, but David still had to bear the painful consequences of his behavior for the rest of his life.

After the death of Absalom, there was a movement to return King David to Jerusalem, which did take place. On the way, a man named Shimei, who cursed David upon leaving Jerusalem, publicly admitted that he was wrong, and David spared him from the hand of one of his men. Thereafter, all other enemies were subdued. Then, a census was taken, for which David repented, and a sacrifice was offered to the Lord, which averted a plague in Israel.

As King David grew advanced in years, he could not stay warm. The time to die seemed imminent. His son Adonijah, who was next in age to Absalom, pronounced that he would be the king's successor (1 Kings 1:5). King David offered no objection to it. However, David's men did not side with Adonijah. One of them went to Bathsheba. He asked her to go unto David and remind him of his promise that Solomon would be his successor.

As a result of that encounter, King David renewed his vow before God and those around him that Solomon would succeed David as king (1 Kings 1:30). As the time of death drew near, David charged his son, Solomon: "Be strong; be courageous and keep the charge of the Lord your God" (1 Kings 2:2-3). Thereafter, David died at perhaps some seventy years of age, and he was buried in the city of David.

King Solomon

When David declared Solomon as the king to succeed him, he ordered Zadok the priest and the prophet Nathan to anoint him as ruler over all of Israel at the Gihon Spring just a few yards east of Jerusalem, the city of David. It was fulfilled as pronounced by King David. It transpired in a festive procession upon David's own mule with the sound of pipes, trumpets and rejoicing people, while everyone joyously exclaimed: "Long live King Solomon" (1 Kings 1:39).

After the removal of opposing people from high levels of office and making a marriage alliance with Pharaoh's daughter from Egypt, Solomon proceeded to Gibeon. He offered many offerings on the altar there. On a night when he was there, the Lord reportedly appeared to Solomon in a dream with the words: "Ask what I should give you."

Solomon apparently said to the Lord:

> You have shown great and steadfast love to your servant, my father, David. Even though I am but a young one and do not know how to go out or come in, you have made me your servant king in the place of my father, David. Therefore, give me an understanding heart to discern what is right in governing your great people — so numerous that they cannot be numbered or counted.　　　　　　　　　　　　— 1 Kings 3:6-9

When given the choice of gifts from God, Solomon humbly asks for wisdom, by which his reign begins with tremendous success including the construction of the temple — his greatest achievement. In building the temple, preparations had to be made. Wood must be imported from Lebanon. Solomon's laborers are skilled in stone and not in timber. However, King Hiram of Lebanon has craftsmen from Gebal, known as Biblos today. Therefore, Solomon's men in conjunction with Hiram's people construct the temple in Jerusalem.

When the building operations are finally completed, Solomon's treasury is empty. In order to refill it, Solomon finds it necessary to sell twenty cities in Galilee to Hiram for a huge amount of gold. Since gold is a soft metal, it would be useless in warfare. Thus, Solomon added the gold to beautify the edifice and enhance the glory of the whole area.

With Minas of gold on decorative shields, a great ivory throne overlaid with the finest gold, drinking vessels and every other vessel made of pure gold, nothing like it ever had been made in any kingdom. In addition, people throughout the region brought objects of silver, gold, as well as garments, weaponry, spices, horses and mules. Furthermore, Solomon gathered together an amazing number of chariots and horses. Thus, King Solomon reportedly excelled all kings at that time in riches and wisdom (1 Kings 10:14-26).

It could be a good thing for the Israelites to have riches and wisdom, but that is far from the real purpose for the people of God. According to the Bible, the highest goal in human life is to obey God.

As a result, life soon began to unravel during the reign of Solomon. The Lord grew increasingly upset and warned Solomon about it. This downward trend started, according to scripture, when Solomon took on many heathen wives to solidify foreign agreements (1 Kings 11:1-4). In fact, Solomon accumulated hundreds of wives. These foreign spouses had their own gods, which they brought with them. Moreover, Solomon provided for the cult of these gods and began to lean in this direction himself.

Solomon no longer followed the one, true God, named Yahweh, as his father David did all of his life. Solomon's heart was turning away from God. He began following

Astarte, the goddess of the Sidonians; Milcoln of the Ammonites and the gods of the foreign women whom he loved.

This led the hearts of the Israelites to become cold toward God's covenant with them on Mount Sinai. This led to the ruin of families, the government and eventual destruction of the nation. Moreover, the people took on the bad qualities of the false gods that were worshiped. They grew more cruel, power hungry and sexually perverse.

Solomon tended to work and tax his people excessively, which alienated him from his own people. However, those from distant lands journeyed from afar to admire him and his accomplishments. Following that, adversaries began to revolt against Solomon. For example, Edom was conquered by David, but a young Edomite prince, Hadad, fled toward the desert of Midian. Eventually, Hadad intermarried with Pharaoh's house, returned to Edom upon hearing the deaths of David and Joab and revolted against Solomon.

Also, King David thoroughly defeated Syria, but a man named Rezon escaped and became a bandit thief when the weaker King Solomon ascended the throne. As a result, Rezon was able to establish an independent state at Damascus, which remained an opponent of Israel for a long time.

Then, Jerobaum, an Ephraimite from Zeredah, was given the supervision of forced labor in Ephraim, the house of Joseph. From his rebellion against Solomon, he was forced to flee into Egypt where he remained until the death of Solomon. At that time, Jerobaum returned to rule the northern kingdom of Israel.

After many decades of reigning over the twelve tribes of Israel, a dejected Solomon died and was buried in Jerusalem, the city of his father, David.

Kings in a Divided Nation
Following King Solomon's death, his son, Rehoboam, who was born from one of the foreign wives of Solomon —

an Ammonite, proceeded to Shechem for the purpose of being crowned the king. Upon arrival at Shechem, Rehoboam met before the assembly of Israelites including Jerobaum, who had returned from Egypt after escaping from the rebellion that he led against Solomon.

Rehoboam was greeted by these words from the assembly of Israel: "Your father, Solomon, made our yoke very heavy. Now, therefore, lighten the hard service of your father upon us, and we will serve you." Rehoboam responded: "Go away for three days, and then come again to me."

In the meantime, Rehoboam sought counsel from two groups of people — older men who had attended Solomon and the younger men who had grown up with Rehoboam and attended him now. The older men advised Rehoboam: "If you will be a servant to these people and speak good words to them, they will be your servants forever."

His buddies, the younger men, thought rashly and told Rehoboam to become more forceful with his words and demeanor, which he accepted. As a result, when Rehoboam met with the assembly three days later, he stated to all of them: "My father made your yoke heavy, but I will add to your yoke; my father disciplined you with whips, but I will discipline you with scorpions" (1 Kings 12:1-14).

When all of Israel saw that Rehoboam would not listen to them, ten of the twelve tribes walked away and separated themselves from the other two tribes, Judah and Benjamin. Benjamin soon merged into one with Judah. From that point forward, two kingdoms existed: One to the north henceforth called Israel, and one to the south named Judah. Jerobaum reigned as king of Israel, while Rehobaum was king of Judah that would be called the Jewish people.

Jerobaum approached Jerusalem to fight the people of Judah and to restore all twelve tribes of Israel, but a man of God named Shemiah expressed words to Rehoboam: "Thus says the Lord: You shall not go up or fight against other people of Israel. Let everyone go home" (1 Kings 12:24), which evidently transpired on both sides.

From that point onward, there were two kingdoms among the Hebrew people until each was carried away into captivity. The northern kingdom of Israel was captured and then taken to Assyria by Shalmaneser. The southern kingdom of Judah was carried off into captivity in Babylon by Nebuchadnezzer. During the interim before captivity and afterward, a formidable rise of prophets occurred that produced further pronouncements from God to the people.

CHAPTER 7

PROPHETS OF ISRAEL AND JUDAH

When the monarchy under Saul arrived upon the scene, the charismatic leadership of the tribal confederacy, as described in the Book of Judges, gave way to the new office of prophet. The prediction and best description of being a prophet is found in Deuteronomy 18:8, "I the Lord God will raise up for the people and among the people — a prophet, and I will put my words in his mouth, and he shall speak to them all that I command."

Thus, the prophet was called directly by God to proclaim the divine word to Israel. Prophets in the land that was promised by God to the Patriarchs of Abraham, Isaac and Jacob were unique people, according to the Bible. They literally were one of a kind.

In fact, the prophetic movement is the most astounding phenomenon in the history of Israel and has no parallel anywhere else in human history. Nowhere in the world has there ever been such a succession of extraordinary personalities whose message was both relevant to the needs of the moment as well as possessing exceptional value for human beings throughout the ages.

What is special about these prophets in contradistinction to all other religious communities who may even upon occasion use the same name? In simple language, what is the difference between a true prophet and a false one? For one thing, the prophets of Israel and Judah are not at all like the seers and diviners of the pagan cultures with their heathen practices of sorcery, divination and necromancy.

Furthermore, these prophets were not bound by ancient traditions, cultic patterns, hereditary ties or royal appointment. Also, they were not limited merely by self-induced ecstatic experiences or hypnotic suggestion. Instead, the prophet was called by the one, true God to proclaim the divine word to the people. The immediacy and directness of the relationship by which the prophet received this divine communication produces a mission often contrary to the cultural thinking of the people and the propensity of their leaders.

Jeremiah best describes this phenomenon: "If I say, 'I will not mention God, or speak any more in God's name,' there is in my heart, as it were, a burning fire shut up in my bones, and I am weary with holding it in, and I cannot" (Jeremiah 20:9).

Moreover, the immediacy of the relationship, by which the prophet received the divine communication in giving it to the people is graphically described in 1 Kings 22:13-18. Yahweh presides over the heavenly council of the heavenly host standing beside the Lord. The prophet shares in this higher fellowship as an earthly representative. He hears what goes on, is appointed the messenger of the verdict and expounds it to the people.

Therefore, the prophet chiefly was a representative of the heavenly court. He was divinely appointed to proclaim the living word of God directly to God's people. The prophet's life was completely directed and dominated by the one, true God of heaven and earth. As a spokesman purely for God to the covenant community, he advised kings and exhorted the nation to obey the laws and do what God commands in accordance with God's will.

It clearly is summed up in Amos 3:7, "Surely the Lord God does nothing without revealing the message to God's servants — the Prophets."

The time of such prophecy occurred from approximately 1020 BC to 350 BC and peaked prior to the exile and right afterward. Distinguishing marks of the prophets included their call directly from God as well as their teachings involving God, the Word, Ethics and the Ultimate Victory.

"The call" was the basic, fundamental experience in the prophet's life. It gave legitimacy to his office, authority to his message and urgency to his preaching. Also, the call was the distinguishing mark between the true and the false prophet. The call for the prophet was the valid expression of God's will for his life, the certain assurance that God had reached down to take hold of him and make him acutely aware of his mission. When false prophets so often opposed the divinely appointed messenger, it seemed valid proof enough that their words were not from Yahweh (Jeremiah 14:14; 23:21-22; 28:15).

The call of the prophet was not a mystical experience but a convulsive moment that changed the prophet's whole life. By this unique, divine intervention, the prophet was set apart from other people and brought into a special relationship with God. It was for the purpose of serving as an intermediary of the divine word to the nation and the world.

That call, the circumstance and the mission varied from person to person. In no way did this lessen the validity of the call. In fact, it only seemed to strengthen it. Therefore, this unique experience of the call was the impelling force in the life of the prophet, giving urgency to the message and confident assurance in the face of hostile opposition.

In addition, the basic characteristic of prophecy in the Bible was the centrality of God. For the prophet, the one, true God was everywhere — in his life, in his message and in history. Because of his faith, the prophet saw the reality of God in all that happened. Catastrophes were punishments; deliverance transpired because of God's love for the people. Therefore, the historical event manifested God's presence for judgment or salvation.

The message of the prophet is the living word of God and distinguishes the prophet from the priest and the wise person. Teaching, instruction or sacrifice on behalf of the people to deity belongs to the priest; counsel to the wise one, but the word of God belongs exclusively to the prophet. This divine word, which the prophet proclaimed, was active and powerful. It was creating and destroying, comforting and disquieting. The success of this word, as communicated by the prophet, is assured by no one except God.

Ethics for the prophet is rooted and grounded in God, who is the defender of what is right and good. The prophets were the first to preach morality, which is above cultic purity. Their pleas for mercy and charity to the poor and the oppressed, as well as their strong condemnation of the greedy oppressor and religious hypocrite, are well known. Therefore, according to the prophets, the one, true God named Yahweh is holy, just and righteous and demands that people be holy, just and righteous too.

Last but not least, the prophets speak about the ultimate victory. They are convinced the climax of history is in the future when God would destroy evil and usher in the age of bliss. This will be manifest in several ways: 1) The "day of the Lord" when people will be judged for their sins (Amos 5:18; Joel; Zephaniah; 2) a "remnant" shall return, be saved and form a new community (Isaiah 6:13; 7:3; 8:16; 10:20-23; 28:5; 37:32); 3) a Davidic leader, who is the Messiah (Isaiah 9:6-7,11:1-5; Micah 5:2-4; Jeremiah 23:5, 33:14-18; Ezekiel 34:23-24; Zechariah 9:9-10); the "son of man," an apocalyptic figure, coming with the clouds of heaven (Daniel 7:13-14, 18).

Finally, a completely different figure is portrayed in the "suffering servant," who brings true faith throughout the earth and instructs all people in God's way. Unlike any other figure, this one accomplishes God's mission through suffering and dying for others that they may be justified (Isaiah 50:6; 52:13—53-12; Zechariah 12:10; 13:1).

All of these figures, each in their own way, are linked to a coming time when human hearts will be changed forever and brought into God's will, peace and righteousness, which will cover the earth as waters cover the sea. These thoughts lead to a biographical sketch of how these prophets were manifest in their own way during this remarkable period of history.

Former Prophets

Moses is the archetype and ideal of the prophets. He set the tone and propelled the message of God through the reported voice of Aaron to the people at that first, most critical juncture in the history of Israel. His relationship with God and the people was direct, fiery and forthright. He remained close to God throughout a tumultuous time for the Israelites and stayed true to his prophetic call and mission throughout his days. It was not because he wanted or chose to do it, but because God had chosen him. He was to lead the way for an overwhelming number of people on their journey out of Egypt to the Promised Land.

Next, there arose what was known as a band of prophets — first recorded in the Bible at the time of King Saul (1 Samuel 10:5-10; 19:20). These bands of prophets apparently had the prophetic gift. They lived together in communities of spiritual fellowship where they cultivated their own spiritual lives and went forth to instruct people in reviving faith in Yahweh throughout the land.

As stated in the Bible, these bands of prophets were understood as those who were possessed by the Spirit of God. This led to some frenzy and ecstatic movements — accompanied by musical instruments such as harp, tambourine, flute and lyre. Obviously, contagious enthusiasm affected many people who came in contact with them.

Then, there is Samuel, who was the connecting link between the judges and the new era of prophecy at the time of the kings. In fact, Samuel was known as the last judge in Israel. Also, as a man of God, Samuel apparently possessed supernatural powers to reveal secrets and foretell future events (1 Samuel 9:6-11). Also, he went from place to place as a prophet to revive and strengthen the people's faith in Yahweh (1 Samuel 7:15-17).

Totally rejecting the priestly system at Shiloh, Samuel associated himself with the ecstatic prophets instead (1 Samuel 19:20) and fostered the faith in Yahweh at local sanctuaries. He preached, taught (1 Samuel 12) and advised the king on spiritual matters (1 Samuel 13:8-15; 15:17-31). By his insistence upon obedience to the word of God rather than upon sacrifice, Samuel set the course of prophecy for centuries to come.

Samuel was born in Ephraim at the time of the judges but served God as a prophet under two kings — Saul and David, whom he anointed. His mother, Hannah, dedicated Samuel to God's service through a priest named Eli. Eli's death marked a decline in the influence of the priesthood and the rise of the prophets in Israel under the eventual leadership of Samuel.

According to the Bible (1 Samuel 3:1-11), Samuel's calling took place in this way: As a young boy, Samuel was serving the Lord under the priest in the temple named Eli during the later years of Eli's life. Three times while Samuel was sleeping on the floor of the tabernacle in the evening where the ark of God was placed, Samuel was awakened by the words: "Samuel! Samuel!" He ran to Eli stating: "Here I am, for you called me."

Eli replied: "I did not call; lie down again." Nevertheless, Eli realized the third time that the Lord may be calling Samuel. So, he told Samuel: "If you are called again, say: 'Speak, Lord, for your servant is listening.' " When Samuel did respond in that manner the next time, the Lord said to him: "I am about to do something in Israel which will make the ears of anyone who is listening — tingle."

That was the beginning of Samuel's powerful journey as a prophet, which included many times when the people would not listen to him. At the same time, respect for him grew wider and stronger through the years simply because Samuel was a trustworthy prophet of the Lord (1 Samuel 3:19-20). Samuel was a man of prayer who finished the work of the judges, began the school of the prophets and anointed Israel's first kings. He like others was not immune from finishing poorly. Samuel's sons turned away from God; they took bribes and perverted justice. Nevertheless, when Samuel died, all of Israel assembled together and mourned him. Then, they buried him in Ramah.

Nathan, as already is known, was an invaluable prophet during the reign of King David. He was a fearless, but delicately careful confronter and a most trusted advisor. He appears three times in the Biblical record. In the first instance, Nathan seemingly "jumped the gun" so to speak by telling David that he could build the temple for the ark of the covenant. God apparently spoke to Nathan afterward saying that David's successor would accomplish that task, which Nathan did report to the king (2 Samuel 7:2-17).

As already documented, Nathan was able to assist David with seeing his own wrongdoing in his encounter with Bathsheba and her husband, Uriah the Hittite. He showed David that he would not have tolerated such action from anyone else (2 Samuel 12:1-25). Furthermore, Nathan near the end of his life carefully reminded David that he had promised Solomon would succeed him as king over his already self-appointed son, Adonijah, as king (1 Kings 1:8-45).

Therefore, Nathan magnificently lived up to his name, which meant "God has given." Nathan was a most needed and helpful gift from God during the reign of King David. He tirelessly served as God's spokesman to David. He proved to be a fearless friend and counselor, always willing to speak the truth even amidst extremely difficult circumstances.

Elijah emerged as a prophet during the reign of King Ahab in the northern kingdom of Israel during the first half of the century in 800 BC. Elijah became known as the greatest representative of the prophets, especially as recorded in the gospel accounts of the Bible (Matthew 17:3-17; Mark 9:4-13; Luke 9:30-33).

Elijah was born a Tishbite in Gilead but was assumed into heaven on a chariot of fire led by horses of fire, which supposedly was witnessed by his successor, Elisha. Others in a company of fifty or so prophets from a prophetic school ultimately verified this departure in that Elijah's deceased body could not be found anywhere (1 Kings 17:1; 2 Kings 2:12-18).

Elijah's prophetic ministry began with and centered upon his confrontation with King Ahab, whose reign in northern Israel commenced in 874 BC and ended in death at a horrendous battle in 853 BC. Even though Ahab may have been the most evil king among all of them, his wife, Jezebel, apparently was even worse.

Jezebel systematically eliminated the representatives of God in Israel, promoted and funded Baal worship to the point that she relentlessly insisted upon making all of Israel worship her gods and was determined to pursue and kill Elijah. She believed that kings rightfully could do, or have, anything that they wanted. She ruthlessly killed Naboth and confiscated his land when he refused to sell his vineyard to Ahab.

Jezebel wielded tremendous power. She not only managed her husband, Ahab, but also had some 850 pagan priests under her control. In the end, however, she suffered the loss of her husband in combat and her son at the hand of Jehu, who took the throne and became king by force.

126

Nonetheless, even though Jezebel died a terrible death, she still succumbed in the same defiant and scornful way in which she lived.

When comparing Jezebel and Elijah, each one's strength of commitment can be noted. However, the big difference has to do with whom each one was committed. Jezebel was dedicated to herself and her false gods, but Elijah was committed wholly to the one, true God of the whole universe. In the end, by the strength and power of the ever-living God, Elijah was proven to be right.

Elijah's own life demonstrated that to be a fact. First, Elijah predicted drought before Ahab and then supposedly and miraculously supplied food. After reportedly restoring a boy to life, Elijah rebuked Ahab. Unlike King David that looked upon the prophet Nathan as a faithful friend, Ahab saw Elijah as the enemy.

Ahab relentlessly blamed Elijah for bringing him prophecies of judgment. Ahab only wanted to hear good news — especially about his own self. As a result, Ahab only surrounded himself with people who encouraged him to do whatever he wanted to do. He took his wife's evil advice, listened just to the supposed prophets who gave good news and consistently followed the majority opinion that led to his death.

This specifically played out with the confrontation on Mount Carmel between the forces of Ahab's priests supporting the worship of Baal and Elijah alone before the one, true God — Yahweh. Two bulls were placed on separate altars. Each side called upon their deity to light a fire upon the dry wood at their altar, but after many long tries by the Baal worshipers, only the prayerful cry of Elijah to the one, true God produced fire that consumed everything before his altar. Then, all of Israel bowed down before Yahweh, while the priests and prophets of Baal were killed.

As a result, the forces of Ahab via the murderous intent of Jezebel went after Elijah to destroy him, while Elijah ran for his life until he came to a cave far away on Mount Horeb, where Moses at one time supposedly had his fiery encounter with God. In deep depression and despair, Elijah was asked by the Lord: "What are you doing here?" Elijah responded: "I have been very zealous for the Lord, the God of hosts; for the Israelites have forsaken your covenant, thrown down your altars and killed your prophets with the sword. I alone am left, and they are seeking my life — to take it away" (1 Kings 19:9-10).

Here comes the answer of the ages, not only for people in great despondency like Elijah was, but for everyone who wants to know where the Lord is to be found:

> The Lord said to Elijah, "Go out on the mountain, for the Lord is about to pass by." So, there was before Elijah — a great, strong wind, but the Lord was not in the wind; after that an earthquake, but the Lord was not in the earthquake. After the earthquake, there was a fire, but the Lord was not in the fire.
>
> Then, there was sheer silence, and in that quiet moment the voice of the Lord moved into the subtle consciousness of Elijah saying: "Go even to the region of Damascus, and anoint King Hazael over Aram, Jehu as king over Israel and Elisha as prophet in your place, for there are many — even thousands in Israel who have not bowed their knees to Baal nor kissed him."
>
> — Kings 19:11-18

So Elijah reportedly went forth to accomplish what he was called to do.

When Elijah anointed Elisha, Elisha became his servant. Elisha asked only one thing of Elijah when he departed from this life — that Elisha could inherit a double share of Elijah's spirit. According to scripture that was granted to Elisha upon seeing Elijah ascend out of sight. Elisha took Elijah's mantle that was left behind. The company of prophets immediately declared, as Elisha was walking toward them, that "the spirit of Elijah" now rests upon Elisha.

Elisha from that point forward became a formidable leader of God among the prophets of the land from approximately 848 BC to 797 BC and primarily during the reign of King Jehu in Israel. Elisha was a farmer from the tribe of Issachar in the northern kingdom, who became a prophet under the tutelage of Elijah. Both Elijah and Elisha concentrated their efforts on the particular needs of the people around them, but each of them was different from the other in the way they approached the situation.

The fiery Elijah confronted and exposed idolatry head on and thereby helped to create an atmosphere where people could freely and publicly worship the one, true God. Then, Elisha moved forward to demonstrate God's powerful, yet caring nature to all who came to him for help. He spent less time in conflict with evil and much more in showing compassion for the daily needs of people.

The Bible records no less than eighteen encounters of Elisha with needy people, four of the most memorable ones being — the flow of olive oil (2 Kings 4:1-7), the healing of the Shunemite woman's son (2 Kings 4:8-37), the healing of Naaman's leprosy (2 Kings 5:1-27) and the floating ax head (2 Kings 6:1-7).

The purpose of Elisha's ministry was to restore respect for God and God's message. With great courage and prayer, Elisha revealed not only God's judgment on sin but also God's mercy, love and tenderness toward all people who remain faithful.

Moreover, Elisha stood firmly against the evil kings of Israel. Every terrible king in Israel and Judah encouraged idolatry. Of course, an idol then and now is any idea, ability, possession or person who is regarded more highly than the Lord of heaven and earth. These false gods in the time of Elisha represented war, cruelty, power and sex. These disreputable leaders had priests, prophets and the law of God to guide them. They sought only priests and prophets whom they could manipulate to their own advantage.

Only 20% of Israel and Judah's kings followed God. Furthermore, the idolatrous kings were shortsighted. In essence, they thought that they could control their nations' destinies by importing other beliefs, forming alliances with heathen nations and enriching themselves. The good kings, who remained loyal to the one, true God, had to spend most of their time undoing the evil that was accomplished by their predecessors, and as proven over and over again, God will not forever ignore nor tolerate unbelief or rebellion.

It is true that the consequences of rejecting God's commands and purpose for human life are severe, whereas blessings ultimately are granted among those who persevere in their faith and in their action with the one, true God. Why? Because the faithful people are the only ones who genuinely respond with a grateful heart! Others only complain because they think they did not receive more and better than they already have experienced.

After the days of Elisha, there is no evidence that communities of prophets existed any further in time. Of course, the northern kingdom was destroyed in 722 BC for rejecting God (2 Kings 17:7-17), and the fall of the southern kingdom was not far behind. King Hezekiah beginning in 715 BC and King Josiah commencing at 640 BC were able to stem the tide with the downfall of Judah. Both of them repaired the temple and gathered the people for Passover.

During Josiah's reign, a high priest by the name of Hilkiah in 622 BC uncovered a book of God's law in the house of the Lord, the temple. As a result, Josiah eradicated idolatry from the land, but as soon as Hezekiah and Josiah left the Judean scene, the people returned again to living their own way, which led to the fall of Judah in 586 BC. Then, the Jews were carried off into Babylonian captivity.

At the period of time following the days of Elisha, a new kind of prophecy arose in the form of what was called "Literary Prophets." In other words, these people not only spoke their words from God, but also they and/or their followers wrote down these pronouncements. Furthermore, there was a shift of emphasis as to whom the message of God was directed. Instead of focusing their divine pronouncements upon the king, they now were directed primarily to all of the people in Israel, in Judah and everywhere.

Major Prophets

Amos is the first of the literary prophets and therefore the first among the Major Prophets, even though this writing does not even come close to the other three in length. Moreover, Amos sets the overall tone among the vast majority of the literary prophets by raising the specter of God's judgment upon God's own people, who seem to drift farther and farther away from leading the world into what is good, right and just in the sight of God and among human beings.

In addition to the subject matter that is displayed among these literary prophets, the order in which they appear in the Bible and their composition does not necessarily follow logically in thought proceedings or historical lineage. In other words, the message can seem at times to be all jumbled up and perhaps unclear to the modern mind, which is indicative of the times in which these people lived.

Nonetheless, the essential message rings clear through it all: The one, true God remains forever involved as the central figure throughout human life and activity. With this background in mind, the literary prophets themselves now come into the forefront of focus — beginning with Amos.

The prophet Amos grew up in Tekoa, which is located in the rugged sheep country of Judah, ten miles south of Jerusalem. Although Amos was a herdsman, a sycamore-fig grower and pruner from the southern kingdom of Judah, he prophesied in the northern kingdom of Israel — primarily in Bethel and Samaria. According to his own words as recorded in Amos 7:14-15, "The Lord took me from shepherding the flock of sheep and said to me: 'Go prophesy to my people Israel.' "

Around 745 BC, Amos did as he was told, which catapulted him into the kingdom of Israel during the reign of King Jeroboam II, to condemn Israel for five specific sins: 1) selling the poor as slaves, 2) exploiting the poor, 3) engaging in perverse sexual sins, 4) taking illegal collateral for loans and 5) worshiping false gods.

Amos spoke strongly to the upper class. There was no middle class in the country — only the very rich and the very poor. The rich kept religious rituals. They gave extra tithes, went to places of worship and offered sacrifices, but they were greedy and unjust. Most deplorably of all, they took advantage of the helpless.

Illegal and immoral slavery appeared as a result of over-taxation and confiscation of property. Also, there was cruelty and indifference toward the poor. Amos proclaimed with true prophets of all time that God is weary of greed and will not tolerate injustice. Moreover, Amos knew that God hated false worship whereby people do it only for show and merely pretend to be religious.

Amos' message was delivered in an age of unprecedented prosperity in the middle of the eighth century BC. Assyrian invasion of the preceding century had ceased at that moment in time because of internal struggles within that empire. By the time Amos began his public career during the latter part of Jeroboam's reign, Israel had been enlarged to her most extensive boundaries. Judah similarly was prosperous under King Uzziah. An era of luxury like that of Solomon seemed to have returned.

Business was booming. Everyone was optimistic. The opulent members of society were very happy, but with all of the comfort and luxury came self-sufficiency and a false sense of security, because prosperity brought on corruption and destruction. Even though real faith in God may have been abandoned, people still pretended to be religious, but as people like Amos knew, a complacent present leads to a disastrous future.

The purpose of Amos in this time of such glut and success was to penetrate the veneer of self- satisfied complacency into the rotten core of the religious and social life among the leaders of Israel. They proudly assumed that their prosperity was evidence of their cultic observances. In the midst of this overwhelming prosperity, Amos foresaw a coming rude awakening in a deadly "day of Yahweh." It would mean a punishing worldwide judgment, which undoubtedly would produce the destruction of the nation at the hands of a God-empowered invading enemy.

The situation looked almost hopeless to Amos unless possibly they turned to seek the Lord. Thereby, a "remnant" of the nation might avoid the coming death or exile into a foreign land (Amos 5:6, 15, 24). It was with a sense of God-impelled, divine urgency that Amos proclaimed that "the lion had roared" in the hope that at least a few might escape this death-dealing leap, which caused the prophet to speak (Amos 3:8).

So, Amos proclaimed the keynote to his whole prophetic speech before the well-to-do Israelites at the royal chapel in Bethel, as recorded in Amos 5:21-24,

> I hate, I despise your festivals, and I take no delight in your solemn assemblies. Even though you offer me [the Lord] burnt offerings and grain offerings, I will not accept them; I will not look upon the offerings of the well-being of your fatted animals. Take away from me the noise of your songs; I will not listen to the melody of your harps, but let justice roll down like waters, and righteousness like an ever-flowing stream.

Such pronouncements and more produced a violent reaction, as might be surmised. Amaziah, the high priest of Bethel, sent word to Jeroboam saying: "Amos has conspired against you at the very center of the house of Israel. The land is not able to bear his words, when he states: 'Jeroboam shall die by the sword, and Israel must go into exile away from this land' " (Amos 7:10-11).

This reaction did not affect Amos in the least, because he was not intimidated by priest or king. He strikes back with further words of judgment by adding striking metaphors from his shepherding and farming experience such as an overloaded cart, a torn lamb, fat cows and a basket of fruit (Amos 8:1-2). The prophetic ministry of Amos ended 10 years after he began. It was some 22 years before the northern kingdom of Israel fell to the Assyrians.

Isaiah is the result of what sometimes has been called a dual personality. Without a doubt, Isaiah is one of the greatest prophets of all time. His insight into the nature of the world around him and his devotion to the one, true God in a high, unique way make him a one-of-a-kind person to be admired and respected throughout all time.

What about this dual personality business? That is related directly to the circumstances in the book of the prophet Isaiah itself. There are at least two parts in the Book of Isaiah, divided almost down the middle. The first 39 chapters are set in the period of approximately 740 BC to 700 BC, whereas chapters 40-65 are dated in the era somewhere between 536 BC and 530 BC, which is a differential of some 300 years.

Obviously, Isaiah is not the same person throughout this whole span of time, but there is more unity here than might be expected via some phenomenal editorializing in some unknown fashion. The unity is found throughout the whole Book of Isaiah through the eyes of faith found in the person of Isaiah and all of his followers, which is evident in every line that is scrolled.

Only the first Isaiah is a specifically known person, but that in no way detracts from the second Isaiah, or even possibly a third Isaiah as some try to speculate. In fact, the second and conjecturally speaking — a third Isaiah may be even stronger and more revered than the first, because the temperament is much more palatable to those who read that portion of the Bible. The different sounding of the words clearly is differentiated at the breaking point between the first and second Isaiah.

Listen to these words now for yourself: "Hear the word of the Lord of hosts: Days are coming when all that is in your [King Hezekiah's] house, and that which your ancestors have stored up until this day, shall be carried to Babylon; nothing shall be left" (Isaiah 39:5-6).

Then, "Comfort, O comfort my people says your God. Speak tenderly to Jerusalem, and cry to her that her warfare is ended, that her iniquity is pardoned" (Isaiah 40:1-2).

In essence, the dominant note in the first 39 chapters in the Book of Isaiah is God's judgment. Even though chapters 40-65 include judgment throughout the text, there also is a leaning toward hope in God's caring and redemptive goodness well into the future.

Furthermore, there is a clear difference between the setting of the first Isaiah and the second. In the first portion of the book, Assyria is the major world power. Jerusalem and Judah are hard pressed to defend themselves, their city and the temple against the invading enemy. Isaiah, who is a lifelong resident and official in Jerusalem, warns the people about their possible capture by the Assyrians, which did not materialize as did happen in Israel to the north.

In chapters 40-55, however, Babylonia is the world ruler. Cyrus and the Persians are soon to take over the whole area. The Jews live in Babylonian exile but ultimately will be freed by Cyrus the Persian while the city of Jerusalem and the temple lie in ruins. Then, in chapters 56-66, the exile is over; the Jewish community is restored, and the people try to settle down into a new life in the land of their forbearers.

The only clearly delineated person of Isaiah is found in the first 39 chapters of this Biblical book. He was born in the city of Jerusalem, the son of Amoz, about 770 to 760 BC, lived there all of his life and died not long after 700 BC. His name means: "Jehovah is salvation."

Isaiah was called into prophetic ministry around 740 BC and was married about the same time. He had a son named Shear-jashub meaning "a remnant shall return." A second son named Maher-shalal-hash-baz was born around 735-734 BC, whose name meant "swift spoil" or "quick prey."

Isaiah was born of noble birth, lived among noble Jewish people. He was well respected and an honorable man all of his days. Therefore, he acutely was aware of the political circumstances and even had great influence upon the affairs of Jerusalem and Judah. His ministry lasted throughout his adult life during an excruciating period of Jewish life.

Because of Isaiah's location, his involvement in the affairs of state and his influence, the focal points throughout the Book of Isaiah involve Jerusalem and the Davidic dynasty. Moreover, Isaiah prophesied during the reign of the kings in Judah including Uzziah, Jotham, Ahaz and Hezekiah. His visions were about Judah and Jerusalem, and he spoke on behalf of the Lord, which has had a tremendous impact upon people to this very day.

Isaiah's prophetic insight into the divine purpose for human life is made abundantly clear in one of the finest literary presentations in the history of the entire world (Isaiah 6:1-13): "In the year that King Uzziah died, I saw the Lord sitting on a throne, high and lofty, and the hem of his robe filled the entire temple."

Probably at a festival ceremony for the divine king near the time of 742-740 BC, when most people were going through the normal ritualistic practices in a meaningless way, Isaiah suddenly became aware of the divine reality behind that symbolism. In an instant, the vivid color, pageantry and music of that ancient ceremony faded into the irrelevant background, and the Lord appeared to him in a deeply personal and abiding way.

In that supreme moment, Isaiah was alone with God in a most uplifting and edifying manner. An overpowering realization came upon him that he was in the presence of the Majesty from on high.

Immediately after that, Isaiah proclaimed: "Woe is me! I am lost, for I am a man of unclean lips, and I live among people of unclean lips." Here was an overwhelming encounter with personal inadequacy.

Almost as soon as Isaiah's words of confession were uttered, the prophet felt the touch of God upon his lips, saying: "Your guilt is taken away; your sin is forgiven, and I will remember it no more." It is blotted out forever. The unshakable assurance of divine mercy is given, which can bring undeniable hope to any and all human beings.

Afterward, Isaiah heard the unmistakable voice of the Lord saying: "Whom shall I send, and who will go for us?" And Isaiah responded: "Here am I; send me!" And God said: "Go and speak to the people." Isaiah did and never turned back from that point onward.

First Isaiah is called to reveal the disobedience of Judah and to proclaim disaster. Isaiah is shown a picture of a desolated land, of exile and destruction and of further ruthless judgment on those who survive. The statement that the holy seed is a stump or sacred pillar means ultimate disaster to Judah and Jerusalem at the hands of the Babylonians many years later. Also it would show in that disaster that the working out of a purpose of grace for God's people could lead to a new and better relationship.

In Isaiah 9:1-7, the darkness finds its answer in a word of hope — the restoration of the Davidic kingdom. Over this reestablished Davidic kingdom, there will rule an ideal king, who is acclaimed as a "wonder of a counselor," one whose counsel will be effective for the people's well being; a "divine" hero — "mighty God"; an "everlasting Father" of God's people, and a "prince" who brings peace and prosperity. The Lord's rule will be established forevermore, and character will be justice for all.

The hope centered upon a reestablished Davidic kingdom with an ideal king is projected even further with Second Isaiah in the coming of a messianic age when God's people will become a light to all of the nations including the Gentiles. These people will be a remnant of cleansed and purified ones who return to Jerusalem and shine forth with the glory of God within them for people everywhere (Isaiah 40-55).

The only way to accomplish this new way of life among the remnant people is to put away from them all idolatry, which is the worship of all things ahead of God. In fact, the makers of idols are in dismay because God is with the Jewish people and all of Israel.

The gods of Babylon are rendered powerless, and Babylon's love of "magic" will be to no avail. Even winning support from allies will not help Babylon. They cannot even protest because the purpose of God is declared: It is to save God's people in order that the whole world may know who God is. In fact, the nature of God, according to Isaiah in the Holy Bible, now is revealed in historic events — the rise of the foreigner, Cyrus the Persian, under God's authority and the deliverance of God's chosen people — Israel. Therefore, the hidden God of Israel presently becomes known to the whole world.

In chapters 56-66, or Third Isaiah, it is proclaimed that God will make Jerusalem, or "Zion," the center of the universe. The nations will throng to Jerusalem and bring back even a scattered Israel. The wealth of the nations will help in the rebuilding of the city of Jerusalem and will bring a new

138

kind of beauty there that God will accomplish. Moreover, all of the people will share in the salvation that God brings to them. The new city and the new people will be like a crown for all to see.

Although this victorious celebration may have been properly focused and with a much needed jubilation following years of misery in Babylonian captivity, it did not last forever as may have been surmised. Nevertheless, that hope was well grounded, never was obliterated and became the chief characteristic of the prophetic writings in the Book of Isaiah along with judgmental and destructive pronouncements. Most importantly, such hope may have become true and manifest at a later period of history in God's own perfect timing and in God's own way, according to some scripturally minded analysts — centuries later.

Jeremiah on occasion has been called the weeping or sorrowful prophet. Whether that is true or not often has been debated, but there is no doubt that Jeremiah functioned as a lonely prophet. He was timid and introspective with an apparent lack of self-confidence. Sometimes he even felt as if he were God's victim. He definitely felt that he had been denied the privilege of wife and children.

Jeremiah's prophetic literary contribution is found in his confessions (Jeremiah 15:10—20:18), according to some scholars. This portion of scripture makes the move in Judaism from a focus upon the nation and actions within the whole body of people to the individual and each person's attitude of mind. Thus, Jeremiah is the father of personal spirituality in the Bible. God speaks to the nation henceforth through a personal relationship with God, which seems best expressed in Jeremiah 31:31-34:

> The days surely are coming, says the Lord, when I will make a
> new covenant with the house of Israel and the house of Judah.
> It will not be like the covenant that I made with their ancestors
> when I took them by the hand in bringing them out of Egypt.

139

This is a covenant that I will make, says the Lord, in which I will put my law within them, and I will write it on their hearts. No longer shall they teach one another, or say to each other, "Know the Lord," for they shall all know me, from the least to the greatest.

What Jeremiah showed the world is that it is possible to know God personally, to speak with God face-to-face, to see God eye-to-eye and individually to be in communion with God (Jeremiah 32:4). As a result, Jeremiah produces a new type of devotional literature in which tenderness, compassion and peace are found in nearness to God. Therefore, Jeremiah becomes the father of true prayer also.

Jeremiah was born in Anathoth, a place four miles northeast of Jerusalem. His father, Hilkiah, was of the priestly family there in the tribe of Benjamin. According to the first ten verses in the Book of Jeremiah, God had appointed Jeremiah to be a prophet even before he was born, but his actual commissioning by the Lord transpired sometime around 628-627 BC.

Recorded very simply in verse 9 of the first chapter, "The Lord put forth his hand and touched my mouth saying to me: 'Behold, I have put my words in your mouth.' " There is no human reflection or speculation here. What Jeremiah is called to proclaim comes directly from God and not from himself.

Furthermore, his mission is not just to Israel alone but to the nations. His hesitancy to accept the appointment is overcome by the firm assurance that God will be with him and deliver him — assumingly from all who come against him. That is all Jeremiah needs to hear. It truly is enough for that point in time.

The calling to be a prophet took place at a moment when a wave of optimism about the nation's future ran high, emotionally speaking. When Jeremiah immediately and repeatedly spoke of an invasion from the north and insisted that

Judah was far away from receiving any good will from Yahweh, he created quite a stir to say the least. When the original edition of the Mosaic Law was found in the temple, a national reformation was instituted based upon these principles five years later in 623-622 BC, and Jeremiah's warning of imminent judgment seemed totally irrelevant.

Jeremiah was dismissed as unimportant by many prophets in Israel. Therefore, Jeremiah entered into obscurity for some fifteen years — from the time in his life as a teenager to being well over thirty years of age. During this extensive period of time, Jeremiah even had doubts about himself (Jeremiah 15:15-18; 20:7-10).

When Pharaoh Neco killed King Josiah in battle at Megiddo, he took Josiah's son, Jeboahaz, as his captive and put another son, Jehoiakim, as his vassal around 609 BC, Jeremiah arose as a prophet of significance. About the time of Jehoiakim's coronation, Jeremiah declared in the temple court that unless Judah changed her ways, the temple would be destroyed (Jeremiah 7:1-15; 26:1-6). This prophecy caused a riot. Only the intervention of a few nobles prevented Jeremiah from being killed by the angry mob (Jeremiah 26:7-24).

Nonetheless, Jeremiah stubbornly continued in the same vein. In 605-604 BC after one outburst among the people, the temple authorities tried to silence him with a flogging and a night in the stocks (Jeremiah 20:1-2). Since that had no effect, they refused to allow Jeremiah in the temple. Jeremiah responded with a new idea: He produced his prophetic utterances by dictating them to a friend, Baruch, and sent him into the temple to read them. After 598 BC, Jeremiah voiced his disgust with popular tendencies in returning to heathen practices and with the attitude of the newly rich. They were the bad figs of chapter 4 in the Book of Jeremiah.

When in 593 BC a group of ambassadors met in Jerusalem to plot further rebellion, Jeremiah publicly opposed alliance with Egypt, opposed any rebellion against Babylon, recommended a lengthy residence in Babylon and was against the man, Hananiah ben Azzur, who was prophesying success in taking action against Babylon. That rebellion did not take place. Possibly Jeremiah's determined opposition helped. Revolt, which was bolstered by Egyptian promises, did break out against Babylon in 589 BC, however.

By January 588 BC, the Babylonians and their allies overran the country and were settling down to besiege Jerusalem. Jeremiah stayed in Jerusalem throughout the siege. In its early months, King Zedekiah sought counsel from Jeremiah (Jeremiah 21:1-4), who told the king that surrender to the Babylonians was the only way to save himself and the city. Nevertheless, Zedekiah could not even hope to have his nobles embrace such a thought.

The Egyptian army moved up into Palestine, and the Babylonians turned from besieging Jerusalem to meet the challenge of the Egyptians. When Jeremiah attempted to leave the city to visit his family property, he was accused of deserting to the Babylonians and was imprisoned (Jeremiah 37:11-15). Prisoner though he was, Jeremiah continued to urge surrender from the barracks in which he was held.

The exasperated military leaders threw Jeremiah into an empty cistern to die, but an Ethiopian, probably helping in the king's household, rescued him. Jeremiah was returned to the barracks where he remained for the rest of the siege. When the siege dragged on, a kinsman offered to sell Jeremiah a plot of family land in Anathoth.

Since the future was so uncertain, it was a most unattractive proposition, but Jeremiah bought it. Moreover, he insisted upon paying the full market price as a testimony to his faith that Judah had a future in the promises of God (Jeremiah 32:1-25). This incident particularly is significant because it shows that the message of hope truly was part and parcel of Jeremiah's pronouncement: After punishment would be restoration.

The city of Jerusalem fell in 586 BC. Babylonian intelligence evidently had taken note of Jeremiah's support for their cause, because the local commander received orders to allow Jeremiah his freedom. Jeremiah chose to remain with the new governor, Gedaliah. When Gedaliah was assassinated and survivors fled to Egypt, Jeremiah and Baruch were carried along with them.

The last we hear about the prophet is in the country where Jeremiah vigorously protested against the possibility that Egypt could provide a satisfactory home for the Jewish people. Instead, Jeremiah asserted that Nebuchadnezzer of Babylon would conquer Egypt as he had done throughout the rest of the Fertile Crescent. Jeremiah died in the companionship of his faithful Baruch at the spot which he so strongly detested.

Ezekiel lived approximately in the years that spanned from 593 BC to 571 BC, according to the Biblical record. Other than that, little is known about this person. Evidently, Ezekiel was preparing to be a priest in the temple at Jerusalem when he was carried away into Babylonian captivity.

There, Ezekiel was called to become a prophet, which propelled him forward in faithfulness to God's calling for some 22 years. In the process, people under the prophetic leadership of Ezekiel, which was given to him directly from God, became what the name Ezekiel meant: "God is strong" or "God makes strong." The whole Book of Ezekiel is summed up in this basic message: In spite of the whole troublesome, deprecating experience in Babylonian captivity, God's sovereign strength prevails. Yahweh will judge his enemies and restore the people who remain faithful to God.

Ezekiel is known as a prophet of individualism as well (Ezekiel 9:4-6; 14:12-23; 18:1-32; 33:1-20). He heralded divine love for each person. His message centered upon the pronouncement that God loves the sinner and therefore warns the sinner through the prophet Ezekiel. Far from being a recluse or living in a remote imaginary world, Ezekiel was a man who mingled freely with people and felt their every mood and need.

Most of the material in the Book of Ezekiel is poetry, even though some of it is prose. Therefore, people listened to Ezekiel out of appreciation for aesthetic beauty, but they did not heed his teaching. Their minds were too engrossed with selfish passions (Ezekiel 33:30-32). Nevertheless, truth and beauty rarely have been combined so magnificently throughout all of Hebrew literature as here with the prophet Ezekiel.

With all of this somewhat fragile data in mind, it comes as no surprise that Ezekiel was called to be God's prophet. Nothing in his previous experience had prepared him for such an overwhelming display of God's presence and power. As recorded in the first and second chapters in the Book of Ezekiel, the glory of the Lord appeared to Ezekiel like a bright light and dazzling fire. He fell to the ground overcome by the vast contrast between God's holiness and Ezekiel's own sinfulness and insignificance.

The immortal God addressed Ezekiel by calling him mortal, which thoroughly emphasized the distance between the two of them. However, when God recognized Ezekiel's open, responsive and willing attitude, the Lord filled him with the Spirit of God and gave him power for the tremendous task ahead.

Ezekiel's vision of God, who is seen as seated upon a throne and borne aloft by four living creatures, is recognized in a mighty storm cloud with flashing bolts of lightning streaming across the sky. Falling down in awe before the realization and manifestation of God's overwhelming glory, Ezekiel is raised up by the Spirit of God to receive the di-

144

vine message, which is written upon a scroll. The command to eat the scroll emphasized the necessity of fully absorbing the word of God as well as the absolute objectivity of God's word given to the prophet Ezekiel. In this process, Ezekiel found God's word to be as sweet as honey (Ezekiel 1:1; 3:21).

All of the symbols in Ezekiel's ecstatic vision have come to represent very powerful events for the prophet as well as for the people of Judah: The stormy wind from the north meant that the great armies of Babylon were reaching toward Jerusalem as God's instrument of judgment upon the nation of Judah. The four living creatures in the mist of the great cloud, which projected a brilliant light, showed that Jerusalem's destruction was God's punishment for Judah's sins.

Each of the four living creatures apparently was meant to represent God's perfect nature, according to some analysts — the lion for strength; the ox for diligent service, the human for intelligence and the eagle for divinity. The wheel within a wheel probably is a scene of two wheels at right angles to each other — one on a north-south axis and the other on an east-west axis. Showing the ability to move anywhere, these wheels are placed in such a position as to say that God is present everywhere and is able to see all.

Moreover, the wheels by themselves signify that God travels right along with Judeans into and through captivity. Therefore, God in truth rules all life and history. Ezekiel relayed this message, which he received directly from God in the midst of the storm of national defeat, which utterly devastated the people. He announced that even Jerusalem would not escape destruction. In addition, Ezekiel had to endure his wife's death during this terrible time.

Then, in chapters 25-32 in the Book of Ezekiel, the prophet proclaims to the surrounding seven nations that God will condemn and judge them for their sinful actions as well. No doubt, the people in these nations had proclaimed that

God was too weak to defend the people of God and the city of Jerusalem.

The Book of Ezekiel concludes with a proclamation of hope for God's people because of God's faithfulness. Future blessings for God's people are foretold as well, which is summed up in verses 22-24 of chapter 36:

> Thus says the Lord God: It is not for your sake, O house of Israel, that I am about to act, but for the sake of my name. I will sanctify my great name, which has been profaned among the nations, and which you have profaned among them also. The nations shall know that I am the Lord when through you I display my holiness before their eyes. I will take you from the nations, gather you from all the countries and bring you into your own land.
>
> See, I am for you. I will multiply your population, the whole house of Israel — all twelve tribes of you. The towns shall be inhabited, and the waste places rebuilt. I, the Lord God, will multiply human beings and animals upon you. They shall increase and be fruitful. I will cause the land to be inhabited, as in former times, and do more good to you than ever before.
>
> — Ezekiel 36:8-10

These pronouncements further were illustrated in the imagery with the valley of dry bones when the Lord said to Ezekiel: "Prophecy to these dry bones," which obviously referred to all of the people of Israel at this point in time. Ezekiel did as he was told, and the bones came together; skin was placed upon them and breath was blown into them. Behold, they lived, stood upon their feet and became a vast multitude (Ezekiel 37:4-10).

At this point, as recorded in chapters 40-48 in the Book of Ezekiel, a blueprint for the restored community is outlined. It includes dimensions and activities for the restored temple in Jerusalem, land boundaries throughout the nation and legalistic requirements for every person. It is stated further that if these requirements are met, further tragedy could be averted.

This procedure involves proper prayers, tithing, multiplicity of sacrifice and then even more sacrifice beyond that. As a result of these written requirements, Ezekiel is termed the father of legalism. Normative, mainline, faith-filled Judaism followed the line of what was begun by this prophet in the Book of Ezekiel, and it never has dimmed since that time.

In the process, God's faithful people throughout all of Israel were cleansed after seventy years of captivity, were given a new heart, a new spirit and were endowed with a freshly felt sense of greatness in the sight of God.

In summation, what Ezekiel proclaims as a prophet of the one, true God is the coming doom of Jerusalem, individual responsibility, being a watchman for the people as well as the restoration of Israel through mechanically and ritualistically formulating a new way of life for God's people. So, the prophetic ministry of Ezekiel concludes in 571 BC with a detailed vision of a new temple, a new city and a new people that would shine forth with God's holiness in the land of their forbearers.

Minor Prophets

Hosea is the first of the Minor Prophets, so-called "minor" simply because of the length in their writings. The extent of their scrolls generally are much shorter than their "major" counterparts, which does not in any way suggest that they are less valuable or more inferior than the others. In some ways, these literary prophets may be uniquely positioned to express what needs to be heard by people of the one, true God — even at this present moment in time. Overall these expressions are significant for the whole world to receive and understand.

Hosea, the son of Beeri, was born and raised in Ephraim, located in the northern kingdom of Israel. He lived during the prosperous, yet perverted, reign of King Jeroboam II and in the same era of the prophetic pronouncements against the king by Amos the prophet. Hosea's activity spanned the years, roughly speaking, from about 753 BC to 715 BC, but his prophetic approach was totally different from other prophets. In fact, the message of Hosea is not found anywhere else in the Biblical record until one person, Jesus of Nazareth, appears upon the scene many centuries later.

The mind and heart of God reportedly changed during the prophecy of Hosea from primarily focusing upon judgment of the people to that of mercy and love for human beings (Hosea 9:15-17; 10:10; 11:8-9; 13:2-11; 14:4-7). Of course, love is mentioned somewhat prior to the prophet Hosea and afterward, but not in an all-encompassing, deeply motivated, primal sense as set forth in the Book of Hosea. For this reason, Hosea is one of the more power-packed messengers of the one, true God throughout all time.

It does not mean in any way that there is no judgment with Hosea's prophetic words. On the contrary, there is plenty of gloom and doom pronounced in this portion of the Biblical record. In fact, it might be said that two thirds of the statements in the Book of Hosea are denunciatory in nature.

According to the vast majority of Biblical analysts through the ages, however, the significance of chapters 1-3 and chapter 14 override that of the other nine chapters in quality, authority and significance. That is music to the ears of anyone who wants to live by the truth as recorded in the Bible.

As intimated already, the strong, undeniable message of the prophet Hosea is God's steadfast love, which is proclaimed in the Hebrew word hesed. Hosea, himself, is seen in his writing as a tender, gentle, refined person. He is responsible for the early and sympathetic interpretation of hesed as God's steadfast love and forgiveness (Hosea 6:4; 11:3-4). This formidable message is conveyed in the marriage figure as a symbol of the bond between God and Israel. God is the loving Father (Hosea 11:1-3) and Israel is the loving spouse (Hosea 2:2) who has strayed far away from her marriage covenant.

This imagery comes from the depth of Hosea's own experience. In fact, his prophetic calling arises out of the relationship with his own wife named Gomer. Evidently, Hosea's wife Gomer had a propensity for prostitution and harlotry. Several ways of interpreting this statement in the Book of Hosea have been suggested through the years. It includes such thoughts as: the story itself being just an allegory; that Hosea married a harlot who already had given birth to illegitimate children; Gomer actually was a woman of wifely virtue who was a victim of character assassination.

The most popular thought among scriptural analysts through the years is that Gomer's unfaithfulness did not manifest itself until sometime after the marriage, which Hosea came to suspect after the birth of their first child and recognized it as an expression of a fundamentally corrupt nature.

In any event, Hosea's love for Gomer superseded all of this waywardness and corruption. He was willing to take her back if she genuinely were willing to return. Supposedly, Gomer did realize that life had been better with Hosea in the marriage bond. After a period of living together in isolation, Hosea and Gomer were reunited.

It was this experience that prompted Hosea to reflect deeply upon the relationship of God with God's own people and to accept his call into prophetic ministry. From the bitter experience of a shattered home and a faithless wife, whom he loves nonetheless, Hosea comes to understand God's deep love for faithless Israel. Here, Hosea learns the deeper meaning of love and forgiveness, which is the very heartbeat of his message. God forgives Israel and woos her back to the relationship of the days in the wilderness. God renews the marriage covenant "in righteousness and in justice, in steadfast love and mercy" (Hosea 2:19).

At the same time, Hosea stands in true line with the prophets of Israel by proclaiming the emphatic need to turn away from sinning, from sacrificial offerings on the altar of Baal worship, from reveling in agricultural festivals that produced heavy drinking and sexual indulgence especially with the cult prostitutes of Baal, and most of all — from the idolatry of images created by human hands.

Hosea condemned the social evils of his time: The crimes committed against fellow human beings to satisfy people's own greed, the lust for power, or sheer self-indulgence and especially the corruption of political leaders in high places. In Hosea's opinion, this mindset led to unholy alliances with leaders of other countries, who could care less about Israel and especially the one, true God named Yahweh, who had developed the people in the wilderness and bound them together to God with cords of love.

If people did not turn away from their wicked and sinful ways and turn to the Lord, their demise, doom and destruction most certainly would come and lead them into slavery once again. In chapters 4-13, Hosea's earlier hope for a national conversion gives way to despair. It is the conviction that the nation ultimately is doomed, which in fact did take place at the hands of the Assyrians in 721 BC.

However, in the epilogue of Hosea 14, there is a glimmer of hope and expectation. Even in the midst of doom and gloom, the steadfast love of the Lord will be with the people and precipitate in them — return and renewal. Being firmly rooted anew in God, the glorious result will be repentance, healing and fruitfulness beyond compare.

Micah, the literary prophet, came from a town in Judah named Moreshath-bath some twenty miles southwest of Jerusalem and in the period after the mid-seven hundreds BC similar to Isaiah. Other than that, little is known about this person. The fact that Jeremiah's contemporaries compared him to Micah over a century later may suggest that Micah could have had access to the royal court in Jerusalem, as Jeremiah did.

Also, Micah's words span two different eras, even though that spacing is not anywhere near the distance between the two Isaiahs, and may suggest a dual involvement in Micah's writing too. Nonetheless, Micah's prophetic message is clear: The main purport of Micah's message is that God will destroy the wickedness in the capital city of Samaria in the northern kingdom of Israel and the southern kingdom of Judah, while concentrating his message primarily on the leaders in the city of Jerusalem. Micah condemns the national sins of God's people, the well-paid prophets and judges and the greed of many people. His primary concern is the enrichment of the upper classes at the expense of the poor. In the process, Yahweh will be departed from God's people (Micah 3:4), and Judah will discover the eclipse of God.

The final blow and last outrage occurred upon the completion of Micah's scathing, well-deserved and highly accurate message from God. It strangely was directed to the heads of the house of Jacob, the rulers of Israel, which included all of the priests and prophets. In their totally insensitive and impudent response, all of them had the audacity and gall to claim: "Is not the Lord in the midst of us? No evil shall come upon us" (Micah 3:9-12)!

Although coming from a later time, Micah additionally anticipates the future restoration of the Davidic monarchy as a revived political kingdom — as well as the restoration of the temple in Jerusalem. By employing poetic allusions to Jerusalem in the Book of Micah 4:8, this prophet declares that Judah's lost place among the nations will be renewed.

It is not at all shocking, therefore, that this Davidic ruler will come from Bethlehem where King David grew up. It is amazing, however, that this new ruler and deliverer "shall be one of peace" (Micah 5:5), even though it may be connected against false prophets of the time, who cried "Peace" themselves (Micah 3:5). That genuine peace would come from the line of one, who solely had been a military leader, which is contrary to all ordinary expectations. Nonetheless, it was stated to be true — directly from God via the prophet Micah, according to the Biblical record.

Furthermore, in what has been claimed to be one of the most beautiful and poignant pictures of the coming, long-to-be-awaited Messiah - is the statement in the Book of Micah 5:4: "He shall feed his flock in the strength of the Lord, in the majesty of the name of the Lord his God. And the people shall live secure, for he shall be great to the ends of the earth."

Finally, in the coming of the messianic age when all conflicts have passed, Judah no longer will need to trust in military resources (Micah 5:10-11), for again the people will be led by one of peace. The Book of Micah concludes by pronouncing that hope and expectation have displaced despair. Confession and trust inspire a new vision.

As humiliation was a mark of God's judgment, so defeat of the enemy will signal salvation. Here, Micah does not dwell on humiliation by the enemy, which possibly means Babylon, but focuses positively and with enthusiasm upon the restoration of the forsaken city, Jerusalem. "That they will come to you in that day" pictures the risen city presiding over a new order in peace and prosperity by the very hand of the Lord (Micah 7:10-17).

Thanksgiving is offered for the forgiveness of sins and the lifting of the burden of guilt. The past is redeemed. Over against divine judgment proclaimed by Micah from God, there appears the overwhelming love of the forgiving God. The jubilant words: "Who is a God like thee?" is the very meaning of the prophet's name, Micah. This is in vast contrast to the presumptuous previous claim of the leaders and rulers of Jerusalem, as recorded in Micah 3:9-12.

The enemy is trodden down, and nothing can be compared to the knowledge that God will tread all of our iniquities under foot (Micah 7:18-20)!

Zephaniah was a prophet in the southern kingdom of Judah, who probably was called into prophetic ministry sometime in the decade between 640 BC and 630 BC. That was during the time when King Josiah was young, which was some eight years into his reign before he even began thinking to "seek the God of David his father" (2 Chronicles 34:3-8). Moreover, Josiah was twelve years into his regal post when he began to undertake Deuteronomic reforms. Again, it was in his eighteenth year between 623 BC and 622 BC when those excellent reforms were brought to fruition, and Zephaniah's prophetic ministry ended some months later around 621 BC.

Zephaniah was a contemporary of Jeremiah and Habakkuk and a descendant of the royal house of Judah. As boldly stated in the Book of Zephaniah 1:1, "The word of the Lord came to Zephaniah — son of Cushi, son of Gedaliah, son of Amariah, son of Hezekiah — in the days of King Josiah, son of Amon of Judah."

Then with the valuable assistance of many fellow writers, Zephaniah immediately proclaims even more succinctly:

> The day of the Lord is near, near and hastening fast. The sound of the day of the Lord is bitter; the warrior cries aloud there. That day will be a day of wrath, and day of distress and anguish, a day of ruin and devastation, a day of darkness and gloom, a day of clouds and thick darkness.   — Zephaniah 1:14-15

Nevertheless, in the midst of this pronouncement of terror and apparent punishment to come, there also is a measure of hope with a whispered promise proclaimed in the very next chapter:

> Seek the Lord, all you humble in the land, who do God's commands. Seek righteousness; seek humility, and perhaps you may be hidden on the day of the Lord's wrath.
> — Zephaniah 2:3

> Furthermore, there will be a "remnant in the house of Judah," who will be restored.
> — Zephaniah 2:7

Finally in chapter 3, the quiet refrain grows into a great crescendo of God's salvation and deliverance for those, who are faithful to the Lord, as Zephaniah declares:

> Sing aloud, O daughter of Zion; shout O Israel! Rejoice and exult with all your heart, O daughter Jerusalem! The Lord has taken away judgments against you. God has turned away your enemies. The king of Israel, the Lord, is in your midst. You shall fear disaster no more.
> — Zephaniah 3:14-15

Therefore, the reader of this portion in scripture from the Book of Zephaniah is to listen carefully to the words of judgment: God does not take sin lightly; it will be punished. However, be encouraged by words of hope, for God reigns, and the Lord will rescue God's own people. So, humbly worship; obey God's commands, and be part of the joyful, faith-filled remnant of God's people!

Nahum is a poet and not a reformer like other literary prophets. Nevertheless, he is a highly motivated patriot, a skilled artist in his literary composition and most of all — an indignant nationalist.

The Book of Nahum consists of a fragmentary song and a triumphal ode, which Nahum composed in August of 612 BC, when Ninevah, the capital of Assyria, was destroyed (Nahum 2:3—3:39). The ode of Nahum is a poem of joy celebrating the downfall of the Assyrian empire and is ranked by some Biblical analysts as one of the two or three best poems in the Bible.

154

It is a known fact that the northern kingdom of Israel and the southern kingdom of Judah had suffered more from the harsh and relentless Assyrians than from any other oppressor. For two-and-a-half centuries, Assyria had harassed them, driven the northern kingdom into cruel captivity and demolished Judah by forcing her kings into rigorously enforced subservience. Now at last, the end of Assyria was at hand. As Nahum proclaimed Assyria's defeat, he seemed to speak loudly for all of Israel and the one, true God called Yahweh.

Who Nahum the literary prophet was, no one seems to know. Even the stated town of his birth, El-Kosh, actually is unknown, while some people would speculate that it was located somewhere in the region around the Sea of Galilee. However, Nahum's poetic writing lives on.

In fact, it is most probable that the Book of Nahum was employed for liturgical use in the temple at Jerusalem and was shared publicly there in official ceremonial celebrations between 612 BC and 609 BC. This is when Judah was forced into submission by the Egyptians, who would have suppressed any open exultations. Nonetheless, the beauty of this expression remains in the heart and mind of God's people yet today.

Habakkuk is another literary prophet not known for who he was or where he lived. Nonetheless, he is a literary prophet of unusual importance. The Book of Habakkuk reveals that he is a person who seriously questions the Lord in the midst of terrible times. Then in a reflective way he gains an answer, which seems appropriate for a while. When an even more harsh reality sets in and new questions arise, new reflective answers are produced in the presence of God. Through it all, Habakkuk gains new insights, which propel him and the people forward.

Apparently, Habakkuk begins to prophesy around 607 BC and his ministry supposedly ended around 589 BC.

Moreover, a dual personality may be manifest with the prophet Habakkuk — one who responded during the time of Jehoikim (609 BC to 598 BC) and the other during the time of Zedekiah (597 BC to 586 BC).

There is no doubt that these were horrendous times, especially for the people in Judah when Habakkuk was a prophet. Pharaoh Neco of Egypt had killed King Josiah, subdued Judah, deposed Josiah's elder son and offered the throne to his second son, Jehoiakim, at a price of complete subservience. That was accepted for the sole purpose of pursuing his own ruthless internal policies, which led to the demise and destruction of Judah.

From what can be gathered in the Biblical record, Jehoiakim had a character totally opposite from his father Josiah. He allowed the hard-won gains of Deuteronomic reform to lapse. He forsook all morality, which was based upon God's covenant, by oppressing the poor more cruelly than ever before. One of the worst forms of economic oppression during that period involved the retaining of pledges in lieu of unpaid loans or services.

At this time of international crisis, Jehoiakim built a pretentious palace with taxes squeezed out from his own subjects. All of his efforts seemed to be for the glorification of Jerusalem to his own credit and at his subject's expense. Habakkuk cried out against this to the Lord.

In 604 BC Jehoiakim was forced to submit under Babylonian control, when Nebuchadnezzer drove the Egyptians back to their border. For three years, Jehoiakim served under Nebuchadnezzer. In yielding to enticements by Egyptian ambassadors, Jehoiakim threw off the Babylonian yoke, which precipitated inevitable retribution. Jehoiakim died while Nebuchadnezzer's army was besieging Jerusalem in 598 BC but not before treating the prophets, who dared to reprove Jehoiakim, with harshness and deep contempt.

Into this ugly scene Habakkuk was thrust. He personally wonders before the living presence of the one, true God: Why do the wicked prosper (Habakkuk 1:12-17)? The response Habakkuk received was that the wicked shall be destroyed, but righteous ones of God shall live by faith (Habakkuk 2:1-5). A list of woes against the nation that conquers and against those who are greedy, idolatrous, intemperate, cruel and bloodthirsty follow (Habakkuk 2:6-20).

Finally, as Habakkuk witnessed the devastation wrought by the Babylonians and as his prophetic ministry draws to a close, he was driven to prayer. That prayer became the most deeply spiritual utterance in the whole book and one of the noblest of the kind throughout the Biblical record. Glorious language in Habakkuk 3:1-19 expresses the overwhelming majesty of the Lord.

God is like the sun, filling the whole earth with God's glory and shaking the mountains with rage. All enemies of Yahweh are vanquished, as God goes forth in behalf of the people's salvation. Then, in the prophet's own experience at that moment in time, Habakkuk's inspiration rises to its highest exaltation.

The divine manifestation makes Habakkuk tremble at the core of his very bones. The approach of calamity and God's wrath leaves him helplessly weak and exhausted. More than that, it gives him the calm assurance that no matter how severe the trials may be, the high purpose of the Lord will be carried out against invaders.

These thoughts lead the prophet at the end to rejoice in the God of salvation. Whatever Habakkuk may suffer, whatever may be taken from him, he will continue to be joyful in this great God over all creation. As a result, Habakkuk becomes a prime example of a righteous person who lives by faith!

Haggai is listed as the first one of the Minor Prophets among the sixth century BC leaders, but he is not alone.

Zechariah was a literary prophet right along with Haggai at that time. In fact, people often associate Haggai and Zechariah together because they were committed to the same task, even though each one's approach may have been somewhat different.

There are other leaders who felt called to the same end also, even though they were not literary prophets. Their names were Zerubbabel, Joshua the high priest, Ezra and Nehemiah. They were leaders in the Jerusalem area after the Babylonian exile too. All of these people were committed to rebuilding the destroyed temple area in Jerusalem.

The first and largest group of Judeans journeyed back to the Promised Land after Cyrus the Persian had set free the Judeans from Babylonian captivity in 539 BC. It was for the purpose of rebuilding the temple in Jerusalem. A descendant of King David named Zerubbabel with excellent leadership capabilities seemed to be right for the task in 538 BC.

Nonetheless, when the altar was rebuilt and when the temple foundation was completed and celebrated, fear prevailed. With outside pressure from hostile neighbors and disappointment over the less than grand appearance of the temple in comparison with King Solomon's accomplishment, the work came to a grinding halt in 530 BC. The people concentrated upon building their own homes instead.

That is where Haggai, the prophet, as well as Zechariah came into the picture. Called by the Lord in 520 BC, Haggai sensed that everyone's priorities were out of order. In August of that year, Haggai conveyed the message that people needed to hear: "Is it a time for you to live in your comfortable, well-paneled houses, while the house of the Lord lies in ruins" (Haggai 1:4)?

The people of God were called into action by Haggai's proclamation, which came directly from the God of all creation, "Thus says the Lord of hosts: Consider how you have fared! Go up to the hills, bring wood and build the house of the Lord, so that I, the Lord, may take pleasure in it and be honored" (Haggai 1:7-8). As a result, this message from the Lord via Haggai became the catalyst for finishing the work of rebuilding the temple, and Haggai encouraged the people in the process all along the way. He continually assured them that God was with them throughout their effort and final victory as well.

Although little is known about Haggai himself, his name does mean "festal," which conveys that he probably was born on a feast day. That he was a member of the "Great Synagogue," which became the first college of learned scribes that produced interpretation of the covenantal law forward to later rabbis, suggests that he may have been influential in the community as well as being well qualified as a literary prophet.

Haggai truly was a practical man, but what moved him and therefore his people forward — was hope. He was able to sense the movement of the presence of God in events around him and communicate that sense of God's presence daily among the people. As a result, the rise of the sanctuary walls from the pits of Jewish despair enabled everyone to see that God was acting mightily again, and people were able to rejoice. This means that Haggai's festal name did influence others in truth to the glory of God's great and wondrous name!

Zechariah, as literary prophet, held fast to God's proclamation of rebuilding the temple in Jerusalem along with Haggai. In fact, they overlapped in relaying the same message for two months together. When Haggai concluded his work, Zechariah continued for two more years and in the process expanded the message even further.

First, Zechariah's approach to the building of the temple does not appear to be as direct as Haggai's seemed to be. Speaking in more figurative language, this prophet elicits how God's purpose, which from his perspective is hidden

159

in the maze of human history, will be manifested and fulfilled. Zechariah expresses divinely revealed designs that seem almost too elaborate and sweeping for ordinary minds to grasp. Angels are sent to explain their meanings, according to Zechariah, but the statement at the outset in the Book of Zechariah is without a doubt — the underlying message of this literary prophet: "Thus says the Lord of hosts: Return from your evil ways and from your evil deeds" (Zechariah 1:4).

In addition, Zechariah speaks of a coming Messiah, who upon first reflection could have been Zerubbabel, but such thoughts were dashed for some unknown reason. Nonetheless, the prophecy itself seems to coincide amazingly and substantially with later Biblical writings as recorded in Matthew 21:4-9; Mark 11:1-9; Luke 19:30-39; John 12:12-15.

Verses 9-10 in the Book of Zechariah 9 seem to be declared over 500 years before the scriptural recordings previously cited. Here they are as follows:

> Rejoice greatly, O daughter Zion! Shout aloud, O daughter Jerusalem. Lo, your king comes to you; triumphant and victorious is he, humble and riding on a donkey, on a colt, the foal of a donkey. He will cut off the chariot, the war horse and the battle bow — from Ephraim and from Jerusalem, and he shall command peace to the nations; his dominion shall be from sea to sea and from the River to the ends of the earth.

Thus, it was believed that the rebuilding of the temple would be just the first step ushering in the messianic age. Ultimately, the victory of God over all nations would prevail in leading the world to universal peace. To Zechariah, the one God demands in the final sense — one world. According to the Book of Zechariah, God will not rest until all things are under his feet. "On that day, the Lord will be one and his name one" (Zechariah 14:9).

In Zechariah's prophetic words, the Lord will be one king over one people and known by one name. Therefore, in Zechariah's divine vision Israel at last is a kingdom of priests. In every home sacramental bread is broken; the family hearth is familiar to the presence of God, and even the bells of the horses, freed from battle, ring in tune with God's heavenly glory (Zechariah 14:9-21).

Supposedly born in Babylon, Zechariah was a fairly young man when he returned to Jerusalem in 538 BC. Being sympathetic to the priesthood, especially through Joshua the high priest, he shared leadership with Zerubbabel as prince and builder of the temple. That made him a priest-king (Zechariah 3:1-5; 6:14). In fact, Zechariah formerly may have been a priest himself. Whatever the situation, Zechariah became a true prophet of the one God of the whole universe and over all history.

The meaning in the Book of Zechariah, whose Hebrew name is "the Lord remembers," can be summed up as follows: Prophets and kings pass away, but the purposes of God are firm, inescapable and enduring!

Malachi became a literary prophet around 450 BC, which was some seven decades after the era of the previous two prophets, and times were quite different. Rebuilding the temple during the post-exilic period had been completed by 515 BC, and malaise settled in among the Judeans.

The excitement over the return from exile and the construction of the temple had long since passed. Jewish people, as a poor and struggling community, were losing their identity (Malachi 2:11). Drought and locusts continually struck the farmers (Malachi 3:10-11), but the worst ills were social.

Disintegration of Jewish family life became highly manifest in divorce (Malachi 2:16) and adultery (Malachi 3:5). Divorce not only was common, but it also occurred for no reason other than a desire for change. Men, who were the only ones able to separate from their spouses in that culture, divorced their faithful wives to marry younger, pagan women. As a result, they flaunted God's law about marriage and threatened the religious training of the children. Pride had hardened their hearts.

Moreover, the rich again oppressed the poor and victimized the helpless with impunity (Malachi 3:5). Dishonesty was the keynote of business success (Malachi 3:15). The sacred principle of covenant, which absolutely is essential to a responsible society, continually was disregarded (Malachi 2:4, 10, 14).

It was bad enough for the country to be overrun by lawless men, but it appeared as if God now favored the so-called outlaws even within their own society (Malachi 2:17). To be cynical, godless and corrupt appeared to be more beneficial than anything else. The mood of the hour simply was: "What's the use of trying" (Malachi 1:13)? Therefore, the heart of the Jewish predicament was not hard times per se, but the loss of the presence of God (Malachi 3:1).

Furthermore, neglect in the worship of God and perfunctory performance by the people, most especially by the priests, produced irresponsibility everywhere, according to Malachi. The priests' teaching function with regard to traditions of the past and consultation of sacred omens vastly and cynically was abused. To Malachi, the failure of the priests in this critical time of undependable, secular authority was principal cause for corruption throughout society.

If priests were unfaithful, how could they lead the people? They had become stumbling blocks instead of spiritual leaders. Malachi singled out the priests for condemnation, because they knew what God required. Their sacrifices were unworthy; their service was insincere, and they were lazy, arrogant and insensitive. A mere casual attitude toward the worship of God prevailed and thereby with the observance of God's standards in the covenantal relationship.

In addition, the failure of the priests to keep the covenant of responsibility in the presence of the Lord (Malachi 2:8) caused God to withdraw from the people (Malachi 2:2, 9; 3:5, 18).

The people equally had been guilty. In the broader context of their responsibility, they had taken advantage of the laxity among their leaders by bringing maimed offerings (Malachi 1:13), by divorce (Malachi 2:14), by failing to tithe (Malachi 3:8) and by oppressing the helpless (Malachi 3:5). Moreover, when the people say, "What good does it do to worship God?" what really is asked: "What good does it do for me?" The focus is purely selfish and not in any way to honor God. When God truly is worshiped, the Lord will bless the people mightily (Malachi 3:10-11).

Malachi, which means God's personal messenger, firmly believed that the ceremonies of the priests among the people must be performed properly in dignity and reverence to God's majesty (Malachi 1:14). The ideal priest is one who takes God seriously (Malachi 2:5). In answer to those who insist: I cannot endure solemn assembly and forego iniquity, Malachi strongly proclaims: If you really kept your solemn assembly, you would not perform iniquity!

The message of the prophet, Malachi, is: Return to God, and God will return to you (Malachi 3:7). Even more than this, if people meet their responsibilities to God, the windows of heaven will be opened and multiple blessings will come (Malachi 3:10).

Since priests are custodians of the temple, Malachi calls upon them to lead the return to God (Malachi 1:5; 2:1, 7). They are challenged by this one question from the prophet: Do you really believe God is there (Malachi 1:13; 2:2; 3:1)? Those people who do not respect the worship of God will not respect God's commands (Malachi 1:13; 2:8).

Malachi strongly insists that the priest is the messenger of God (Malachi 2:7). Therefore, this points toward the end of the institution of prophecy, because God will provide access to his word henceforth through a cleansed and active priesthood. As God speaks from the temple, there no longer will be the need for a prophet. The doomed pronouncements and obscure visions of spirit-seized prophets will vanish in the light of perfect law.

Therefore, it is not surprising that the next movement from a teaching priesthood would be a codification of laws in order to stabilize justice. Half of a century later, Ezra would become a priestly scribe where his sole authority is the Law of Moses and interpreters of the law. The prophets never would emerge as the key personnel in Judaism anymore.

The rational-minded Malachi becomes the transition point between prophet and the priesthood. Divinely inspired prophecy ceases with Ezra, and reliance upon the Law of Moses then emerges as the wave of the future. At this present moment in time, however, Malachi ends his literary expression in true prophetic style with words of doom and gloom from the Lord of hosts. He points to a great and terrible day of judgment when the land may be stricken with a curse (Malachi 4:1-5).

Even then, however, that is not left without hope, as stated in Malachi 3:1: "I, the Lord, am sending my messenger to prepare the way for me, and the Lord, whom you seek, suddenly will come to his temple. The messenger of the covenant, in whom you delight — indeed, he is coming, says the Lord of hosts." Why? Because God still loves the people (Malachi 1:2), and God's love never ends!

Obadiah lived as a literary prophet somewhere between 586 BC at the fall of Jerusalem and 350 BC. It probably is closer to the earlier date than the latter, but no one knows for certain when he prophesized. Not much else is known about Obadiah other than what is contained in the scripture and that his name means: "servant of the Lord" or "worshiper of Yahweh."

The Book of Obadiah is the shortest book in Biblical scripture among the Hebrews. It primarily is a denunciation of Edom, the people descended from Esau, who was the brother of Jacob. Their land was located south of the Dead Sea, and the Edomites were subjected under the reign of King David. Thereafter they continued to be under the dominion of Judah. When the Edomites succeeded in the revolt against King Ahaz, it became merely an exchange of masters, because Edom soon became a vassal of Assyria.

At the destruction of Jerusalem in 586 BC, the Edomites aided the Babylonians. Understandably they took advantage of the opportunity in gloating over Judah's problems, capturing and delivering fugitives to the enemy and looting the land of Judah. Presumably, that is the reason for which Obadiah spoke so strongly on behalf of God against Edom and why Edom came to symbolize any power hostile toward Yahweh. In fact, the Book of Obadiah becomes a dramatic example in how this prophet portrays the divine response toward anyone who would harm God's children.

Obadiah reportedly is called to give a scathing message against the people of Edom, because of their indifference and defiance of God, their cowardice and pride, their treachery against brothers and sisters in Judah and all of God's people (Obadiah 1:10-14). Accordingly, they stand condemned and will be destroyed by God.

The Book of Obadiah begins with the announcement that utter disaster is coming upon Edom (Obadiah 1:1-9). Despite their impregnable cliffs and mountains, Edom will not be able to escape God's judgment. This pronouncement proceeds further with a description of the "day of the Lord" whereby judgment will fall upon all who have harmed God's people (Obadiah 1:15-21). Obadiah concludes with an insistence that all of those who defy God will meet their doom as Edom did.

Joel appears upon the scene as a literary prophet around 350 BC at the prompting of a locust plague, which devastated the land of Judah. In true prophetic fashion, Joel interprets this plague as from Yahweh signaling that the "day of the Lord" in judgment is near (Joel 1:15-20).

Nonetheless, Joel holds out hope of deliverance if Israel turns to God wholeheartedly (Joel 2:12-14). In that way, a turning point does occur. God becomes jealous for the people (Joel 2:18). They are assured of prosperity, an outpouring of the spirit and victory over nations in a final battle.

The only information that is given about Joel himself is that he was the "son of Pethuel" (Joel 1:1). His familiarity with the temple liturgy suggests that he may have been associated with personnel in the temple in some particular way. Also, his interest in Jerusalem may imply that he could have lived in or near the city.

The dominant motif in the Book of Joel is that of lamentation. It is evident early on, through Joel's urging of Israelites to assemble and mourn over the invasion of the locusts (Joel 1:15-20). A great variety of literary expressions in these laments is evident throughout this portion of scripture. There is admonition (Joel 1:2-3), the summons to lament as already mentioned (Joel 1:5-7, 11-12, 13), complaints (Joel 1:16, 19; 2:17), alarms (Joel 2:1; 3:9), oracles of assurance reportedly from the Lord (Joel 2:19-27) and conclusions of a theological nature. In fact, this great variety of lamentations is combined eloquently into one, whole, meaningful, theological message with ramifications well into the future.

From lament, the prophet Joel leads the people of God into the turning point for anyone and everyone seeking a better way of life:

Yet even now, says the Lord, return to me with all of your heart.
Rend your hearts and not your garments. Return to the Lord,

your God, for the Lord is gracious and merciful, slow to anger, and abounding in steadfast love.   — Joel 2:12-13

"Then afterward" says the Lord your God in whom there is no other, "I will pour out my spirit on all flesh; your sons and your daughters shall prophesy; your old ones shall dream dreams, and your young ones shall see visions. In those days I shall pour out my spirit upon everyone who calls upon my name."
          — Joel 2:28-32

According to the reported speech of Peter, the disciple and apostle of Jesus – whom he called the Christ, that pouring out of the Spirit began at Pentecost nearly 400 years later (Acts 2:16-21). Furthermore, the outpouring of the Spirit historically has been verified ever since that time when people gather together in the name of the Lord.

Jonah is unlike any other person among the prophets. History, fact, autobiography and even just plain biography do not seem to fit into this prophetic writing, and yet tale, legend, folklore, myth or mere story does not characterize the Book of Jonah either. Authorship and date present a tremendous problem as well, but none of these descriptions interfere with the powerful message portrayed therein.

In fact, the Book of Jonah — even if viewed somewhat as a dynamic parable that Jesus of Nazareth employed for people then as well as now — is one of the most significant scripts throughout the whole Bible. Nowhere else does such a written thought appear before a reader like this one. It includes: a human being trying to run away as far as possible from God's calling, finally doing what was asked in the first place, not understanding why good results transpire among hostile enemies in darkened regions, being angry and upset about it all and then in the end supposedly realizing how critically important God's merciful way is for all people.

Specifically speaking, Jonah was called by Yahweh, the one, true God of the Hebrew people to go into enemy territory of the Assyrians, the worst oppressors of the Israelite and Jewish people, even to their wicked capital city of Ninevah. There, Jonah is to pronounce God's judgment of impending doom upon them, but he refused to go to Ninevah. Instead, he went as far away as he thought possible from that horrible task in an extremely undesirable spot. He boarded a ship at the Mediterranean seaport city of Joppa, which presumably was bound for Tarshish in Spain.

Through a multiple set of disastrous events at sea, Jonah ended back on land heading toward Ninevah. In the process of being on board ship, however, the pagan, Gentile sailors during a violent storm recognized the judgment of Yahweh upon them, their vessel and cargo — apparently because of Jonah. As a result, the sailors cried out to the one, true God of the Hebrew people: "Please, O Lord, we pray, do not let us perish on account of this man's life" (Jonah 1:14)!

Thus, the sailors turned to the Lord of the Hebrews, "the God of heaven, who made the sea and the dry land" (Jonah 1:9), while the Hebrew, Jonah, still was being totally disobedient to God's calling. The sailors reportedly picked up Jonah, "threw him overboard into the sea, and the sea ceased from its raging," which seemingly made the sailors fear the Lord even more. As a result, the sailors "offered a sacrifice to the Lord" (Jonah 1:15-16), while Jonah was caught in the deep blue sea for three days and three nights" (Jonah 2:3).

With the flood of waters, waves and billows surrounding Jonah in the heart of the sea and with life ebbing away, Jonah ultimately remembered the Lord, called out to God in his distress and prayed the prayer of his life. It was answered by finally delivering him upon dry ground (Jonah 2:3-9). When the Lord spoke to Jonah a second time with the command to go to Ninevah and speak prophetically, Jonah did not hesitate. He went! (Jonah 3:1-3).

168

When Jonah reached Ninevah and cried out: "Forty days more, and Ninevah shall be overthrown" (Jonah 3:4)! At that, everyone — from the king to the very last person throughout the city supposedly repented and turned away from their evil ways, even from the path of violence that was in their hands. At that point, their only hope reportedly was that the Lord would relent, have a change of mind, turn from wrath toward them, and they would not perish (Jonah 3:8-9). They also prayed mightily to God that this event would come to pass. Even the unnamed king of Ninevah evidently repented, which was in stark and favorable contrast to the impenitent Hebrew king Jehoiakim.

Reportedly when God saw what they did and how the Ninevahites turned from their evil ways, God did change thoughts about the calamity that should have come upon the Ninevahites, and the Lord did not do what was projected. At that, it might be surmised that Jonah would rejoice with exceeding great joy. After all, a whole city full of people supposedly was converted to the one, true God, which would make Jonah the most successful missionary of all time in a feat never before recorded in the annals of history, but it did not affect him in that manner at all.

In fact, Jonah grew exceedingly upset over the whole scenario. He became grossly resentful, simply because the Assyrians did not deserve God's forgiveness, mercy and love. Jonah 4:1-2 reveals the real reason behind being against such a thing: Instead of God forgiving the Ninevites, Jonah in his intense indignation really wanted them to be destroyed. He did not understand that this gracious and generous action of the one, true God of Israel was meant for the whole world. Jonah's self-centeredness, along with all of his people, had caught up with him.

Jonah, all of his people and anyone like them throughout the world, had to learn a most critical lesson. Again, the Lord was ripe and ready for such a challenge in a subtle, most convincing and irrefutable way. After Jonah expressed his indignation before the Lord and asked to die rather than face what seemed to him such a terrible indignity, God's response was: "Do you really have a right to be angry" (Jonah 4:4)?

Instead of answering the question, Jonah went out of the city to sit down, supposedly still sulking, and see what further might happen to Ninevah. In the process, a bush grew up rather quickly on the spot where he stayed and gave Jonah shade over his head in the heat of the day. This saved him from an immense amount of discomfort and made Jonah very happy (Jonah 4:5-6).

However, when Jonah awoke in the morning, a worm attacked the bush, and it withered and died. A very sultry east wind reportedly followed, and the sun beat down upon Jonah's head so that he was faint enough to wish that he could die. The dialogue of the ages commenced between the Lord and Jonah, which rings true down through the centuries — even to this very day.

The Lord questioned Jonah forthrightly again saying:

> "Is it right for you to be angry about the bush?" Jonah without a moment's hesitation supposedly answered: "Yes, angry enough to die!" Here comes the punch line directly from the Lord of hosts: "You are concerned about the bush, for which you did not labor and which you did not grow. It came into being in a night and perished in a night. Therefore, should I not be concerned about Ninevah, that great city, in which there are more than many thousands of people, who do not even appear to know their right hand from their left." — Jonah 4:9-11

In other words, all people by nature wish that judgment and destruction would come upon sinful people, whose wickedness seems to demand immediate punishment. However, God is more merciful than any human being possibly can imagine. According to the Book of Jonah, God always feels compassion for sinners, and the Lord forever seeks ways to enfold them into God's own self.

Therefore, no one is beyond the redemption of God. God's message of love and forgiveness was not meant for Jewish people alone, but for all people — even the Gentiles. The Assyrians did not in any way deserve God's love, but God supposedly spared them — even Israel's worst enemy — when they repented, and even if there is no evidence that it occurred.

Jonah evidently did not understand before his encounter with the one, true God and with the people of Ninevah that the God of Israel was meant for the whole world. Furthermore, Jonah was upset that God had spared Ninevah, but he already had forgotten that God had spared Jonah's own life. It took this long hard knock in his own mind even to begin comprehending the extraordinary reaches of God's love.

That the one, true God of the Hebrews reaches out even further to the Gentiles is demonstrated in the Book of Acts over many hundreds of years later and still spreads wider and wider throughout the earth to the glory and majesty of the one, true God who lives and reigns forever.

Prophetic Aftermath

Daniel is claimed as a prophet of a unique sort also. Some Biblical accounts even have placed him among the Major Prophets, but the text itself defies that listing — having been divided into two contrasting sections: chapters 1-6 and chapters 7-12. The first six chapters show Daniel as a wise judge of events, which his name Daniel implies. He not only is able to declare the meaning of dreams but also what those dreams are themselves. The last six chapters, however, are another situation entirely. Here, Daniel describes in the first person the ultimate triumph of God over cruel nations to end all evils and giving the kingdom to "one like the son of man" (Daniel 7:13-14). In highly visionary form, the use of hidden, often extreme, symbolism prevails.

As a result of this differential, the overall writings of Daniel belong to what is known as "apocalyptic" writings in Biblical literature and not at all to prophetic expressions. For this reason, the Book of Daniel is classified in the third category with the Hebraic listing of scripture known as the "Writings." In contrast with that of the other two, namely the Law and the Prophets, it adds to the fact that Daniel does not belong in the category of prophet.

Nevertheless, it is a very important narrative that thoroughly belongs in the Bible, even though some analysts have disagreed about that assessment throughout the ages. On the other hand, there are others who wonder why it is only one of two apocalyptic books in the Bible namely Daniel and Revelation, because of the popularity of this kind of thinking and writing during the Inter-Testament and New Testament periods.

The times helped to fuel this new apocalyptic mindset. No era was fraught with as much persecution and oppression since perhaps the years spent in Egyptian slavery. The length of this misery contained in the Book of Daniel covered events from 605 BC to approximately 160 BC, which ultimately led to Roman rule after Pompey captured Jerusalem in 63 BC. This was followed by Julius Caesar in 48 BC as well as Augustus Caesar from 27 BC to 14 AD.

What a dreary shadow is cast over the person named Daniel and the Jewish people in those intensely accelerated and darkened times. However, some of them, like Daniel, appeared to be equal to that terrible situation by their unflinching devotion to the one, true God. As a result, they made it through a fiery torment (Daniel 3:1-28), a lion's den of iniquity (Daniel 6:1-24) and every raw measure that they ever faced — seemingly with the Lord always among them and with them.

Moreover, by the gift and grace of God, Daniel also was able to foresee a time in the future – of resurrection (Daniel 12:1-3, 13), and the apocalyptic "Son of Man" reigning supremely over all evil (Daniel 7:13-14). As a result, Daniel finds in these visions a divine plan for human history: 1) The triumph of heathen nations, and then 2) their destruction and triumph of the Jewish nation or the people of the one, true God.

Unparalleled catastrophes will herald the kingdom of God, which is the main point of all apocalyptic writing. In the Apocalyptic Philosophy of History by direct contrast to the Deuteronomic Philosophy of History previously cited, the strong message every time seems to be: After the Gentile empires all have run their course, one like unto a "Son of Man" will appear on earth from clouds of the heavenly realms. God first will judge the Gentiles and then give eternal dominion to the Son of Man, the Jewish nation and those of the one, true God. The new Israel will enjoy an intimate and uninterrupted relationship with God forevermore.

Ezra, as already mentioned among the literary prophets, became a priestly scribe upon returning to Jerusalem after supposedly leading a second wave of exiles out of Babylon. Now that they had been freed from captivity by the Persians (Ezra 7:11-14), Ezra's main purpose, according to the Biblical record, was to study the law of the Lord and to teach these statutes and ordinances to the Jewish people.

Upon arriving in Jerusalem, Ezra became acutely concerned about people, even priests and Levites, intermarrying with pagan women of foreign nations. They were holding the worship of idols in high esteem too. Ezra was extremely upset because he was a purist — especially in relation to what was proclaimed as God's law.

So, Ezra prayed what has been regarded as one of the great prayers of confession and intercession throughout the Bible. Ezra reviewed the past sins of the people, which reportedly brought on their suffering and humiliation under foreign rulers. Moreover, even when their condition became better under the beneficent rule of the Persian kings, the people had forsaken the commandments of God (Ezra 9:6-15).

On a cold and rainy day, Ezra addressed the people and made it abundantly clear that they gravely had sinned. Furthermore, because of the sins of many persons, all now were under God's condemnation. Ezra's public and prayerful proclamation ended on a note of fear: God no longer could do anything for the people. It produced an immediate effect, which Ezra really had hoped would transpire.

The people wept bitterly because of their sins, made a sacrifice to the Lord and sent away those who had transgressed what intensely was believed to be God's law (Ezra 10:1-19). This initial effort on Ezra's part set the stage for what would become accomplished under Nehemiah.

Nehemiah is one of the most clear-cut personalities throughout the entire Bible. He was a cupbearer, one of the highest positions and most trusted people in any land throughout the mid-eastern countries. He served in the Persian court under King Artaxerxes I at the capital city of Susa around 445 BC. At that time, Nehemiah's brother, Hanani, and a group of his companions came to Nehemiah from Judah with troubling news. The wall of Jerusalem had been breached and its gates destroyed by fire (Nehemiah 1:1-11).

Overcome with grief at the shocking news of these tragic conditions in Judah, Nehemiah first and foremost prayed to the Lord of heaven. Then, evidently Nehemiah's downcast countenance, in contrast to his usual upbeat demeanor, was quite noticeable to the king when he was being served wine. When the king inquired of Nehemiah about his unusual look of sadness, the king was told about what had happened in Judah. Then, he offered to grant any request that Nehemiah might have. As a result, Nehemiah graciously and most generously was given leave to proceed to Jerusalem and rebuild the walls (Nehemiah 2:1-9).

In the process, Nehemiah gave the king a specific time to complete the task, which was fulfilled, but not without many problems and threats against the whole effort. There even was refusal to continue with the project on the part of many fearful, weary and obstinate people. None of these setbacks deterred Nehemiah from his mission and the task before him.

Nehemiah was a stalwart leader of the people in commitment, prayer and strategy. Diligent enemies were in opposition to him. The Jewish community was frustrated constantly, but workers consistently were encouraged by Nehemiah. He was first to labor at the task both day and night.

When wealthy Jewish people were profiteering from the plight of their working countrymen, Nehemiah confronted the extortionists face-to-face by stating forthrightly:

> Let us stop this taking of interest. I, my brothers and my servants already are helping them with money and grain. Restore to them this very day — their fields, their vineyards, their olive orchards and their houses, as well as the interest on money, grain, wine and oil that you have been exacting from them.

Then, the rich people replied: "We will restore everything and demand nothing more from them. We will do as you say" (Nehemiah 5:10-12). At that, Nehemiah called the priests and made those people take an oath to do what they had promised. Then, in shaking out the fold in his own garment, Nehemiah exclaimed: "So may God shake out and empty everyone from house and property, who does not perform this promise." Everyone evidently responded: "Amen." Then they praised the Lord together. Most importantly, it was reported that the people did as they had promised (Nehemiah 5:13).

Thereafter, opposition against rebuilding the wall continued, but Nehemiah persisted to downgrade all threats as mere fear in halting the people from the work. He prayed: "O God, strengthen my hands" (Nehemiah 6:1-9). As a result, the wall was finished in 52 days. Furthermore, Nehemiah gave instructions for guarding the wall, led the people in the act of prayerful confession, helped to establish policies in occupying the restored city of Jerusalem, made arrangements for supporting the Levites and sought to purge the people from what seemed to him and others as detrimental foreign influences (Nehemiah 7-13).

After some twelve years of administration as the Persian governor among the Jewish people, Nehemiah returned to Persia. Upon hearing of irregularities later back in Jerusalem, Nehemiah returned there in 432 BC to remove from the temple quarters the instigator, who had opposed the rebuilding of the wall, and all of his belongings. Nehemiah brought drastic action in shutting down the gates of Jerusalem on the seventh day of each week and in keeping the Sabbath holy.

The Book of Nehemiah fittingly closes with a prayer for God's remembrance and goodness, which not only sustained Nehemiah and his people, but all people who are so inclined and so dedicated.

Esther should be a book that is placed before the Book of Nehemiah in the Bible. The dates of the events that supposedly are described in this writing precede Nehemiah by some thirty years in an era between 483 BC and 471 BC. Moreover, even though many strong reasons have been cited throughout the centuries for not including the Book of Esther in the Biblical canon, one of which involves the dating and circumstances having been much later than this writing, it has an extremely important message for the whole world.

According to the Biblical account in this portion of scripture, Esther was a beautiful Jewish woman. She probably was born in the Persian capital city of Susa among Jewish parents who had been freed from Babylonian captivity. Her parents for some unknown reason evidently died while Esther was very young. However, Esther's older cousin named Mordecai adopted her, became her guardian and raised Esther as one of his own children.

The Book of Esther opens with the king of Persia, Ahasuerus, also known as King Xerxes I (486 BC to 465 BC), who deposed his queen named Vashti for disobedience. Vashti simply refused to obey an order from her husband. So the king removed her from the scene and began the search for a new queen. He sent a decree throughout the land to gather all of the beautiful women in the empire and bring them into his royal harem.

Esther became one of those young women who was chosen, even though the king probably did not know that she was a Jewess. However, King Ahasuerus evidently was so pleased with Esther that he made her his new queen. At the same time, Esther's older cousin, Mordecai, became a government official, while a man by the name of Haman was appointed as the prime minister.

Haman was a descendant of King Agag, a bitter enemy of all Jewish people. In his lust for power and extreme sense of pride, Haman grew determined to have Mordecai bow down to him in subservience. When Mordecai refused to do so or to show any kind of reverence toward the prime minister, Haman grew furious. He had his mind totally set upon destroying Mordecai and all of the Jewish people.

To accomplish this vengeful deed, Haman deceived King Ahasuerus. He persuaded him to issue an edict condemning the Jews to death, which supposedly would produce a holocaust for thousands upon thousands of Jewish people. Mordecai evidently told Queen Esther about the edict. She decided on the spot to risk her own life by attempting to see the king when he had not requested her presence. There was no guarantee that King Ahasuerus even would see her. Although Esther was queen, she apparently still did not feel secure — especially knowing the fate of the former queen.

Therefore, Esther made her plans carefully. She began by asking the Jewish people first and foremost to fast and to pray with her before she went to the king. Then, on a chosen day, Esther approached the king. He did ask her to come forward and speak. Instead of issuing her request directly, however, Esther invited the king and Haman to a banquet. During that feast, the king asked Esther what she wanted. He promised to give her anything that she requested, but Esther simply invited both King Ahasuerus and Haman to another banquet the next day. At that the king seemingly was astute enough to realize that the queen really had something important upon her mind.

Overnight, a miracle apparently transpired. Unable to sleep, the king flipped through some records in the royal archives and read of the assassination plot against him, which Mordecai had thwarted. Realizing that Mordecai never had been properly rewarded for saving the king's life, Ahasuerus asked Haman what should be done to thank a hero properly. Surmising that the king must be talking about himself, Haman described a lavish reward, and the king thought it to be a marvelous suggestion.

According to the Biblical script, Haman was in great shock when he learned that Mordacai was the person to be so honored. When the king asked Esther again what she desired at the second banquet, she replied that someone had plotted to destroy her and her people, and she pointed the finger at Haman as the person. At that, the king immediately sentenced Haman to die, which was accomplished on the very gallows that Haman had built for Mordecai.

Afterward, Mordecai was promoted to prime minister, and the Jewish people throughout the land were guaranteed protection. Ultimately, the feast of Purim on February 28 became the celebration of this event and has remained so to this very day. As a result, the message rings clear to every one of the Lord's people: Racial hatred always and utterly is sinful. It must be stopped whenever and wherever it raises its ugly head. Genuine people of the one, true God always are called to stand against any form of racism.

If it can be accomplished in the manner achieved by Esther and her associates, that would be wondrous to behold, but whoever is involved in such activity always belongs to the elect of the one, true God. Why? Because God created each and every person with intrinsic worth!

Furthermore, the Jewish people were and still are a minority in this world. Therefore, it takes great wisdom to survive in such an environment. When outnumbered and powerless, it is natural for those in a minority position to feel helpless. Esther and Mordecai resisted this temptation and acted with courage instead — to their eternal credit.

It is not enough to know that God is in control. Self-sacrificial courage and action are necessary. Praise to God should be given for all of those people who live to make such a real difference in this existence!

Judas Maccabeus and his younger brothers, Jonathan and Simon, as well as John Hyrcanus and Aristobolus belong to what is known as the Inter-Testament period or writings in the Bible commonly called the Apocrapha. These books are not found in every Bible. In fact, only a few copies of the Bible include the Apocrapha, but it is the only Biblical record available between the prophetic era and the Gospel according to Matthew. Furthermore, the First and Second Books of the Maccabees, each in their own way, cover the Jewish wars of resistance against the Syrian power from 175 BC to 135 BC.

What is critical in knowing the lives of the Jewish people during this period is to understand about the times that led up to the leadership of the Maccabees as well as afterward.

It should be noted from the outset, however, that the vast majority of those associated with the nation of Judaism were scattered everywhere beyond the borders of the Promised Land following the edict of King Cyrus, which permitted the Jewish people to return into their homeland.

Throughout succeeding generations, the Jewish people always looked upon Jerusalem and the nearby area as their home. It forever felt like being their "mother," but the nature of that place was quite different after the Babylonian captivity. Under the influence of the prophet named Ezra, the spiritual landscape of Jerusalem had changed. People there, though smaller in number, became more "strict" and "orthodox" than those living elsewhere in diaspora. Furthermore, each group of Jewish settlers clung to their particular customs.

In 334 BC, Alexander the Great of Macedonia, or of the upper part in Macedonia, began his vast conquest, which soon included Palestine. At Alexander's death in 323 BC, that enormous empire split into sections. Various generals seized power wherever they could. Ptolemy seized control of Egypt, and Seleucus established his rule at Antioch, north of Palestine. Judea lay between those two powers and became a prize that each one wanted to seize and control.

The Greeks continually sought to propagate their culture everywhere. It was quite different from the eastern, more oriental way of life and thinking to which the Jewish people were accustomed. The philosophical thought of Socrates and Plato was made available in every center of the Greek empire. In addition, Aristotle's passionate interest in what we now term scientific analysis and classification of phenomena was well known among educated people everywhere.

Moreover, the Greeks sought to promote their way of thinking with missionary zeal, because they fervently believed that their form of civilization and culture was the highest that the world ever had seen. In the midst of this new approach to life, Palestine had its share of these Greek cities with their Greek names, language, culture and religious way of life too, but little whatsoever is known about what actually was happening in Judea during the third century BC.

Furthermore, two intellectual movements can be noted among the Jewish people in that era. First, there was tremendous activity in Biblical studies at Jerusalem. Prophetic material evidently was collected and edited along with the Psalms and other writings. Also, the temple ritual had grown to become highly elaborate.

The second movement was quite different in nature, but it had a tremendous impact upon the Jewish people for generations upon generations to come. Realizing that their Hebrew language was hidden from the rest of the world, the Jewish people in Alexandria, Egypt, took an extremely bold initiative. They asked the Jerusalem scholars to help them in translating their scriptures into the Greek language. As a result, the Septuagint evolved into being.

In the meantime, the Jewish people in Jerusalem and Judea sought to "put a fence around the Law" and keep themselves "unspotted from the world." Of course, an inevitable clash between the Jewish people in Jerusalem and those in Alexandria transpired, and it happened during the time when the First Book of the Maccabees was recorded.

By 198 BC, the Seleucids, who were centered in Antioch, grew into a stronger Greek kingdom than the one in Egypt. The change in rulers seemed to make little difference at first. Then a crisis suddenly arose between the Greeks to the north and the Judeans. However, the Jewish people seemed equal to the occasion. For the first time in centuries, Israel was aroused to unprecedented heights of valor and faith, due primarily to King Antiochus IV. He ascended to the throne in Syria, or the Seleucid Empire, in 175 BC.

Antiochus IV was described in the First Book of the Maccabees as "a sinful root" (1 Maccabees 1:1-10), and 2

Maccabees called him a "murderer and a blasphemer." The Book of Daniel said that Antiochus gave himself the name Epiphanes, which means "God made manifest." To the Jewish mind, this was blasphemy. Once they experienced the ferocity of his ways, they called Antiochus IV "Epimanes," which meant "mad man."

The trouble began when a foolish party in Jerusalem revolted against Antiochus IV at the very same moment that the Romans had become a thorn in his flesh. Being unable to come to grips with the Romans, Antiochus IV took out his vengeance against the Jewish people. Within a matter of three days, some 80,000 men, women and children of the Jewish nation were brutally slain by soldiers of Antiochus IV (2 Maccabees 5:11-14).

Antiochus himself stormed into the temple, plundered its riches, tore down the curtain that hid the Holy of holies and entered where no one excepting the high priest would dare to go and even at that — only once a year (2 Maccabees 5:15-16).

Then by force, Antiochus IV sought to do what the Jewish people in Jerusalem had resisted for over a century and a half: They were made to adopt Greek culture totally. All distinctiveness of Judaism was to be eliminated. People were to think only the same Greek thoughts as he did. Jewish worship was ordered to cease. Reading of the Law was forbidden. All scrolls were to be destroyed. Also, circumcision and observance of the Sabbath were no longer permitted.

Worst of all, Antiochus ordered an altar to be set up on which swine, the most unclean animals to the Jewish people, were to be sacrificed to the Olympian god Zeus in utter repudiation of the one, true God named Yahweh. There could have been no greater desecration of the temple in Jerusalem. Later generations remembered this act as "the abomination of desolation" or as "the desolating sacrilege."

The resistance to this horrendous sacrilege immediately clustered around the family of one man named Mattathias. With his own hands, this old priest slew the king's officer, who had come to enforce the royal decree. He also murdered a Jewish neighbor, who had become a traitor for the Selucids. Afterward, this little group fled to the hills. Mattathias died almost instantly, but his five famous sons and descendants became the nucleus of resistance.

The eldest son, Judas, as the new leader, was given the name of "Maccabee," which probably meant "hammer." With him at the helm, a guerrilla war was waged against the Greek forces of Antiochus IV until that small Maccabean army succeeded and rededicated the temple in Jerusalem to the glory of Yahweh. This celebration is remembered to the present day as the festival of Hanukkah, which occurs each year during the month of December.

According to legend as recorded in the Talmud of the Jewish people, a small jar of oil was found by the Maccabees when the temple was rededicated. It was sealed by the high priest's seal and was meant for the kindling of the menorah, the candelabrum. The jar reportedly contained sufficient oil for only one night. Miraculously it lasted eight nights until fresh uncontaminated oil could be produced.

Thus, there arose two separate ideas surrounding the celebration of Hanukkah: 1) The victory of the Maccabees, and 2) the miracle of the oil. However, it was the miracle of the oil that subsequently captured the imagination of the Jewish people.

Some learned people suggest that the emphasis on the oil is due to the disillusionment of later generations with the Maccabees. Also, the victory itself evolved to become interpreted in terms of the spiritual power that belonged to the Torah. It was symbolized by the oil that burned miraculously, even when, by the natural order of things, the light should have been snuffed out. It should be noted as well that some Jewish people to this day refuse to accept this Talmudic story as "legend." To them, it always and forever should be viewed as historical fact.

Even at that, the recovery of Jerusalem by a band of Jewish people, which was led by Judas Maccabeus, did not mean total freedom for all of the Jewish people. The war went on. Antiochus IV died the next year, but the struggle was continued by his successors. When Judas Maccabeus was killed in battle, his brother Jonathan stepped forward to carry on leadership with the fighting, which by this time in 160 BC no longer had become a religious war — only a nationalistic one.

In 143 BC, Jonathan was murdered, and his brother Simon, took over. Finally, in 142 BC according to 1 Maccabees 13:41, "The yoke of the Gentiles was removed from Israel." Judea became a completely independent nation. Also, Simon Maccabee became the ruler of this new independent state of Judea.

During the period of the so-called Maccabean Wars from 175 BC to 135 BC, the pure fires of zeal for the law, which existed since the time of the prophet named Ezra, had subsided greatly. That happened with the ascension of this royal line descended from Judas Maccabeus. Moreover, Jewish religious leadership split into parties. The two major parties were the Sadducees and the Pharisees. In addition, there was the Qumran community.

Eight years after Simon became political ruler of Judea, he was murdered. His son, John Hyrcanus, succeeded him and conquered most of Palestine. However, he forcibly proselytized many. At the same time, the Pharisees gained a wide following in opposition to the aristocratic Sadducees. In 104 BC, Aristobolus I replaced Hyrcanus and conquered Galilee. From that point onward, however, Jerusalem and Judea suffered desperately at the hands of a number of ferocious rulers.

In 103 BC, Alexander Janneus followed his brother Aristobulus I. He issued coins with the title of king, which sparked a great controversy. It led to a revolt against Janneus by the Pharisees that ended when Janneus reportedly crucified 800 rebels. Finally, Janneus died in 76 BC. His widow, Alexandra, ruled as queen, who favored the Pharisees.

When Alexandra succumbed, she bequeathed rule to her elder son, Hyrcanus II, but the younger brother Aristobulus II, who was backed by the Sadducees, seized the crown by force. Incited by Antipater, an Idumean, Hyrcanus II besieged Jerusalem. Both Antipater and Hyrcanus II sought Roman support. In 63 BC, Pompey captured Jerusalem for Rome, and Hyrcanus II was appointed high priest. As a result, Jerusalem and Judea lost their independence for the last time.

Interestingly enough, however, some very succinct messages are recorded in 2 Maccabees including physical resurrection (2 Maccabees 7:9, 11, 14; 14:46), prayer for the dead (2 Maccabees 12:43-45) and intercession of saints (2 Maccabees 15:12, 14). Also, vivid pictures of the intervention of angels in human affairs (2 Maccabees 3:25-26; 5:2-3; 10:29-30; 11:6-8) and the important role of the martyr first appear here (2 Maccabees 6-7; 14:37-46), as well as the doctrine of creation out of nothing (2 Maccabees 7:28). All in all, 1 and 2 Maccabees give somewhat of an insight into events leading to the next portion of scripture.

John the Baptist from all available resources in the Bible is known forthrightly as forerunner of the Messiah and of the Messianic age. Any other caricature of this unique person just does not seem to fit. Even presupposed ideas of what such a predecessor might be like falls far short of what normally might be imagined.

Most people would think of one who prepared the way for royalty — even in the divine sense of the term — as being civil, good looking and decent (Matthew 11:8; Luke

185

7:25), but John the Baptist was anything but that. He arrived upon the scene from the wilderness and is described as a wild-looking man. He was uncouth, ate locusts and wild honey and dressed in camel's hair with a leather belt strapped around his waist (Matthew 3: 4; Mark 1:6).

At the same time, John the Baptist reportedly gathered a great following around him that lasted for many years after his death. Some people even saw John the Baptist as a prophet (Matthew 11:14; John 1:24). That thought was quickly dispelled in the Biblical record when it was proclaimed that more than a prophet is found in John the Baptist (Matthew 11:9; Luke 7:26-27).

Moreover, the message proclaimed by John the Baptist during his ministry does not even come close to what normally might be expected in announcing the coming of any kind of royalty. John the Baptist was loud, brash and demanding with a denigrating sound to his voice in pronouncing repentance for the forgiveness of sins (Mark 1:4). He unabashedly proclaimed: "Repent, for the kingdom of God is coming near" (Matthew 3:2; Luke 3:3).

Perhaps surprisingly as a result, people from the whole Judean countryside, the city of Jerusalem and throughout the region around the Jordan (Luke 3:3) "were going out to see John the Baptist, flocking to hear him, being baptized by him in the river Jordan" (Mark 1:5) and "confessing their sins" (Matthew 3:6).

This description of John the Baptist is not all that could be said about him. He was born in the hill country of a Judean town (Luke 1:39) to older parents, Elizabeth and Zechariah, who had no children. He was dedicated as a Nazarite, or one completely set apart for God's service, but contrary to Samson, who was so conceived and so dedicated many years previously, John the Baptist remained faithful unto that calling to his very last breath.

186

Why did people respond so favorably and so numerously to John the Baptist? It simply was because he spoke the truth! For this very same reason, many other people fiercely resisted the message of John the Baptist and deeply resented him personally. This included ones such as the Pharisees (John 1:24), Sadducees (Matthew 3:7), King Herod Antipas of Galilee and Perea and most especially Herod's wife, Herodias, and her daughter.

Herod and Herodias despised John the Baptist because it was known throughout the land that King Herod Antipas illegally took Herodias, his brother Phillip's wife, away from him and married her. Phillip was king over the northeastern region of Palestine. King Herod Antipas hated being told straightforwardly by John the Baptist that he was wrong in this action and in all of his evil ways (Mark 6:17-18; Luke 3:18-20). So, the king arrested John the Baptist and put him in prison, but he feared doing anything further with John the Baptist because of his popularity among the people (Matthew 14:5; Mark 6:19-20). In addition and strangely enough, King Herod Antipas enjoyed listening to John the Baptist (Mark 6:20).

An opportunity did arise to rid John the Baptist from the whole scene when King Herod Antipas gave a banquet on his birthday for his courtiers, officers and leaders in Galilee (Mark 6:21) somewhere around 27 AD to 28 AD. At this time the daughter of Herodias reportedly danced before the company. She pleased Herod Antipas so much that he promised on an oath to grant her whatever she might ask (Matthew 14:7; Mark 6:21).

At that, the daughter of Herodias reportedly went out and confided with her mother; "What should I ask for?" Herodias apparently replied: "The head of John the Baptist on a platter" (Matthew 14:8; Mark 6:24). Supposedly, the king grieved at that request. Yet out of his regard for his oath and for the guests, King Herod Antipas commanded that it be given to her. So, he sent to have John the Baptist beheaded in prison (Matthew 14:9-10; Mark 6:25-27).

When a soldier of the guard brought the head of John the Baptist on a platter, King Herod Antipas gave it to the girl. She in turn gave it to her mother (Matthew 14:11; Mark 6:28). When John's disciples heard about it, they came and took his body, laid it in a tomb and buried it (Matthew 14:12; Mark 6:29).

CHAPTER 8

JESUS OF NAZARETH

Contrary to what many people have projected through the ages, the man named Jesus of Nazareth was a real, genuine human being. From the very beginnings of the Christian movement, there have been many individuals and groups who have denied his manly characteristics.

Several ideas about this person have been touted over the centuries such as: He just appeared on earth without being born; he did not have a physical body — only seemed to have one; he was not crucified. He did not die or even become buried. Instead, Jesus somehow was assumed into heavenly realms.

Those people, who believed any or all of these thoughts to be true, ultimately were declared to be heretical by a growing Christian movement, but seemingly that did not halt the continual onslaught of this kind of thinking. Every generation had those people who could not fathom the fact that this man from Nazareth was a true, down-to-earth, human being.

In December of 2010, a group of well-to-do people flaunted the thought on billboards across the United States of America that the Bible, especially as it related to the person of Jesus, was purely a myth. Not only scripture was declared as being without any substance, which in and of itself was an unverifiable statement, but also it was insisted that all people should join them in thinking the exact same way that they did.

Evidently, this modern message did not receive any more attention in the twenty-first century than it did in the first two centuries AD, because there appeared to be more people genuinely interested in the message that Jesus has to offer in the world today than ever before this time. It no way means that all who rally around this man from Nazareth always have acted as he did. In fact, some of the worst atrocities in human history have occurred in his name and for his sake. Even at that, however, his name and deeds as a human being on the face of the earth have not been snuffed out but keeps on growing.

What about this man named Jesus of Nazareth? What characteristics, according to the Bible, did he possess along with every other human being on earth? That which immediately arises from the scriptural account, especially in the gospels of Matthew and Luke and even more so in the gospels of Mark and John, is that Jesus of Nazareth was born in Bethlehem of Judea, lived some 33 years during a time span between 6 BC and 30 AD, was crucified in the environs of Jerusalem until dead and was laid in a borrowed tomb to decompose for three days.

Even more directly speaking, Jesus legally was born to a mother (Mark 15:40) and a father (John 6:42) in what appears to be a wonderful, but poor family — full of brothers and sisters (Matthew 12:46, 13:55; Mark 3:42; 6:3). He grew up at a recognizable place in northern Palestine, which to this day is known as Nazareth. He spent three well-known adult years ministering to the needs of people and speaking to individuals as well as among crowds of people. Most of this took place around the Sea of Galilee in northern Palestine in what is referred even today as the Middle East.

He chose disciples. He called and invited people to follow him. At the same time, Jesus had his detractors and even unrelenting, vengeful enemies. He ate and drank (Matthew 11:18; Luke 7:34), walked (Matthew 4:18; Mark 1:16, 11:27; John 6:66; 10:23; 11:54) and rode on a donkey (Matthew 21:2-7; Mark 11:2-7; Luke 19:30-35; John 12:5). He felt the gamut of human emotions including anger, sorrow, fatigue, betrayal, loneliness, joy and gratitude.

His thinking not only was thoroughly human but breathlessly exceptional. In subtle but formidable ways, Jesus used parables or examples from the real-life situations of his time and place — to make his point irrefutably clear for people of all time. In high prophetic fashion, he employed direct words to confront people. In this manner, he allowed no excuses to prevail at any time or in any situation. Jesus truly was a genius in every manner of speaking, which is attested by learned people who have studied his statements over many generations.

This man from Nazareth was exceptional in other ways as well. He reportedly brought healing to people who were sick and infirmed. He supposedly was involved in miraculous happenings. He even forgave sins. All of these actions not only drew people to him but also repulsed others — especially those in political and religious positions of human power and authority. They questioned him at every turn and did not like what they heard.

This diabolical reaction to Jesus began with the forgiveness of sins because no human being, only God, could forgive sins. Strong resentment against him escalated from this point. When this man from Nazareth was elevated beyond just being a rabbi or teacher, physician and prophet, as controversial as all of that may have been — to Son of God, Messiah, King, Lord and Savior, it was too much for any opposition to swallow. Therefore, they sought to entrap him, convict him, kill him and forever dispose of him and his message, according to the Bible, just as had been accomplished with those who preceded him — including John the Baptist.

The Gospel according to Mark, which is the first written message about Jesus of Nazareth, states it best. This account begins with his entrance into ministry as an adult and proceeds in staccato fashion directly to his death by crucifixion. No frills, no elaborate explanations, no fanciful allusions are presented here — just strong, hard facts as the writer of this gospel perceives them.

Nonetheless, all opposition did not in any way deter this man Jesus. He kept on going through thick and thin with his words and actions, which not only were formidable, but never to be forgotten — even if they might have been exaggerated over time. Why? It has to be because what he said and did, even as reported about him, is true. In other words, according to the Gospel of John, Jesus is the incarnate word of God — the truth for all human existence.

There was absolutely no falsehood, fiction or deceit in Jesus of Nazareth. Furthermore, the incarnated truth in him may slumber and lie dormant within people for a while — even over an extended period of time but cannot be extinguished. Because Jesus by his own recorded testimony is the truth, people who believe in him can be set free. In fact, that is the only way human beings are able to be liberated to live the quality of life, which was meant for them from the beginning.

What does that mean for people in this existence even today? The answer is found in the life of Jesus himself as recorded in the Bible from the onset of his adult ministry. That began with his baptism by the person known as John the Baptist. It is true that the first known act of Jesus, as an adult, occurred when he traveled from Nazareth of Galilee to the place where John the Baptist was baptizing people along the River Jordan, an event recorded in all four gospel accounts of Matthew, Mark, Luke and John.

Prior to that time, John the Baptist told the people gathered there: "I baptize you with water for repentance, but one, who is more powerful than I, is coming after me. I am not worthy to carry his sandals. He will baptize you with the Holy Spirit" (Mark 1:7-8). Furthermore, it was reported that the one, true God, who sent John the Baptist to baptize with water, said to John: "He, on whom you see the Spirit descend and remain, is the one, who baptizes with the Holy Spirit" (John 1:33).

When John the Baptist saw Jesus of Nazareth coming toward him, John declared: "Here is the Lamb of God who takes away the sin of the world" (John 1:29)! Furthermore, what John said to Jesus was: "I need to be baptized by you, and do you come to me?" (Matthew 3:14). However, Jesus is recorded as replying: "Let it be so now, for it is proper in this way to fulfill all righteousness," to which John the Baptist assented (Matthew 3:15).

To fulfill all righteousness meant to accomplish God's mission in forgiving all sin, as already stated, to lead all people into righteous living, quality existence, a whole new, totally different way of life and to begin the process of ushering in the Kingdom of God.

At the baptism with Jesus of Nazareth via John the Baptist, what was predicted ahead of time actually did transpire, according to the record. It occurred in a manner that apparently was visible to everyone, remained with Jesus throughout the rest of his life, made an unequalled impact upon the lives of people who followed him and was fulfilled in every way that was stated ahead of time.

Specifically speaking, as recorded in the Bible, "When Jesus had been baptized and had been praying, the Holy Spirit descended upon him in bodily form like a dove and alighted upon him" (Luke 3:21). The Holy Spirit never left Jesus of Nazareth until he brutally expired upon a wooden cross by Roman act and decree (John 19:30).

Jesus with all of the power of the one, true God within him was tempted by the evil forces in this world commonly attributed to Satan or the devil, but Jesus ultimately and humanly was equal to that seeming alluring test. It came in three scenarios. Without any food upon a barren landscape over an extended period of time, Jesus first was tempted to command a stone to become a loaf of bread (Matthew 4:3) but responded by saying: "One does not live by bread alone, but by every word that comes from the mouth of God" (Luke 4:4).

Second, Jesus was shown instantaneously the kingdoms of the world in all of their splendor and was promised to be given all of them outright if he would just worship the evil one of this world (Luke 4:5-6). Jesus answered: "It is written, 'Worship the Lord your God, and serve only the one, true God' " (Matthew 4:10).

Third, Jesus was taken to the pinnacle of the temple in Jerusalem with the words: "If you are the Son of God, throw yourself down from here, for it is written that God will command angels to protect you, and on their hands they will bear you up" (Matthew 4:5-6). Jesus replied: "Again it is written, 'Do not put the Lord your God to the test' " (Luke 4:12).

At that, Jesus reportedly commanded: "Away with you evil one!" When all tests were completed, wickedness departed from Jesus until a more opportune moment arrived during the time of betrayal, trial, denial and desertion. Angels came and ministered unto him (Matthew 4:10-11).

During this same period, Jesus accordingly worked together with John the Baptist following the baptism. He even shared some of the same disciples with John the Baptist until there finally was a parting of the ways. That separation apparently transpired over the issue of which came first — the pronouncement of God's judgment upon people, or the primary emphasis upon the Kingdom of God coming to the people beginning with Jesus, the now-anointed Son of God.

Apparently, John the Baptist refused to give up his belief in pronouncing the judgment of God prior to any manifestation of the Kingdom of God. In order not to make any further trouble with John the Baptist and out of deep respect for him, Jesus removed himself from the scene and retreated to his hometown of Nazareth until the imprisonment of John the Baptist.

Then, Jesus emerged anew to proclaim that the Kingdom of God now is at hand. By the amazing and total power of God the Holy Spirit, he performed all of the signs and wonders of this kingdom before the eyes of everyone. He gathered followers, some of whom formerly were disciples of John the Baptist. Thus, it is not at all surprising that John the Baptist from his prison cell supposedly questioned whether Jesus really was the Messiah as he first had recognized him to be.

John the Baptist sent some of his envoys to ask if Jesus really was the one, or should people wait for another person? (Luke 11:20). Jesus masterfully answered that question indirectly before John's emissaries and yet fully in keeping with his commitment in elevating the Kingdom of God far above the pronouncement of God's judgment upon the people.

Since many people had just been cured of diseases, plagues and evil spirits by Jesus, and sight had been given to many who were blind (Luke 7:21), Jesus answered the emissaries of John the Baptist: "Go and tell John what you hear and see: the blind receive their sight, the lame walk, the lepers are cleansed, the deaf hear, the dead are raised, and the poor have good news brought to them" (Matthew 11:4-5).

In other words, fruits of the Kingdom of God already were made manifest only to be furthered by those who exhibited their own fruitful actions in Jesus of Nazareth. Therefore, people have a choice even today of whether to follow the denunciating judgmental words and actions of John the Baptist and those who preceded him, or to show forth the beautiful and wondrous fruits of the Kingdom of God in Jesus of Nazareth.

Jesus drives this point home with his words to the people gathered around him after the departure of John the Baptist's followers. Jesus said to those with him: What did you see in John the Baptist? A prophet? Yes and more than a prophet!"

Paraphrasing the scripture at this point, Jesus continued by saying: I tell you that of all people on earth, no one fulfilled his God-given purpose in this life better than John the Baptist! "And yet the least in the Kingdom of God is greater than he" (Luke 7:28).

In other words, quite simply and stronger than anything else that can be said: Those who follow after Jesus to further the Kingdom of God in this life, even in the least amount possible, are much greater than those who pronounce doom and gloom in anticipation of the Kingdom of God, as John the Baptist and all of his predecessors did. Wow! As Jesus himself would say, those who have ears to hear, let them hear. Even more importantly, let them act accordingly.

It is well known from the Biblical record that Jesus began his ministry of only a few years in length at his hometown of Nazareth in northern Palestine (Luke 4:16-19). After learning that John the Baptist was imprisoned, Jesus picked up the scroll in the synagogue that he attended regularly on the Sabbath and read from what we know today as Isaiah 61:1-2:

> The Spirit of the Lord is upon me, because he has anointed me; he has sent me to bring good news to the oppressed, to bind up the brokenhearted, to proclaim liberty to the captives and recovery of sight to the blind, to comfort all who mourn and to proclaim the year of the Lord's favor.

At that, Jesus rolled up the scroll, gave it back to the attendant and sat down. The eyes of all in the synagogue were fixed on him. Then, he began to say to them: "Today this scripture has been fulfilled in your hearing." All spoke well of him and were amazed at the gracious words that came out of his mouth (Luke 4:20-22).

However, that was not the end of this beginning in his hometown. When asked to do miraculous things before the home crowd, now that the Spirit of the Lord was upon him,

Jesus replied: "No prophet is accepted in that one's hometown" (Luke 4:24), but that was not all. Jesus proceeded even further, which ultimately antagonized everyone.

He firmly stated:

> The truth is: There were many widows in Israel in the time of Elijah, when there was a severe famine over all the land, yet Elijah was sent to none of them except to a widow at Zarephthath in Sidon. There were also many lepers in the northern kingdom of Israel at the time of the prophet Elisha, and none of them were cleansed except Naaman the Syrian.
> — Luke 4:27

In other words, when the people of Nazareth wanted Jesus to perform miraculous acts before the home crowd, as he reportedly had done elsewhere, Jesus downplayed the whole thought to the point of asserting that such was meant for outsiders, foreigners, even Gentiles but not for them. This infuriated the people of Nazareth to the point of rage. To even suggest that their enemies, those outside of themselves, who were the descendants of Abraham, Isaac and Jacob — the chosen ones of the one, true God, would be more worthy of miraculous acts than they was unthinkable.

When Jesus implied that his hearers in Nazareth were as unbelieving as citizens in the northern kingdom of Israel during the time of Elijah and Elisha, which was a time that was notorious for its great wickedness, the people rejected him, drove him out of town, wanted to throw him off a cliff, but he narrowly escaped (Luke 4:28-30).

After that, Jesus began his ministry in earnest with great authority and with the ruling force of the Holy Spirit that prevailed with him throughout all of the rest of his days. He moved to Capernaum near the northwestern part of the Sea of Galilee. It had been a thriving city with great wealth in the near past, but now it was beginning to be in decline. Because it was the headquarters for many Roman troops, word could spread throughout the Roman Empire.

Jesus spoke in the synagogue there and elsewhere throughout the region, because itinerant rabbis always were welcome to speak and teach to those gathered each Sabbath in synagogues. He called disciples, some twelve in number, and invited others to listen to what he had to say and to follow him. Moreover, great crowds of people did just that, but it did not stop him from focusing upon an individual person all along the way.

What did Jesus preach and teach about a dawning of the Kingdom of God in human life via his own leadership? What was unique and different yet predicted to take place among people of the one, true God? What was the Kingdom of God genuinely like?

Jesus turned the whole world upside down when he said the Kingdom of God was unlike any other kingdom upon the face of the earth. The Kingdom of God was one of peace, healing, love, joy and full of faithfulness, hope and concern for others. There would be no war, hatred, violence, shiftiness, selfishness and greed in this kingdom.

The blessed ones would be "the poor in spirit" (Matthew 5:3), "those who weep and mourn" (Luke 6:21, "the meek" (Matthew 5:5), "those who hunger" (Luke 6:21) "and thirst for righteousness" (Matthew 5:6), "the merciful" (Matthew 5:7), "the peacemakers" (Matthew 5:9), "those who are persecuted for righteousness' sake" (Matthew 5:10), "those who are hated, excluded, reviled and defamed on account of Jesus" (Luke 6:22).

They would be those who love God (Matthew 22:37), love Jesus (John 21:15-17), love, honor and rejoice in the Holy Spirit (Luke 10:21; John 4:23-24; Romans 8:6), love the word of the Lord (Luke 10:42), love themselves in truth (Luke 10:28), love their neighbor (Mark 12:31, 33), love one another (John 13:34-35), love their enemies (Matthew 5:44) and care for those in need (Luke 10:30-37).

They would do good to those who hate them (Luke 6:27), bless those who curse them (Luke 6:28), pray for those who persecute them (Matthew 5:44) and turn the other cheek when struck upon one side of their face (Luke 6:29). They do good wherever they go (Luke 6:35, 45), go a second mile when forced to go one (Matthew 5:41), give their shirt also when someone takes their coat (Matthew 5:40) and give to those who beg without expecting anything in return (Luke 6:30). Most important of all, people belonging to the Kingdom of God do unto others as they would wish to be treated themselves (Matthew 7:12).

They give good gifts to others (Luke 6:36), do not judge others as if they never would be judged (Matthew 7:1-2), do not take the speck out of another person's existence without dealing with the gigantic log in their own way of looking at things (Luke 6:41-42) and do not place a gift upon the altar before seeking to be reconciled with a brother or sister (Matthew 5:23-24).

Instead, people in the Kingdom of God show mercy (Luke 10:36), forgive others (Matthew 18:21-22), build their lives upon the solid bedrock and foundation of God's presence (Luke 6:48-49), endure the storms of life (Matthew 7:24-27), produce good fruits out of the goodness of their own heart (Matthew 7:16-20), let their light shine before others and give glory to God (Matthew 5:16). They work prodigiously and as quickly as possible in coming to terms with an accuser (Matthew 5:25) and live not by mere words but by deeds worthy of the one and only God (John 5:29).

They actively ask, seek and knock for assistance from the Lord and refuse to remain passive or lethargic (Matthew 7:7-11), do not worry about anything — even tomorrow (Matthew 6:25-34), take the narrow, straight pathway to life

(Matthew 7:13-14) and always move forward toward perfection in God's love (Matthew 5:48).

In addition, Jesus used parables of the Kingdom of God to reinforce and strengthen his message everywhere including what is commonly known as the hidden treasure (Matthew 13:44), the pearl of great price (Matthew 13:45), the scattered seed (Mark 4:26), the mustard seed (Mark 4:30), the hidden yeast (Luke 13:20), being as a child (Luke 18:17), invitations to the wedding feast (Matthew 22:2), ten bridesmaids with their lamps (Matthew 25:1-13), the loaned money (Matthew 25:14) and laborers in the vineyard (Matthew 20:1).

All people within this Kingdom of God exist in vast contrast to the kingdoms of this world. Jesus said as much at many points along the way. More importantly, he always acted wholly consistent with the way in which he spoke.

Where did all of that get him? Evidently, nowhere fast! Trouble and opposition seemed to be the outcome everywhere he turned, even though crowds of people apparently gathered around him continually and followed him almost everywhere. That antagonism and even the desire to kill Jesus of Nazareth apparently came from every direction including such people as the scribes, Pharisees, Sadducees, Herodians, chief priests, people of the Jewish nation, elders of the people, the Gadarenes, Gentiles and ultimately Judas Iscariot, one of the disciples of Jesus in the supposed high office of treasurer with the group, the temple police, Caiaphas the high priest and his father-in-law Annas, Pilate who was the appointed prefect of Judea by Tiberius Caesar of Rome, King Herod Antipas of Galilee and the Roman soldiers.

Reasons for resentment against Jesus were many and varied as well: Jesus healed people on the Sabbath, which was against the law — especially according to the Pharisees. Jesus and his disciples plucked heads of grain on the Sabbath, which was unlawful too. Resentment began to escalate even further when Jesus forgave sins. As recorded early in the first written Gospel of Mark, sins could only be forgiven by God. For the man Jesus to forgive sins was utter blasphemy to them (Mark 2:6-7).

This man from Nazareth spent time eating with tax collectors and sinners, which was disgusting to scribes and Pharisees, because they alone were the righteous ones and deserved all of the attention, and it unsettled them no end (Mark 2:16-18). Jesus told the parable of the wicked tenant farmers who killed messengers and even the owner's son, who were sent to collect the rent. In the process, the religious leaders including the chief priests and scribes realized that Jesus was talking about them, and they sought to destroy Jesus like they had done with all who did precede him. Realizing the truth of what Jesus said, these religious leaders sought all the more to rid themselves of him by putting Jesus of Nazareth to death (Luke 20:1-19).

After Lazarus was raised from the dead, a dinner was given in honor of Lazarus at his home. Jesus and his disciples were there as well. When people heard that Jesus and Lazarus would be there, a crowd came to see them. As a result, many Jewish people were deserting their Jewish heritage to believe in Jesus. So then, the chief priests planned to put Lazarus to death along with Jesus (John 12:1, 9-11).

On the very next day, a great crowd who had arrived at the festival heard that Jesus was coming to Jerusalem. They took branches of palm trees and went out to meet him exclaiming: "Hosanna! Blessed is he who comes in the name of the Lord, the King of Israel" (John 12:12-13). As a result, the Pharisees reportedly said to one another: "You see! We can do nothing. Look, the world has gone after him" (John 12:19).

Nevertheless, the saga does not end there. The next day, Jesus upset the tables of the money changers in the temple by angrily proclaiming: "It is written, 'My house shall be called a house of prayer for all nations,' but you have made it a den of robbers," and the chief priests and scribes looked for a way to kill him (Mark 11:17-18).

Around that same time Jesus was confronted in the temple area by some of the Jewish people, which resulted in even more heightened reasons against Jesus of Nazareth. Jesus was asked point blank by them if he was greater than their father Abraham (John 8:53) and Jesus unhesitatingly answered: "Very truly, I tell you, before Abraham was, I am." So, they picked up stones to throw at Jesus, but he hid himself and went out of the temple area (John 8:58-59).

Jesus said to the Jewish people gathered around the portico of Solomon in the temple area at Jerusalem: "The Father and I are one," and they took up stones again to stone him (John 10:30-31). In the process, they stated: "We are going to stone you for blasphemy, because you, though only a human being, are making yourself God" (John 10:33).

Jesus replied: "If I am doing the works of my Father in heaven, even though you do not believe me, believe the works, so that you may know and understand that God the Father is in me, and I am in the Father," but they did not even believe that much. Instead they tried to arrest Jesus once more, but he escaped from the intent of their murderous hands (John 10:38-39).

Therefore, it seems to be a well known fact, according to the Bible, that Jesus severely criticized each and all of the religious and political figures, which obviously brought strong retaliation from them — against him. Since they seemingly could not succeed in any debate with Jesus, no matter how hard they deviously had tried, the only answer that apparently was left for them was to physically silence him by putting him to death.

Even that was not easy. Jesus was able to escape their wrath and physical harm many times before they finally were able to arrest him. Ultimately, however, all of those who opposed Jesus were able to accomplish that horrendous deed in the springtime around 30 AD and put him to an ugly, torturous, gruesome death.

It commenced toward the end of that same week in Jerusalem. After a meal on Thursday evening, Jesus went out to pray in the Garden of Gethsemane not many paces east of the city of Jerusalem. When he rose from those agonizing prayerful moments, in which Jesus ultimately put his whole existence in God's hands, Judas Iscariot came with a large crowd armed with swords and clubs. Judas Iscariot betrayed Jesus with a kiss into the company of those armed persons. One of the people with Jesus drew his own sword, but Jesus insisted that he put back his sword saying that those who take the sword will perish by the sword (Matthew 26:47-52).

According to the Gospel of John (18:12-24), the soldiers, their officer and the Jewish police arrested Jesus, bound him and took him first to Annas. Even though the Romans had appointed to the position another high priest, Caiaphas, the son-in-law of Annas, the office of high priest itself was held for life, and Annas still was the official high priest in the eyes of the Jewish people. Annas interrogated Jesus first, but when a policeman standing nearby did not like the way that Jesus spoke to Annas, he struck Jesus. At that, Annas sent Jesus to Caiaphas.

The ones who had arrested Jesus took him to the house of Caiaphas, the high priest, where chief priests, scribes and elders were assembled (Mark 14:53). There the council was looking for some testimony against Jesus in order that they might put him to death, but they found none. Many gave false testimony against him. Even their testimony did not match with one another. Some heard Jesus say: "I will destroy this temple made with hands and in three days build another one not made with hands," but even on this point their testimony supposedly did not agree. Caiaphas stood up and proclaimed to Jesus: "Have you no answer?" Jesus reportedly was silent (Mark 14:55-61).

At that Caiaphas stated these words directly to Jesus: "I put you under oath before the living God, 'Are you the Messiah, the Son of God?' " Jesus proclaimed: "I am" (Mark 14:61-62) or "You say that I am" (Luke 22:70). Caiaphas tore his cloths and exclaimed: "He has blasphemed! We need no other witnesses. You, here, have heard this blasphemy. What is your verdict?" Reportedly, all of them condemned him as deserving death (Mark 14:63-65). Then, they spit in his face, struck him and slapped him (Matthew 16:63-68).

Afterward, they sent Jesus to Pilate, the Roman Governor of Judea. According to the Gospel of Luke, the assembly did bring Jesus before Pilate and accused him by proclaiming: "We found this man perverting our nation and saying that he is the Messiah, a king." Pilate asked Jesus, "Are you king of the Jews?" Jesus answered: "You say so." Then, Pilate said to the people there, "I find no basis for accusation against this man," but they were insistent saying: "He stirs up the people by teaching throughout Judea from Galilee where he began" (Luke 23:1-5).

When Pilate heard this, he asked Jesus if he were a Galilean. When he learned that Jesus was a Galilean under the jurisdiction of Herod Antipas, Pilate sent Jesus off to Herod Antipas, who was in Jerusalem at that time. When Herod Antipas saw Jesus, he was glad because he had wanted to see him for some time hoping that Jesus would perform some miraculous sign. However, Jesus gave Herod Antipas no response whatsoever while others there treated Jesus with contempt and mocked him. Herod Antipas sent Jesus back to Pilate (Luke 23:6-12).

According to the Gospel of Matthew, a governor at the time of the Passover festival was accustomed to releasing one prisoner who could be anyone whom the crowd would wish. At that time, there was a notorious criminal in prison

204

named Barabbas, who had committed heinous murder. After the people had gathered, Pilate asked the crowd: "Whom do you want me to release to you — Barabbas or Jesus, who is called the Messiah?" They said: "Barabbas." Pilate continued the question: "Then, what shall I do with Jesus?" All of them exclaimed: "Crucify him" (Matthew 27:15-22).

Since Pilate could find nothing wrong with Jesus of Nazareth; since Jesus was claimed to be a king, this set him up against the emperor, Tiberius Caesar, according to the crowd. When Jesus had no army or earthly government to back him up, the only option remaining from this point onward for this crowd of authorities and disgruntled people was to mock Jesus, have him flogged, beaten and handed over to be crucified, which did happen.

Moreover, it did take place in spite of the fact that the wife of Pilate sent word to the governor: "Have nothing to do with that innocent man, for today I have suffered a great deal because of a dream about him" (Matthew 27:19). Furthermore, this ordeal only meant unjustified, unwarranted and unequalled shame, humiliation and degradation for Jesus of Nazareth because of his declared innocence from everyone and coming from every conceivable direction. He was all alone in this ordeal of seemingly relentless suffering and subjugation. No one came to his defense to support him.

According to the Gospel of John, Pilate took Jesus and had him flogged. The soldiers wove a crown of thorns and put it upon his head, and they dressed him in a purple robe. They kept coming up to him one after another, cynically bowing and mockingly proclaiming: "Hail, King of the Jews!" They struck him on the face. At that, Pilate again went out to the crowd reportedly saying: "Look, I am bringing him out to you to let you know that I find no case against him" (John 19:1-4).

When Jesus came out wearing the crown of thorns and the purple robe, Pilate announced: "Here is the man!" When the chief priests, the crowd and the police saw him, they shouted: "Crucify him! Crucify him!" (John 19:5-6). Pilate spoke to them again, "Why, what evil has he done?" They shouted all the more, "Crucify him!" So, wishing to satisfy the crowd, Pilate released Barabbas for them and washed his hands of the whole affair. After flogging Jesus again and stripping him of the purple cloak, Pilate handed him over to be crucified (Mark 15:14-15).

As they led Jesus out to be crucified, a passerby coming into Jerusalem from the country named Simon of Cyrene was compelled to carry Jesus' cross. According to the Gospel of John, they took Jesus to what is called The Place of the Skull, which in Hebrew is named Golgotha. There, they crucified him with two criminals, one on his right side and one on his left.

Pilate also had an inscription written and put on the cross of Jesus. It read: "Jesus of Nazareth, the King of the Jews." Many Jewish people apparently saw this inscription, because the place where he was crucified was very near the city of Jerusalem. Moreover, it was written in Hebrew, Latin and Greek. Therefore, the chief priests of the Jewish people expressed to Pilate: "Do not write, 'The King of the Jews,' but, 'This man said, I am the King of the Jews,' " Pilate answered: "What I have written, I have written" (John 19:17-22).

According to the Gospel of Luke, when they crucified Jesus, he said: "Father, forgive them; for they know not what they are doing." The people stood watching as the leaders scoffed at him saying: "He saved others; let him save himself if he is the Messiah of God, his chosen one!" The soldiers mocked him too by offering him sour wine and saying: "If you are King of the Jews, save yourself!" (Luke 23:34-38).

One of the criminals, who hanged there, kept deriding Jesus and saying, "Are you not the Messiah? Save yourself and us!" The other criminal, however, rebuked him saying,

206

"Do you not fear God since you are under the same sentence of condemnation? Indeed, we have been condemned justly, for we are getting what we deserve for our deeds, but this man has done nothing wrong" (Luke 23:39-41).

That same fellow turned to Jesus and said: "Remember me when you come into your kingdom." Jesus reportedly replied: "Truly, I tell you, today you will be with me in Paradise" (Luke 23:42-43).

It was about noon when darkness came over the whole land until three in the afternoon. When the light of the sun faded, the curtain of the temple was torn in two. Jesus crying out with a loud voice proclaimed: "Father, into your hands I commend my spirit." Having said this, Jesus of Nazareth took his last breath and died (Luke 23:44-46).

When the centurion and those with him, who were keeping close watch over Jesus of Nazareth and saw what had taken place, they said: "Truly, this man was God's Son!" (Matthew 27:54; Mark 16:39).

Of course, Peter, who was a disciple of Jesus, was the first person in the Bible to voice this statement about Jesus of Nazareth. As recorded in the Gospel of Matthew, when Jesus came into the district of Caesarea Philippi, he asked his disciples: "Who do people say that I am?" They replied: "Some say John the Baptist, but others say Elijah, and still others — Jeremiah or one of the prophets." Jesus asked another question of them: "But who do you say that I am?" Simon Peter answered: "You are the Messiah, the Christ, Son of the living God."

Jesus reportedly said to Peter:

Blessed are you, Simon son of Jonah! Flesh and blood has not revealed this to you, but my Father in heaven. I tell you, you are Peter, and on this rock I will build my church, and the gates of Hades will not prevail against it. I will give you the keys of the kingdom of heaven, and whatever you bind on earth will

be bound in heaven, and whatever you loose on earth will be
loosed in heaven.   — Matthew 16:13-19

From that point forward Jesus as the Messiah, the Christ, the Son of the living God – as well as King of the Jews, Lord, Savior, the highest priest after the order of Melchizedek and even King of kings became the normative way of referring to the person, Jesus of Nazareth. All kinds of people in all sorts of ways and in all types of settings used these additional names of the man, Jesus of Nazareth. In fact, the suffix Nazareth very quickly dropped entirely out of sight among all people and hardly — if at all — returned to the vocabulary and mindset of human beings. Even more striking is the fact that the name Jesus Christ was turned around to be posited in even stronger nomenclature by referring to this person as Christ Jesus in order that his divine nature would come first in people's mind.

As expressed in the Biblical record itself, people no longer looked upon the man Jesus as being merely and only human but as the divine Son of God (2 Corinthians 5:16). This had been attested by all kinds of people following what now is known as the great confession of Peter (Matthew 16:16), a disciple and apostle of Jesus. In addition, there were basically two radically different and opposing responses to his divinity at that time, as already documented from the Biblical record.

Some people straightforwardly and reverently claimed Jesus as the Messiah, the Christ, the Son of God, as Peter did — as well as the centurion when he witnessed Jesus in taking his last breath, but others held utter distaste and disdain for Jesus! Moreover, these expressions did not cease following his death. They kept spreading and multiplying throughout all of the time to come — even to this very day.

Nonetheless, whether these names are employed contemptuously or reverently, the reality of Jesus as the Mes-

208

siah, the Christ, the Son of the living God does not go away. It is a most haunting thought but even more than that! It involves the destiny of every human being upon earth, and that destiny is related directly to the complete biography concerning Jesus of Nazareth.

The biography of all people from the beginning of their existence ends with their death. They may live on in people's memory but never physically or in bodily form. Like every other individual who ever lived, Jesus succumbed too. According to the Biblical record, when Jesus expired, a man named Joseph of Arimathea near eventide did proceed boldly to Pilate and asked for the body of Jesus.

Pilate reportedly summoned a high-ranking Roman soldier and asked if Jesus really was dead. The simple answer came in reply that he had been dead for some time. As a result, Pilate did grant the body of Jesus to Joseph of Arimathea (Mark 15:42-45).

Then Joseph bought a linen cloth. After that, he reportedly took down the dead body of Jesus from the cross where he had expired. Joseph wrapped the corpse in the linen cloth and laid it in a new tomb, which recently had been hewn out of rock in a garden place near where Jesus had been crucified. Mary Magdalene, the other Mary and women who had come with Jesus from Galilee followed Joseph and the other officials. They saw where and how the body of Jesus was laid by Joseph of Arimathea. A heavy stone was rolled against the tomb (Mark 15:45-47), and the women returned to houses and prepared spices and ointments (Luke 23:57).

At the same time, chief priests and Pharisees gathered before Pilate with a concern that the tomb of Jesus really ought to be made secure. Evidently, Pilate forcefully replied: "You have a guard among the Roman soldiers! Go, and make that tomb totally secure." They went with a guard and made the tomb secure by sealing the stone against the entrance to the tomb (Matthew 27:62-66).

Is that the end of the person Jesus of Nazareth? Does his biography stop at this point just as it transpires with everyone else? There are people who say so. They will not have a thing to do with anything beyond this point — basically for one of two reasons.

It is thought by some people that the life and example of Jesus are enough for any and all of us to follow. There is no need to consider anything else — hardship, suffering, despair, sinfulness, evil, or any other matter, even among those who seek to follow Jesus. Such thoughts are either non-consequential or simply unimportant. All that might be added here is: Try telling that to those followers who have experienced the same exact horrific measures in life as Jesus did.

On the other hand, there are those such as the ones who opposed Jesus and his way of existence until death — who claimed and still clamor to be correct. In other words, all harmful action by tyrants and deceptive human beings is okay. For example, it was reported via worldwide media in early 2011 that Muslim imam authorities told their constituents that it was acceptable to cheat, lie, steal and murder others for the sake of their religious belief.

Do the naïve or overt forces who are contrary to Jesus and what he stood for — win? They always seem to persist, continue to appeal among many human beings, attract others to their ways and point of view, destroy lots of things and people. Moreover, tyrants never seem to dissipate permanently from the face of the earth. When many of them are gone, others seem to take their place.

At the same time, they do not seem to secure the final blow in this life and reign supremely, even though they continually try to accomplish that feat. The way is open for something else to transpire. The immediate thought would be that no individual or group can dominate others. Sooner or later contrary forces rise up against them and even overcome what appears to be wrong on occasion, but that does not last forever.

A biography that extends beyond birth and death in the natural order of things is needed, and what could be better than the one, true, eternal God who is creator, sustainer and redeemer of the world and all human beings therein?

That is just what is proclaimed in the Bible with the resurrection of Jesus of Nazareth at the dawn of the third day following his death and burial. In fact, the Biblical scriptures are full of this event from every conceivable vantage point. At the same time, no one knows how the resurrection of this person occurred. There is no record of it whatsoever, but there are three strong evidences that such an event did transpire: the empty tomb, the amazing transformation among the disciples of Jesus — as well as the living Christ who is manifest in people's lives ever since that resurrection occurred.

Although the resurrection with Jesus of Nazareth has been disputed over and over again throughout the ages, it never has been disproven. On the contrary, the resurrection of this person from the dead has become the most powerful event ever to transpire in the history of the human race. Unprecedented hope is given to any and all people throughout all time, and the destiny of those who accept this person and event as living truth is found to be without end.

Nevertheless, that faith does not come easily to human beings as attested from the very onset of the reported resurrection with Jesus of Nazareth. Resistance was tremendous among everyone even with the most devoted followers of Jesus. They would not believe until they saw the imprint of his nails driven into his hands upon the cross, put their finger in the mark of the nails upon his risen body and have a hand placed upon his wounded side (John 19:34). They would not accept any hearsay whatsoever (Luke 24:11) and went back to their former trades such as fishing (John 21:3), because

211

all that Jesus stood for and did had been for naught to them with his death.

When the ones who finally did come to the knowledge that Jesus had risen from the dead, their first reaction was filled with exceedingly contrasting emotions of fear and great joy (Matthew 28:8; Mark 16:8) that did not subside. They were afraid, because they knew that they would be persecuted to the same extent that Jesus was, but they also were filled with great joy, because they knew that their ultimate destiny was not the grave.

In fact, death no longer held sway over their whole existence. In the risen Jesus, death absolutely had lost all of its power, and they were prepared to live and die solely for him and all for which he stood. Never had anyone known or experienced anything like this. The truth of what they encountered not only sustained them throughout the rest of their lives, but also became a powerful, unprecedented influence upon others and the whole scene around them. They literally turned the world upside down (Acts 17:6) in the name and for the sake of Jesus, the now-resurrected Son of the ever-living God.

Furthermore, they came to believe that with the resurrection of Jesus there eventually would come a time when all things — even the last vestiges of resistance against Jesus and his way would be subjected under his feet. He would hand the kingdom over to God in order that God truly may be all in all (1 Corinthians 15:20-28).

In the meantime, however, that does not stop any opposition to Jesus, his way and the one, true God whom he represents. Therefore, each and every human being has a choice to the very last breath that is taken: Are we with him or against him?

CHAPTER 9

DISCIPLES AND FAMILY OF JESUS

Of course, the responses among those close to Jesus from his birth to his death have been reported as being quite different from one person to the next one. They each varied in personality, where they had lived and their original occupation, but they all were drawn to him like a strong magnet firmly attracts various objects.

At his birth, there were shepherds near Bethlehem who came to adore him (Luke 2:8-16). Wise men journeyed from afar to worship him and present gifts of gold, frankincense and myrrh (Matthew 2:11).

A devout and righteous man named Simeon, who apparently would not see death before he saw the Lord's Christ, was guided by the Holy Spirit to walk into the temple at Jerusalem when the parents of Jesus brought their baby there for the purification rite of circumcision after eight days had passed from his birth. Simeon took the child Jesus up into his arms and praised God saying: "Master, now I can depart from this life in peace, for my eyes have seen your salvation — a light for revelation to the Gentiles and for glory to your people Israel" (Luke 2:25-32).

There was also a prophet named Anna of reportedly some 84 years of age, the daughter of Phanuel, who was in the temple fasting and praying. When she saw the child Jesus, she also praised God and spoke about him to all who were seeking the redemption of Jerusalem (Luke 2:36-38).

When Jesus was twelve years of age, he went with his parents to Jerusalem for the festival of the Passover. On their way back home to Nazareth, the parents of Jesus realized that he was not among the group of travelers. They returned to Jerusalem and ultimately found Jesus in the temple among the teachers who were amazed at his understanding and answers to the questions that were asked (Luke 2:41-47).

As Jesus began his ministry, which primarily encircled the Sea of Galilee and centered in Capernaum, he began by calling what is said to be twelve disciples. Each of them were unique in their own way, but the whole dozen of them apparently dropped what they were doing on the spot and followed Jesus everywhere even to his crucifixion. Their uniqueness is found in fragments that are available in the Biblical record. Sketches of their relationship with Jesus can be found there. Also, it may give us insight into the way that people, such as ourselves, might fit into a pattern of behavior with Jesus today.

Of course, those twelve disciples found in the Bible include: Andrew, Simon Peter, James and John (the sons of Zebedee), Judas Iscariot, Philip, Bartholomew or Nathaniel, Matthew or Levi, Thomas, James the son of Alphaeus, Thaddaeus or Judas the brother of James and Simon the Zealot.

The Twelve Disciples

Andrew was the first recorded disciple of Jesus who also brought his brother, Simon Peter, to Jesus. According to the Gospel of John, Andrew was a follower of John the Baptist as were some others. When he saw Jesus and heard him speak, Andrew immediately went straight to his brother, Simon Peter. He forthrightly proclaimed to Peter: You must come with me and experience what this man has to offer, for it now is known that "we have found the Messiah" (John 1:35-41).

Andrew, like his brother and others, was a fisherman around the Sea of Galilee near Capernaum. In fact, he lived there and presumably was raised on this northern side of the Sea of Galilee. Also, two other recordings in the Bible feature the disciple named Andrew.

214

According to all four Gospel accounts, crowds of some 5,000 people gathered around Jesus, because of the signs he was accomplishing for the sick. When it was time to eat, disciples were asked about feeding the people. One follower of Jesus replied that six months' wages would not buy enough bread for the size of the crowd. Andrew interjected: "There is a boy here, who has five barley loaves and two fish, but what are they among so many people?" (John 6:9).

At that, Jesus took the two loaves. When he had given thanks, he distributed bread with the fish to the many thousands who were seated along the side of the mount or huge hill. When all had eaten and were satisfied, fragments of what was left over filled twelve baskets (John 6:11-13), which Andrew and the other disciples witnessed.

As Jesus was coming into Jerusalem at a time when crucifixion was not too far away, Andrew along with Philip were approached by some Greeks who said: "We wish to see Jesus" (John 12:21). The two of them went directly to Jesus and communicated to him what they had heard. Andrew came to the close of his journey with Jesus in the flesh, just as he had begun, by bringing others to Jesus. Then, Andrew along with the other eleven disciples deserted Jesus at the time of his crucifixion (Matthew 26:56).

Simon Peter, brother of Andrew, was a gross, burly, impetuous fisherman with hidden, powerful leadership possibilities that only Jesus really seemed to perceive from the outset. He was a "bumbling brawn" of a man who could know and speak the truth and then "blow it," because Peter did not understand the actual meaning of what he said. His desire to please, be loyal, defend, follow and help Jesus got him into trouble more often than not.

His reckless abandonment and mood swings could be to his detriment and quickly deteriorate before everyone. That became a great liability for him, but Jesus never gave up on Peter. Even the apparent rebuke of Peter's words and actions

215

did not deter Jesus from staying with Simon Peter. He knew the potential that was in him. He had the power of being the leader that was needed to further the cause of Jesus in a struggling world.

Early in his ministry, Jesus sent his disciples by boat ahead of him after he dismissed the crowds. Then Jesus went up a mountain by himself to pray. By this time, however, the boat was battered by the waves far from land. Early in the morning Jesus came walking toward them on the sea. The disciples, fearing that it was a ghost, were terrified, but Jesus spoke saying: "Take heart; it is I. Do not be afraid."

At that, Peter answered: "Lord, if it is you, command me to come to you on the water." Jesus said: "Come." So, Peter got out of the boat, started walking on the water and came toward Jesus. When he noticed a strong wind, he became frightened and began to sink. He cried out: "Lord, save me!" Evidently, Jesus reached out his hand and caught him saying: "You of little faith; why would you doubt?" When they got into the boat, the wind ceased" (Matthew 14:22-32).

A married man with devoted family ties (Mark 1:29-30), Peter is known most of all, even in the world of today, by his confession on the way into the Gentile district of Caesarea Philippi. As already mentioned: "You [Jesus] are the Messiah, the Christ, the Son of the living God" (Matthew 16:16). Immediately afterward, however, Jesus proclaimed what this meant in "going to Jerusalem, undergoing great suffering, being rejected by the elders, chief priest and scribes, being killed and on the third day to be raised from the dead" (Luke 9:22).

Peter took Jesus aside and began to rebuke him saying: "God forbid it Lord! This must never happen to you" (Matthew 16:22). Turning and looking at the disciples, Jesus rebuked Peter saying: "Get behind me Satan! For you are setting your mind not on divine things, but on human things" (Mark 8:33).

216

The next step in encountering the real Jesus did not fare any better for Simon Peter. It occurred upon a high mountain where Jesus took Peter, James and John. There, Jesus was transfigured before them. His face shone like the sun. His clothes became dazzling white. Suddenly, there also appeared before them – Moses (representing the law) and Elijah (representing all of the prophets) — and they evidently were talking with Jesus (Matthew 17:1-3).

Peter commented to Jesus: "Lord, it is good that we should be here" (Matthew 17:4). "Let us make three dwellings — one for you, one for Moses, and one for Elijah." A cloud overshadowed them, and from the cloud there came a voice: "This is my beloved Son; listen to him!" Suddenly when they looked around, they saw no one with them anymore, but only Jesus (Mark 9:5-8).

In other words, those disciples who were led by Peter, did not recognize Jesus for who he really was — God's one and only blessed Son. Jesus from now on stood by himself. He was to be revered, honored and followed above anyone else.

According to the Gospel of John, Jesus claimed that he was the bread of God that comes down from heaven. He was the blood that grants eternal life, of which those who believe should partake. Many of his disciples commented that this teaching was too difficult to accept. As a result, many of the disciples turned away from Jesus and would proceed no further with him (John 6:33-66).

Jesus asked the twelve disciples: "Do you also wish to go away?" Peter in behalf of all of them answered in a most responsible way at that moment in time: "Lord, to whom can we go? You have the words of eternal life. We have come to believe and know that you are the Holy One of God" (John 6:67-69).

As the twelve disciples came nearer to the time of the crucifixion of Jesus, however, things changed radically

— especially with the apparent leader among the disciples of Jesus, namely Simon Peter. Again, it was the impulsive Peter who drew a sword and struck the high priest's slave with the arrest of Jesus at the Garden of Gethsemane according to John 18:10-11. At that, Jesus said to Peter: "Put the sword back into its sheath, for am I not to drink of the cup [of death] that the Father has given me?"

Then, probably the greatest fallacy and sin of Peter befell him. Evidently, Peter followed Jesus at a distance when Jesus was handcuffed by rope and taken away to be scourged, mocked, beaten and ultimately put to death upon a Roman cross.

Before this time, however, as they were proceeding to the Mount of Olives at the Garden of Gethsemane, Jesus said to his special disciples: "You all will become deserters." At that, Peter exclaimed: "Even though all become deserters, I will not." Jesus retorted: "Truly I tell you, this day, even this very night, before the cock crows, you will deny me three times." Peter vehemently insisted all the more: "Even though I must die with you, I will not deny you!" (Mark 14:27-31).

According to the Gospel of Luke, when the armed guards seized Jesus and led him to the high priest's house, Peter followed at a distance. A fire was kindled in the middle of the courtyard, and Peter sat among those gathered around the fire. A servant-girl, who saw Peter in the firelight, stared at him and proclaimed: "This man also was with Jesus," but Peter denied it. He brazenly stated: "Woman, I do not know him" (Luke 22:54-57).

A little later someone else upon seeing Peter said: "You also are one of them." Peter declared: "Man, I am not!" Then, about an hour later, still another one kept insisting, "Surely this man also was with him, for he is a Galilean." Peter vehemently exclaimed: "Man, I do not know what you are talking about!" At that moment, while Peter was still speaking, the cock crowed (Luke 22:58-60).

The Lord reportedly turned and looked at Peter. Simon Peter remembered the word of the Lord and how he had proclaimed to him, "Before the cock crows today, you will deny me three times." Peter went out from there and wept bitterly (Luke 22:61-62).

As bad as that moment was for Simon Peter, it turned out to be his finest hour, because at long last he realized in his own act of lying — how awful he had been before the incarnate Lord of the whole universe.

James, Son of Zebedee, was another strong leader in the triumvirate of the chosen few among the twelve disciples of Jesus. He widely was recognized as one of the two Sons of Thunder. He was a fisherman who dropped what he was doing on the spot to follow Jesus (Mark 1:20) and exemplified an unrelenting desire to be seated next to Jesus in the highest position during his reign. Thus, this James was extremely ambitious and determined — without realizing what loyalty really meant and the extent to which it would take him.

Even the mother of James and his brother, John, apparently got in the act of promoting her sons to be seated at the right and left hand of Jesus in his kingdom according to Matthew 20:20-21. To her eternal credit, however, the mother of James and John reportedly stayed not only with her sons but also with Jesus to his very crucifixion, even though it may have been at a distance (Matthew 27:56).

James along with his brother came forward to Jesus and brashly said: "We want you to do for us whatever we ask of you." Jesus responded: "What is it that you want me to do for you?" James and his brother continued: "Grant us to sit — one at your right hand and one at your left hand in your glory." Jesus replied: "You do not know what you are asking. Are you able to drink the cup that I drink, and be baptized with the baptism that I am baptized with?"

They answered:

"We are able." Then, Jesus said to them, "The cup that I drink, you will drink, and with the baptism with which I am baptized, you will be baptized, but to sit at my right hand or my left hand is not mine to grant. It is for those for whom it has been prepared by my Father."　　　　　　　　— Mark 10:35-40

When the other ten disciples heard this, they were angry with the two brothers, but Jesus used this opportunity to teach all of them what being a great person was all about. Jesus formed these mighty words to all of them:

"You know that the rulers of the Gentiles lord it over the people, and their great ones are tyrants. It will not be so among you as my followers. Whoever wishes to be great among you must be your servant, and whoever wishes to be first among you must be your slave, in the same way that I came not to be served but to serve and give my life as a ransom for many."
　　　　　　　　— Matthew 20:24-28

One day while Jesus was standing beside the Sea of Galilee, a crowd was pressing in upon him to hear the word of God. Jesus got into one of the boats belonging to Peter, James and John, and he sat down to teach the people along the shoreline from the boat. When he finished speaking, Jesus asked those three disciples to put out into the deep water and let down the nets for a catch, but they commented that they had worked all night only to have caught nothing (Luke 5:1-5).

At the word of Jesus, however, they let down their nets anyway and caught so many fish that their nets were beginning to break. They signaled partners in another boat to come and help them. They assisted them to secure even more fish. All who were with James, John and Peter were amazed at the fish that they had taken to which Jesus reportedly proclaimed: "Do not be afraid. From now on you will be catching people" (Luke 5:6-10).

As Jesus prepared for his final hours before being delivered up to death, he left the region of Galilee, set his face toward Jerusalem and sent messengers ahead of him. On their way, they entered a village of the Samaritans to make ready for Jesus, but they would not receive him there because his face was set toward Jerusalem.

When James and his brother experienced this rejection, these blustery Sons of Thunder exclaimed: "Lord, do you want us to command fire to come down from heaven and consume them?" In one word, James and his brother desired "retaliation," but Jesus would have none of that. Instead, Jesus demanded only complete dedication to the Kingdom of God from everyone (Luke 9:51-62).

At that point, James, as one of the three leaders among the twelve disciples, did not follow anywhere near that kind of commitment upon arriving in Jerusalem. After the Passover meal on Thursday, James and other disciples went with Jesus to the Garden of Gethsemane for what was the most important prayer in Jesus' life.

He made only one request of James and the other disciples: "Watch and pray with me that you may not enter into temptation" (Mark 14:38), but they fell asleep instead. Finally, Jesus commented: "Could you not stay awake with me one hour?" (Matthew 26:40). "Get up; let us be going, for my betrayer is at hand" (Mark 14:42).

James evidently did get up along with the others, but he did not stay with Jesus any longer. Instead, he turned away from Jesus like others did and at best witnessed the horrific events thereafter from a distance.

John, the brother of James and probably the younger one of the two, was similar to his older sibling in many respects. He was a Galilean fisherman and named Son of Thunder too. Even though there is no hard evidence to support it, John traditionally has been regarded as the disciple whom Jesus loved, often mentioned in the Gospel of John. Most of the time, however, John and James were involved in the same activity, as already stated in preceding paragraphs and recorded in the Synoptic Gospels of Matthew, Mark and Luke. There are a few exceptions, however.

One of those occasions arose when John reportedly said to Jesus: "Teacher, we saw someone casting out demons in your name. We tried to stop him, because he was not following us." Jesus interjected saying: "Do not stop him, for no one who does a deed of power in my name will soon afterward be able to speak evil of me. Whoever is not against us is for us. Truly I tell you that whoever gives a cup of water to drink, because you bear the name of Christ, by no means will lose a reward" (Mark 9:38-41).

When the day of Unleavened Bread arrived on which the Passover lamb had to be sacrificed, Jesus sent John and Peter into the city of Jerusalem saying: "Go and prepare the Passover meal for us that we may eat it." John and Peter evidently asked: "Where do you want us to make the preparations?"

Jesus answered:

"When the two of you enter the city, a man carrying a jug of water will meet you. Follow him into the house that he enters and say to the owner of the house: 'The teacher asks you, Where is the guest room, where I may eat the Passover with my disciples? He will show you a large room upstairs, already furnished. Make preparations for us there.' So, they proceeded to find everything as Jesus had told them; and they prepared the Passover meal."   — Luke 22:7-13

Everything, however, did not go well on that occasion. For example, a dispute reportedly arose among the disciples as to which one of them was to be regarded as the greatest

222

(Luke 22:24). What a terrible way to celebrate this sacred meal on such a hallowed occasion with Jesus!

On the other hand, the Gospel of John states that "the disciple whom Jesus loved was one who reclined next to Jesus at this supper" (John 21:20). If that disciple, whom Jesus loved, was John, the son of Zebedee, and there is no reason to believe that this person was or was not John — other than a long-standing tradition that assumes it, then in truth John the disciple of Jesus might be the only one who can be found above the fray of controversy here.

That same thought continues at the scene of Jesus' crucifixion on the very next day according to the Gospel of John. Here again, it is reported that when Jesus saw his mother [Mary] and the disciple, whom he loved, standing beside her, Jesus apparently said to his mother, "Woman, here is your son." He then turned to the disciple, whom he loved, saying: "Here is your mother." Evidently from that hour this disciple took the mother of Jesus into his own home (John 19:26-27).

Again, if that is true, John the son of Zebedee is the only disciple of Jesus who did not desert him or stand at a distance from the scene of his crucifixion. Furthermore, the Gospel of John would be diametrically opposed to the Synoptic Gospels of Matthew, Mark and Luke, who strongly insist that all twelve of Jesus' disciples deserted him at the time of his death.

Whichever way it actually did occur would seem to make little difference in the outcome of this terrible event, but it could point up a distinction between John and the other disciples in that he may have been the only one who expired of natural causes — namely old age. The others met a similar end to their life as Jesus did.

Judas Iscariot raises the greatest question mark among all of the disciples and perhaps becomes one of the greatest enigmas of all time. Who was he? Where did he come from?

How and why did he become involved with Jesus, and what caused him to be the kind of person that he reportedly turned out to be?

No one will ever be able to answer all the queries about him, but there are some suggested clues in the Bible and otherwise that may be taken as possible insights. Even at that, however, the question about Judas Iscariot continues to loom large upon the horizon.

Where do we begin? It would have to be with some of the possibilities that have been expounded over the centuries. For example, the very name Judas "Iscariot" may distinguish him from another disciple — sometimes referred to as Judas the brother of James. Also, the suggestion is that he was from the Judean town of Kerioth, which may have been some thirty miles south of Jerusalem. That could make him the only disciple who was not from the northern region of Galilee. The reason that such a supposition is pronounced could be in part because of the reference to Simon Iscariot. He reportedly was the father of Judas Iscariot, according to the Gospel of John (6:71; 13:2, 26).

It is probable that Judas Iscariot was a very important member in the inner circle of Jesus' disciples. Lists of the twelve disciples in Mark 3:16-18; Matthew 10:2-14; Luke 6:14-16 and Acts 1:13 put his name last, but the fact that he was treasurer of the group (John 12:6; 13:19) and may have been reclining alongside Jesus also at the Passover meal, according to the Gospel of John 13:21-26, contradicts the lowly listing.

The tendency in tradition to reduce Judas to the status of devil may prove that Luke's less biased account of Judas at the Passover meal may contain fact. Also, the relatively recent discovery of the apocryphal Gospel of Judas in Upper Egypt in 1945, which most favorably evaluates Judas Iscariot, becomes by far an extreme exception rather than the rule in characterizing Judas.

This brings us to the huge reason behind the apparent betrayal of Jesus by Judas Iscariot. All kinds of theories have been projected over the years including: 1)The supreme disappointment at the failure of Jesus to manifest his power in the Holy City after Judas doggedly journeyed there for a showdown appearance; 2) At the last, Judas Iscariot sincerely believed that Jesus of Nazareth was a false messiah, a deceiver of the people, who according to the law in Deuteronomy 13:1-11, should be done away; 3) He attempted to force Jesus into a display of power so that the religious and political authorities would be convinced that he was the Messiah. If he was, could he not call upon a legion of angels to deliver him? Then all doubt would be cleared away, and the nation would be won for Jesus.

Fourth, perhaps Judas Iscariot simply was avaricious and dishonest, a man who could not resist an opportunity for personal gain. With a corresponding zeal to uphold the law and institutions of Judaism against the attacks of false prophets and messiahs, this would seem to explain a deed so radical.

It does appear to be true that Judas Iscariot lost his commitment to Jesus for whatever reason. At the beginning, Judas probably was enthusiastic toward Jesus and his message. No doubt, he was as faithful to Jesus as anyone else. It is evident, however, that little by little, moment by moment, decision by decision, Judas let something else, which already has been suggested, dictate his relationship with Jesus.

Many people have written about the subsequent events in the life of Judas Iscariot. One of them impressed me. It included some crafted and paraphrased thoughts as expressed by Judas Iscariot somewhat as follows:

> The magnetic personality of Jesus brought hope to some of us as his disciples — that he would be the one to lead our nation in its struggle for freedom, and it seemed to be a fact that he easily could get the majority of people to follow him, but he did not move in that direction at all. Instead, he tried to hush those who

wanted to speak with others about his miraculous healings and powerful teachings.

Slowly, I began to understand what Jesus was expressing. He was speaking about the coming of a spiritual kingdom that would be alive and reign in the hearts of people. As he emphasized this more, and de-emphasized the healings, his popularity began to fall off. I could not understand why he did not use his healing powers to build up his following. I kept thinking of the great things that he could do politically and religiously if he would just be more aggressive with his powers.

I must confess that there might have been some personal motive in the back of my mind as well. We were having supper with Simon, when this woman came in and poured expensive ointment all over the head of Jesus. He merely said that it was a beautiful thing she had done. I thought that it was a waste of a valuable resource, but he just brushed aside my comment. He also spoke of suffering and being killed. My confusion heightened, and I did not know what to think.

I really was becoming disgusted with him. All of the hopes and dreams that I had for Jesus were fading into bitter disappointment. He was a fool, certainly not a Messiah. He would not fight even for those things he believed. At our last meal together, I left and brought the temple officials to where he was. Then, as the trial progressed, I looked again into his eyes and heard the calm answers. I understood that I had made a mistake. I knew that he really was the Son of God!

I became desperate. I went to the temple officials and told them what I knew, but they just laughed at me. I stood in the background as they nailed him to a cross. I kept hoping that he would call upon God to step in and rescue him, but God did not. He said, "Father, into your hands, I commit my spirit." The crowd was stilled and in silence I heard the centurion at the foot of the cross say what at last I had come to believe, "Truly, this was the Son of God." In my grief, I went off and killed myself.

As far as the author of this book, The Secret of the Bible, is concerned, the reported words of Judas Iscariot poignantly add to what everyone else had emphasized about Jesus: "I have betrayed 'innocent' blood" (Matthew 27:4). Personally speaking again, the saddest matter about Judas Iscariot is that he never was able to witness the resurrected

226

and ever-living presence of Jesus as others reportedly did, but is this all that can be said about Judas Iscariot? Most everyone would say so, but there is one apocryphal story that definitely adds a measure of hope even for Judas Iscariot and others like him. It wholly falls within the compassionate and merciful manner of Jesus as I have had printed already on another occasion.

It comes from Dr. John L. Knight, Past President of Wesley Theological Seminary in Washington DC, with whom I was privileged to be an Associate Minister under his tutelage during the early days of my ministry: Jesus is standing outside the gates of heaven. He is looking longingly, patiently, hopefully and intently for someone to come.

The beloved disciples are inside standing on those celestial and eternal streets motioning for their Master to join them in celebration. They inquire of him: "What are you doing in delaying so?" And Jesus proclaims: "I am waiting for Judas."

Philip is ranked highly upon the listing of the twelve disciples in the Synoptic Gospels of Matthew, Mark and Luke, but that is the only mention of Philip in those three writings. The Gospel of John, however, offers more detail about this special person. In the very first chapter of John's Gospel, Jesus found Philip the next day after Andrew reportedly turned from John the Baptist to follow Jesus. He invited Philip to follow him, which Philip did (John 1:43).

It was stated that Philip was from Bethsaida — located on the north side of the Sea of Galilee, which had been the hometown of Andrew and Peter too (John 1:44). Thereafter, Philip found Nathaniel, who is named Bartholomew in the Synoptic Gospels of Matthew, Mark and Luke and invited him to come and see Jesus as well. As soon as Philip was called to follow Jesus and accepted that invitation, Philip became a missionary himself without a moment's hesitation.

227

Before feeding the many thousands of people, Philip was asked by Jesus where bread could be bought for the people to eat. Philip answered: "Six months' wages would not be enough bread for each person to have just a very little." At that, Jesus reportedly in a miraculous fashion fed the multitudes with but a few loaves of bread and a couple of fish, which in the end resulted with plenty left over to spare (John 6:5-7).

Again, Philip with Andrew, both of whom had grown up in Bethsaida of Galilee, brought Greeks to Jesus. They wanted to see him in Jerusalem at the festival of the Passover just prior to his crucifixion (John 12:20-24).

The most notable encounter of Philip with Jesus reportedly had to do with one of the most often quoted, most beloved passages in the whole Bible — namely John 14. To read that whole chapter again and again is a blessing beyond compare for anyone so led and so motivated in receiving the word of God.

A keynote in that portion of holy writ is found in the recorded proclamation by Jesus: "If you know me, you will know my Father also" (John 14:7). When Philip heard these words, he evidently said: "Lord, show us the Father, and we will be completely satisfied."

Jesus sadly responded: "Have I been with you all of this time, Philip, and you still do not know me? Whoever has seen me has seen my Father also" (John 14:7). "How can you say, 'Show us the Father'? Do you not believe that I am in the Father and the Father is in me? Words that I say to you I do not speak on my own; but the Father, who dwells in me, does his works" (John 14:8-10).

In essence, Philip along with many other followers of Jesus found it difficult, if not nearly impossible, to believe that the God of the whole universe fully was manifest in Jesus, and Jesus really was the incarnated way, the truth and the life within God. Furthermore, that unbelief and total lack of

228

understanding did not seem to subside, especially with the death of Jesus by crucifixion, which led Philip and others to be at an extreme distance from Jesus during that critical time.

Bartholomew or Nathaniel traditionally is believed to be the same person among the twelve disciples of Jesus. The main reason for this assumption is that in all four Gospels of Matthew, Mark, Luke and John, this person is listed immediately after the name of Philip. In the first three Synoptic Gospels of Matthew, Mark and Luke, the name Bartholomew is used, whereas only in the Gospel of John, the word Nathaniel is employed.

Moreover, just as Philip simply is listed just once as a disciple of Jesus in Matthew, Mark and Luke, so is Bartholomew. In the Gospel of John, however, Nathaniel is mentioned a couple of times, which did include the statement that he came from Cana of Galilee. That singular time is the same reported occasion when Philip led Nathaniel to Jesus — with one difference.

When Philip reportedly said to Nathaniel: "We have found him about whom Moses in the law and also the prophets wrote, Jesus son of Joseph from Nazareth," Nathaniel responded: "Can anything good come out of Nazareth?" Philip replied: "Come and see."

As Jesus saw Nathaniel coming toward him, Jesus said of him: "Here truly is an Israelite in whom there is no deceit." Nathaniel responded: "Where did you get to know me?" Jesus answered: "I saw you under the fig tree before Philip called to you." Nathaniel was astounded and proclaimed before Jesus and others: "Rabbi, you are the Son of God! You are the King of Israel!"

Jesus questioned: "Do you believe this because I told you that I saw you under the fig tree?" (John 1:43-49). That open question would be answered in the miraculous signs shown by Jesus after this encounter, as well as beyond his

229

death by crucifixion. In the meantime, this fellow disciple followed along the same path as Philip until a new day could dawn upon his consciousness.

Matthew or Levi is the same person as in the dual listing of the previous disciple but apparently for slightly different reasons. The name Matthew is the predominant name in the accounting of the Synoptic Gospels. In fact, the name Matthew is listed in all three of them — Matthew, Mark and Luke. The word Levi appears only in the Gospel of Mark and Luke, and it is used there in connection with the same story that is expressed in the other scripture. Just the disciple's name is changed from Matthew to Levi. Therefore, it seems more than likely that this disciple is Matthew, who in two instances is referred to as Levi.

However, the important matter here is who this person is and how he uniquely fits into Jesus' calling of the twelve disciples. According to the Synoptic Gospel accounts, the invitation to follow Jesus came to Matthew very early in the ministry of Jesus soon after the calling of Andrew, Peter, James and John around the Sea of Galilee at Capernaum.

The Synoptic Gospels state that as Jesus proceeded from a house in Capernaum and was walking beside the seashore there, he saw Matthew sitting at a tax booth. Jesus said to Matthew: "Follow me." Without hesitation, Matthew dropped everything, got up and followed Jesus (Matthew 9:9). Soon thereafter, it was reported that Jesus sat at dinner in Matthew's home with many tax collectors and sinners, who along with Matthew also became followers of Jesus.

Matthew was a tax collector. He evidently was a Jewish person who was appointed by the Romans to collect taxes from citizens as well as from merchants passing through town. Moreover, Capernaum was a key center for Roman troops. In addition, it was a thriving business community. Several major highways intersected at Capernaum with merchants moving through there from as far away as Egypt to the south and Mesopotamia to the north.

Tax collectors were expected to take a commission on the taxes they collected. Most of them overcharged and vastly enriched themselves. Thus, tax collectors were despised by the Jewish people, because of their reputation for cheating and for their support of Rome. Jewish people also hated to think that some of the money, which was collected, went to support pagan religions and temples.

When Jesus called Matthew to be one of his intimate twelve disciples, it did not go over very well with Jewish people — especially the Pharisees. They looked upon themselves as strict adherers to the requirements that they felt were necessary. In fact, when Jesus proceeded into the house of Matthew to eat and drink with tax collectors and sinners, the Pharisees vociferously complained to some of the disciples of Jesus: "Why would he do such a thing?" (Mark 2:16).

In addition to eating and drinking with the hated tax collectors in this situation, the query of the Pharisees was prefaced by the word "sinners." Here it meant those Jewish people who were not scrupulous in observing the details of the ritualistic law, as supposedly the Pharisees themselves did.

Overhearing this penetrating question of the Pharisees, Jesus replied: "Those who are well have no need of a physician, but only those who are sick; I have come to call not the righteous, but sinners to repentance" (Luke 5:31-32). As a result, it was not long thereafter that the scribes and Pharisees became filled with fury, discussed with one another what they might do to Jesus and began the process of seeking ways to dispose of him. That did not deter Jesus with his stated mission nor did it stop tax collectors and sinners like Matthew from gravitating toward Jesus during his ministry.

231

Thomas, who is referred to as a twin — even though the name of his twin sibling is not known, also is characterized to some extent only in the Gospel of John. The Synoptic Gospels of Matthew, Mark and Luke only cite the name of Thomas as one of the twelve highly selected disciples. Furthermore, only two statements from Thomas, which occur just prior to the crucified death of Jesus, are mentioned in the Gospel of John. Both of them raise further questions about Thomas, his relationship with Jesus and with the other eleven disciples.

The first encounter centers upon the reported death of Lazarus, a close friend of Jesus, while Jesus and his disciples were staying across the River Jordan where John the Baptist earlier had been baptizing. Jesus said to his disciples: "Lazarus is dead. For your sake, I am glad that I was not at Bethany, so that you may believe. But let us go to him." At that point, Thomas apparently proclaimed to his fellow disciples of Jesus: "Let us go, that we may die with him" (John 11:14-16).

In these words pronounced by Thomas to his compatriots, there is a sense of loyalty denoted but also a perceived risk of disbelief in Jesus, according to some analysts. Despite the great sign in raising Lazarus from the dead, it also would bring the final rejection of Jesus. The question is raised as to what Thomas and the other disciples really had in mind here, which is compounded by the natural questioning nature of Thomas anyway.

Not long after that, according to that beloved chapter 14 in the Gospel of John, Jesus proclaimed:

"Let not your heart be troubled. Believe in God, believe also in me. In my Father's house there are many places. If it were not so, would I have told you that I prepare a place for you? And if I go and prepare a place for you, I will come again and take you to myself, so that where I am, there you may be also. And you know the way to the place where I am going."

232

At that point, Thomas questioned Jesus again saying: "Lord, we do not know where you are going. How can we know the way?" (John 14:1-5). Apparently, Thomas, who was a spokesman for many others, did not in any manner understand the way of the cross, the truth that was incarnated in Jesus, as well as the life that would spring up in him from the totality of death. If Thomas ever really would believe that, it only could possibly come after a long, hard reality check.

James, son of Alphaeus, by virtue of his own name is distinguished from the other James, son of Zebedee. According to Mark 2:14 he has the same father's name as that of Levi or Matthew, which could make them brothers. Other than that, only conjecture remains about James, son of Alphaeus. It includes the thought that he may have been tempermentally and perhaps ideologically different from his brother. Why? Because there is no indication that this James was among those who gathered at the feast among tax collectors and sinners hosted by Levi immediately after Levi accepted the call to follow Jesus (Mark 2:15)!

Even though nothing else is stated in the Bible about James, son of Alphaeus, he is listed as one of the select twelve disciples of Jesus in all of the Synoptic Gospels of Matthew, Mark and Luke. Therefore, he cannot be anything other than important in the eyes of Jesus and others.

Thaddaeus or Judas, son of James, also is relatively unknown as one of the twelve disciples of Jesus, with a slight twist to his name as well as that which he expressed on an occasion. Strangely enough, the name Thaddaeus is listed in the Gospels of Matthew and Mark, but the name Judas, brother of James, is found in the Gospels of Luke and John. Furthermore, no one really knows to which James this Judas belongs.

In both the Gospels of Matthew and Mark, Thaddaeus simply is listed with the other twelve disciples in the same manner that James, the son of Alphaeus, was. In the Gospel of Luke, the name Judas, brother of James, is just listed among the twelve disciples in the same manner that Thaddaeus was listed in Matthew and Mark. Only the name is changed.

With the Gospel of John, however, a sliver of new evidence is offered with the same person listed twice as "Thaddaeus" and once as "Judas, brother of James." In John 14:18-31, a unique query is presented before Jesus by the disciple, "Judas (not Iscariot)," which produces an immeasurable impact upon his followers then, now — even forever! The whole scenario unfolds like this. Jesus proclaimed:

> "I will not leave you comfortless and orphaned. I am coming and will come to you yet again. In a little while, the world will no longer see me, but you will see me, and I am and will be in you. Because I live, you will live also. On that day, you will know that I am in the Father, you in me, and I in you. They who have my commandments and keep them are those who love me; and those who love me will be loved by my Father; I will love them and reveal myself to them."
>
> Judas (not Iscariot) said to Jesus: "Lord, how is it that you will reveal yourself to us, and not to the world?" Jesus answered him: "Those, who love me and keep my word, my Father will love them, and we will come to them and make our home with them. Whoever does not love me does not keep my words; and the word that you hear is not mine, but is from the Father who sent me.
>
> "I have said these things to you, while I am still with you. But the Advocate, the Holy Spirit, whom the Father will send in my name, will teach you everything, and remind you of all that I have said to you. Peace I leave with you. My peace I give unto you. I do not give to you as the world gives. Therefore, do not let your hearts be troubled, neither let them be afraid.
>
> "You have heard me say to you, 'I am going away, and I am coming to you.' If you love me, rejoice that I am going to the Father, because the Father is greater. And now I have told you this before it occurs, so that when it does occur, you may believe. I will no longer talk with you, for the ruler of this world is coming. He has no power over me, but I do as the Father has

commanded me, so that the world may know that I love the Father."

Simon the Zealot also is simply named in the Synoptic Gospels of Matthew, Mark and Luke with two words added: "a Canaanite." Those five words "Simon the Zealot, a Canaanite," however, are most significant. That he is a Canaanite and a Zealot suggest that Simon was a member of the extreme nationalistic movement in Palestine, with the intent politically and militarily of guerilla warfare in overthrowing any and all governments that wished to dominate Israel and Judea.

At that particular time in history, it meant the overthrow of the Roman rule. Moreover, the name Canaanite and Zealot were intimately connected. Canaanite was the older form, and Zealot was the newer version of the same intense desire to rid Palestine of any and all rule by foreign governments.

It is interesting to note, however, that this disciple named Simon apparently was not an insurrectionist like the murderer Barabbas, who was released from death row on behalf of the innocent Jesus of Nazareth and who apparently was crucified in his place. Furthermore, there is no evidence that Simon the Zealot abandoned Jesus of Nazareth simply because Jesus was not zealous enough in the attempt to overthrow Roman domination.

This Simon evidently just deserted Jesus with the other eleven disciples and seemed to have been with the other followers after the death of Jesus (Acts 1:13) It is amazing — knowing the propensity toward a political and military role usually associated with "Zealot, a Canaanite," but it does point to an important fact. It is the seeming vast diversity among the twelve disciples called by Jesus and who somehow mysteriously were attracted to him enough to follow him.

The Family of Jesus

Mary, mother of Jesus, by far and away has been, is and will be the most revered woman in all of Christendom and rightfully so. Her unquestioning devotion to God, to her son Jesus and to the rest of her family is unparalleled, but that seemingly did not deny her from possessing human, maternal qualities according to the Biblical record. She was most unusual on the one hand, while being extremely ordinary on the other. With what she said and did, no one ever has been more extraordinary than this "Mary," and at the same time more down-to-earth with whom every other mother, who ever lived, could identify. That undoubtedly is what makes her the greatest lady of all time!

The quality of Mary's life heightened very early as a young teenager when she was approached divinely with the announcement that she would be the bearer of God's only Son. He was to be named Jesus (Luke 1:31-32), because he would save his people from their sins (Matthew 1:21). When Mary was found to be with child (Matthew 1:18), she went with haste to visit Elizabeth, who was six months into her pregnancy with John the Baptist (Luke 1:26, 39).

As Mary greeted Elizabeth, Elizabeth reportedly exclaimed before Mary: "Blessed are you among women, and blessed is the fruit of your womb. Why would the mother of my Lord come to me?" (Luke 1:41-43). Mary responded to Elizabeth with what has been known throughout the ages as the "magnificat" — one of the finest expressions ever to have been recorded:

> "My soul magnifies the Lord, and my spirit rejoices in God my Savior, for he has looked with favor upon the lowliness of his servant. Surely, from now on all generations will call me blessed; for the Mighty One has done great things for me, and holy is his name.
> "His mercy is for those who fear him from generation to generation. He has shown strength with his arm; he has scat-

tered the proud in the thoughts of their hearts. He has brought down the powerful from their thrones, and lifted up the lowly; he has filled the hungry with good things, and sent the rich away empty. He has helped his servant Israel, in remembrance of his mercy according to the promise he made to our ancestors, to Abraham and to his descendents forever." — Luke 1:46-55

After staying with Elizabeth for several months, Mary returned home to Nazareth. Near the time when Mary was to give birth to her first born son, Mary traveled to Bethlehem in Judea, because the Emperor Caesar Augustus sent out a decree that everyone throughout the Roman Empire should be registered in the town where each family originated.

Since their family was descended from the house and lineage of King David, Mary journeyed to Bethlehem with her husband. While they were there, she gave birth to her firstborn son, wrapped him in bands of cloth and laid him in a manger because there was no place for them in the inn (Luke 2:1-7).

Nearby shepherds came to the place where they were to celebrate what they were told was the Messiah, Christ the Lord (Luke 2:8-20). Also wise men, who journeyed from afar, visited where Mary, her husband and the infant Jesus were lodged and knelt down to pay homage to the newborn king of the Jewish people. Then, opening their treasure chests they offered him gifts of gold, frankincense and myrrh (Matthew 2:1-11). Mary, however, kept all of the words with every event and pondered them in her heart (Luke 2:19, 51).

As was their custom each year, Mary and her family journeyed to Jerusalem for the festival of the Passover. Upon returning home, they assumed Jesus, who was twelve at the time, was in the group of travelers, but when they began to look for their son among relatives and friends, they could not find him. Mary and at least part of her family returned to Jerusalem in search of Jesus.

They found him in the temple area, sitting among the teachers, listening to them and asking questions. All who heard Jesus were amazed at his understanding and his answers. When his parents saw him, they were astonished, but Mary accosted Jesus by exclaiming: "Child, why have you treated us like this? Look, your father and I have been searching most anxiously for you" (Luke 2:41-48).

On at least one occasion during the ministry of Jesus before great crowds of people, Mary was standing on the outside of the gathering with others in her family. In the process, she insisted upon personally speaking with Jesus by asserting their privileged status as the mother, brothers and sisters of Jesus (Mark 3:31-35).

Mary was invited to a wedding with Jesus and his disciples in Cana of Galilee, but when the wine ran out, Mary sharply interrupted Jesus by boldly proclaiming: "They have run out of wine." Jesus countered: "What concern is that to you and me?" At that, Mary, the mother of Jesus, turned to the servants stating: "Do whatever he says" (John 2:1-4).

In each of these three situations, it would appear that Mary was not acting as if she were divinely inspired but as an ordinary, somewhat possessive mother. The situation at Cana of Galilee, however, did turn out to be quite a miraculous event. Jesus ordered six stone jars of twenty to thirty gallons each to be filled to the brim with water. In the process, Jesus turned the water into the best wine ever, which was verified by the chief steward (John 2:5-10).

Furthermore, at the time of Jesus' crucifixion, Mary, his mother, along with two other women reportedly stood close to the cross where her son died. Before he expired, Jesus reportedly said to the disciple, whom he loved, and who was standing beside Jesus' mother, Mary, "Here is your mother" from this time forth. Then, to his mother next to that same disciple, he said: "Here is your son," no doubt meaning from now on (John 19:25-27).

This not only appears to be the last word of Jesus in relationship with his mother, Mary, but most importantly seems to supersede all other thoughts and words concerning her in his eyes and among everyone else around him.

Joseph, the husband of Mary and father of Jesus in an unquestionable legal sense of those terms, is the epitome of what a husband and a father should be. He represents what every father and husband ought to demonstrate before his wife, his family, his children and the whole world. Never has there been a better role model for everyone to see than this man named Joseph. As clearly stated in even the scantiest Biblical record about him, Joseph shows everyone what a responsible, caring, good worker, provider and leader is all about.

In addition to Jesus, Joseph was the father of at least four more boys and three girls, according to the Bible, and his wife, Mary, was mother to them as well. Other than the mention of Joseph as the father of Jesus among those who knew both Joseph and Mary living in Nazareth (Luke 4:22; John 1:45; 6:42), Joseph himself only is described during the earliest days in the life of Jesus basically from birth to about twelve years of age.

There is no mention of Joseph after that time including the ministry, suffering and death of Jesus. In all probability, Joseph had died by that time. Nevertheless, what is known about Joseph during those early and formative years in the life of Jesus, as recorded in the Bible, is significant.

When Joseph learned that Mary was pregnant with her firstborn son to be — while Joseph was engaged to her, but not living with her, and evidently without having sexual relations with her (Matthew 1:18, 25; Luke 1:27; 2:5) — Joseph being a righteous man and unwilling to expose Mary to public disgrace, planned to dismiss her quietly (Matthew 1:19).

Just as he had resolved to do this, Joseph was divinely informed in a dream: "Joseph, son of David, do not be afraid to take Mary as your wife, for the child conceived in her is from the Holy Spirit. She will bear a son, and you are to name him Jesus" (Matthew 1:20-21). When Joseph awoke from sleep, he did as commanded of him: He took Mary as his wife, but he had no marital relations with her until she had borne a son; and he named him Jesus" (Matthew 1:24-25).

That was not the end of Joseph being moved by a dream. When wise men from the East found the child named Jesus and paid him homage, they were warned in a dream not to return to King Herod as he requested. So, they left for their own country by another road (Matthew 2:7-12).

When the wise men departed, Joseph had a dream himself, in which he was told: "Get up! Take the child and his mother, and flee to Egypt. Remain there until you are told otherwise, for Herod is about to search for the child and destroy him" (Matthew 2:13). Joseph evidently did get up, took the child and his mother by night and went to Egypt — remaining there until the death of King Herod (Matthew 2:14-15).

After Herod died, again Joseph was told in a dream to get up, take the child and go to the land of Israel, because those who sought the child's life are dead. However, when he heard that Herod's son King Archelaus was ruling over Judea, he was afraid to go there. So, he went away from there to the district of Galilee and made his home in Nazareth (Matthew 2:19-22), as a carpenter.

Also, Joseph took Jesus to the temple in Jerusalem very soon after Jesus was born for the purification rite of circumcision in accordance with Moses' law (Luke 2:21-24). Again, Joseph was involved in retrieving the twelve-year-old Jesus, who stayed behind in the temple area when the entourage headed back to Nazareth following the festival of the Passover. After that, the Biblical record has nothing to say about Joseph.

James, so designated as the brother of Jesus in the Biblical record (Matthew 13:55; Mark 6:3), is most notably known as the first leader among Christians in the church at Jerusalem. Beyond that, questions abound, which never seem to be resolved. Other than his death in 66 AD, only conjecture remains about James, the brother of Jesus.

Reportedly known facts about this person, therefore, would seem to be the best place to start with this highly regarded man in the early Christian community. James, the brother of Jesus, is the first one listed among the brothers and sisters of Jesus in the Biblical record (Matthew 13:55; Mark 6:3). He clearly is noted in the Bible as the earliest leader of the church at Jerusalem (Acts 1:13; 12:17; 15:13; 21:18; Galatians 1:19; 2:12).

In addition, the brother of Jesus, named James, was the recognized leader of the supposed conservative Jewish Christian people within the early church. He probably believed with others that Christians should adhere to Jewish rites, such as circumcision, and looked askance upon Gentile Christians not needing to do so.

However, at the Council of Jerusalem among early Christians, which basically dealt with the issue of Gentile Christians in the fellowship of the church, James, the brother of Jesus, sided with Peter as to the validity of the mission to Gentiles by saying that Jewish Christians no longer should trouble Gentile converts to the Christian faith. A compromise is implied here that circumcision is not required for salvation. Nevertheless, Jewish ritual requirements would seem to be essential to fellowship at that point in early Christianity (Acts 15:13-29).

Other data in the Bible about James is more questionable. When Mary, the mother of James, is cited (Matthew 27:56, 61; 28:1; Mark 15:40; 16:1; Luke 24:10), which Mary and

James are they? Are they Mary, the mother of James, who is the brother of Jesus? When the other Mary is mentioned (Matthew 27:61; 28:1), is this Mary, the mother of James, the brother of Jesus? Furthermore, when the name Judas, son of James, is used (Luke 6:16; John 14:2; Acts 1:13), is this James the brother of Jesus, whose mother is Mary, wife of Joseph? Is James, who is referred to in the letter of James 1:1, James the brother of Jesus?

Even more complicated is why James, the brother of Jesus, became the leader of the early Jewish Christian Church in Jerusalem? Did his mother, Mary, as we already have witnessed in being somewhat "pushy," have anything to do with that decision, or was James just competent in his own right — perhaps because of his own encounter with Jesus following his death? These questions, as valid as they seem, are unanswerable, which means that the facts as presented by the Bible will have to suffice at present concerning James, the brother of Jesus.

Joseph or Joses, brother of Jesus, is an unknown entity other than his name having been cited as a brother of Jesus, whose mother, Mary, supposedly is the same mother to both of them (Matthew 13:55). In the Gospel of Mark, written some fifteen years prior to the Gospel of Matthew, but even at that — less reliable because of Mark's reliance on Gentile Christian sources over the more Jewish bent of Matthew, uses the name of Joses in the same instance (Mark 6:3).

However, the name Joses is employed at the site of Jesus' crucifixion, where Mary, the mother of James the younger and Joses looked upon that whole, horrific event from a distance (Mark 15:40). Mary, the mother of Joses, saw where the body of Jesus was laid in the tomb (Mark 14:47). Who is this Mary? Is she the mother of Jesus, James and Joses or not? Even though this question is unanswerable, it certainly is a very interesting thought.

Judah, Judas or Jude also is unknown other than being listed as a brother of Jesus, of whom Mary is the mother to Jesus as well as to this person (Matthew 13:55; Mark 6:3). Also, the letter of Jude in the Bible is attributed to the brother of Jesus, whose mother is Mary, the wife of Joseph.

Simon is the fourth brother of Jesus, who is only listed with the three other brothers in the Gospel of Matthew 13:55 and the Gospel of Mark 6:3, but he must have been important enough to be named in the Bible. There are sisters of Jesus, who are mentioned immediately after the name of Simon and who remain unnamed (Matthew 13:55; Mark 6:3).

Not only were the brothers and sisters of Jesus mentioned in the Synoptic Gospels, but also in verses 20-21 of the Gospel according to Mark. The charge is made by other people and even by Jesus' own family that he was demon-possessed. Therefore, Jesus' mother, brothers and sisters came to rescue Jesus from the consequences of his "condition" or being "beside himself."

The point here is that literally no one, not even members of Jesus' own family, recognized his true significance as "the Son of God." It also implies that Jesus was unaccepted by his own family at that moment in time.

This thought is furthered just a few sentences later in Mark 3:31-35 and resounds throughout the Synoptic Gospels — when Jesus' mother, brother and sisters came amidst a crowd of people sitting around Jesus. They were standing outside the circle of people insisting upon personally speaking with Jesus. In the process, they seemingly were asserting their privileged status as his mother, brothers and sisters, as already mentioned.

However, Jesus turned this whole situation around and used it as an opportunity to convey to the crowds of people then, as well as to people throughout all time, who his true family is. The question is posed by Jesus himself: "Who are my mother, my brothers and my sisters?" The answer clearly was and is: All of God's people that gather around Jesus, who hear God's word and do it. They are his brother, sister, mother and family (Mark 4:32-35; Luke 8:19-21).

Other Disciples of Jesus

Nicodemus is a person mentioned only in the Gospel of John, but in that one Biblical account he is noted on at least three different occasions — and most significantly so. According to the Bible, he was a Pharisee who was a leader of the Jews and resided in Jerusalem. In fact, Nicodemus is heralded here as a "ruler of the Jews," who sits on the supreme council of the Sanhedrin. He undoubtedly was one of the more liberal Pharisees in contrast to the literalists, because he reportedly was open to new teachings and interpretations.

At the same time, Nicodemus definitely was highly regarded as a defender of the Jewish, cultic, legal system. His fairness and adherence to strict rules of judicial procedure are apparent and stand out like another great Pharisee, Gamaliel, teacher of Saul, who later became Paul. Gamaliel definitely was the protector of rights among early apostolic people and leaders (Acts 5:34-39).

When Jesus came to Jerusalem, many reportedly believed in his name, because they saw the signs that he was doing (John 2:23—3:1). As a result, Nicodemus decided to approach Jesus personally and find out for himself what was going on and what this fellow named Jesus was all about. No doubt, Nicodemus could have sent one of his assistants to see Jesus, but he evidently wanted to examine Jesus for himself and to separate fact from fiction.

Thus, Nicodemus went to Jesus at night (John 3:2). Perhaps he was afraid of what his peers, the Pharisees, would say about his visit, or perhaps it simply was a matter of caution in view of the hostility that Jewish leaders held toward Jesus. Nonetheless, in spite of the marked difference in worldly

244

status between Jesus and Nicodemus, each one respectfully addressed the other by the title of "rabbi" or "teacher" (John 3:2, 10).

One might expect that the conversation between these two would revolve around the problem of whether salvation is possible via keeping the law, because rabbis taught that when all Israel kept the law, the kingdom of God would come. Jesus immediately moved the discussion to a different level. Salvation in the kingdom of God required a new birth, which in accordance with the Greek word means "from above" or from heaven itself.

This birth is not merely of water that John the Baptist evidently offered — but a birth of the Spirit, which is possible only by a belief in the Son of God, Jesus himself (John 3:3-8). To illustrate this teaching, which becomes so incredible to Nicodemus, Jesus employed a sign from Moses, the lawgiver.

When the people of God had sinned in the wilderness through disbelief, they were afflicted with serpents. Many of them died as a result, but through the intercession of Moses God gave them a sign. It was the sign of the bronze serpent. Whoever looked upon it and believed would live (Numbers 21:4-9). So, it also would be with the Son of God when he is lifted up on the standard of the cross, a cursed thing like the serpent itself (Genesis 3:14-15). Therefore, whoever believes in Jesus as the Son of God will have eternal life (John 3:14-15).

This was a revolutionary matter to Nicodemus and to all would be followers of Jesus — that the kingdom of God is not national or ethnic in nature, but personal — with requirements of repentance and spiritual rebirth via the Holy Spirit. Like the wind, the Spirit does blow around and within human beings. Sometimes the breeze of God the Spirit blows stronger than at other times, but the air of God the Spirit is always available to everyone (John 3:5-8).

Nicodemus did not quite understand this new way of understanding and living as proclaimed by Jesus (John 3:4-9), but his respect for Jesus (John 3:2) did turn beyond admiration toward a true acceptance of him as is evidenced in subsequent events. That change within Nicodemus began when the temple police were asked why they did not bring Jesus back to the chief priests and Pharisees under arrest. The temple police replied: "Never has anyone spoken like he does." The Pharisees countered: "Surely you have not been deceived too, have you?" (John 7:32, 45-47).

However, Nicodemus, who was one of them, asked: "Our law does not judge people without first giving them a hearing to find out what they are doing, does it?" The others did not answer that question but instead judgmentally commented to Nicodemus: "Surely you are not also from Galilee, are you? Anyone knows that no prophet ever is to arise from Galilee" (John 7:49-52).

After Jesus was crucified, Nicodemus came bringing a mixture of myrrh and aloes that weighed about a hundred pounds. He joined another man who had received permission from Pilate to take the dead body of Jesus down from the cross and laid him in a new garden tomb. Together, they took the dead body of Jesus and wrapped it with spices in linen cloths according to the burial custom of the Jewish people (John 19:38-40).

That is the conclusion of the Biblical record concerning Nicodemus, but what a marvelous portrait of such an outstanding person that he was and also turned out to be — especially in relation to this man whom he knew as Jesus from the region of Galilee.

Mary Magdalene brilliantly shines as an extraordinary person who has been maligned and denigrated over the years. Through it all, she remains one of the most formidable women ever, according to the Biblical record.

Mary Magdalene has been castigated as a prostitute and a whoremonger. She even has been elevated in fictional ways to become a sensual lover and mistress of Jesus or actually his secret wife who bore children from him. Supposedly that began a royal line of successors to the Messiah. Of course, none of these conjectures ever have been proven to be true.

The only possible inference to any of these suggestions is that the place where her name is associated did have a reputation of prostitution. According to the Bible that does not mean she was one of them any more than Jesus could not have been a prophet, the Messiah or Son of God, because he came from Nazareth.

It is true that Mary Magdalene perhaps came from a place called Magdala or Magadan, located on the western coast of the Sea of Galilee in one of the ten Roman towns known as the Decapolis, but that in no way was the heart and soul of this person described in the Bible as Mary Magdalene.

One of the earliest recordings about her took place when Jesus went through towns and villages proclaiming the good news of the Kingdom of God. The twelve disciples accordingly were with Jesus as well as with some women who reportedly had been cured of evil spirits and infirmities.

Named first among those women was Mary Magdalene, from whom supposedly seven demons went out. In addition, she along with the other women provided for Jesus and the twelve disciples out of their own resources (Luke 8:1-3).

Therefore, it readily can be assumed that Mary Magdalene was a disciple and follower of Jesus. She also was a well-to-do woman of means, who monetarily contributed to Jesus' proclaimed cause concerning the Kingdom of God. Moreover, she accompanied all of those people, who went with Jesus, all the way to his crucifixion. In fact, Mary Magdalene is recorded in the Bible as looking upon the whole ugly scene (Mark 14:40) from a distance (Matthew 27:55-56) and close by (John 19:35).

She saw the dead body of Jesus put in the tomb (Mark 15:47) and returned home to prepare spices and ointments (Luke 23:56). However, Mary Magdalene was not the only woman involved in this pilgrimage with Jesus and other disciples. There were other women in the Biblical record who are recognized right along with Mary Magdalene.

Primarily, Mary, the mother of Jesus, is listed first and foremost among the women who traveled with Jesus and other followers. In addition to Mary, the mother of Jesus, who always was named in close proximity with Mary Magdalene, there also was Joanna, Suzanna, Salome and a seeming host of other women. This included those in general named Mary. They should be considered and elevated strongly along with Mary Magdalene.

Joanna is the first one to be highlighted. She is mentioned twice in the Biblical record. She is lifted up in Luke 8:3 as the wife of King Herod's steward, Chuza, whose name is found in Nabatean inscriptions. However, nothing else is known about Chuza and his office, but this information is most significant in and of itself.

It means without a shadow of a doubt that the wife of an important steward in the intimate court of King Herod Antipas, who ordered John the Baptist beheaded and supposedly interviewed Jesus during his trial in hopes that Jesus would perform something miraculous in his presence — actually joined the followers of Jesus and journeyed from Galilee with other women and persons unto the very death of Jesus (Luke 24:10).

Overall, it shows that there was a vast diversity among committed followers of Jesus — rich, poor; Gentiles, Jews; women, men; those of high standing in the community as well as the lowest of the low people upon the face of the earth. None of them, however, really understood who Jesus really was or what he was all about. Their own preconceptions and personal desires always seemed to get in the way.

Suzanna is mentioned only once in the Bible. That is right along with two other women from the region of Galilee in the Gospel of Luke 8:3. Suzanna becomes the third person listed with Mary Magdalene and Joanna, who accompanied Jesus through cities and villages after being cured of supposed evil spirits and infirmities. She also is accounted as one who provided for Jesus and the twelve out of her resources, but no other reference is made of Suzanne. Evidently, she did not proceed to Jerusalem with the other women of Galilee or did not help out enough to be mentioned any further as Mary Magdalene and Joanna apparently did.

Then, the name Mary, who also is associated with the Galilean region, brings consternation and unresolved answers among Biblical readers. One Mary, who is listed among the women looking upon the crucifixion of Jesus from a distance in Mark 15:40, is the mother of James the younger, or James the less. Who this Mary is seems to depend upon which James is the reference here. Is this James the son of Alphaeus, who is listed as one of the twelve disciples of Jesus? The mention of James, as the less or the younger, could distinguish him from the James, who reportedly was the son of Zebedee and one of the three disciples closest to Jesus.

Moreover, is this James the son of Mary, the mother of Jesus, the brother of Jesus, as well as the first leader of the church in Jerusalem? James the less or James the younger is mentioned in Mark 15:40 along with Joses, who also has been listed in the Bible as a brother of Jesus. That would tend to substantiate this assumption. If this were true, then Mary, the mother of Jesus, would have been among those women from Galilee and supposedly stood at a distance during the crucifixion of Jesus. Again, who really knows?

As already mentioned, there is Mary the mother of James and Joses from Galilee. She is so named in Matthew 27:56;

Mark 15:40, 47, and Luke 24:10 in connection with the crucifixion of Jesus. Mary, the mother of Joses, reportedly saw where the body of Jesus was laid in the tomb as well. Finally, the so-called "other" Mary saw the great stone rolled to the door of the tomb. Again, could this Mary, the mother of James and Joses and stated as the "other" Mary, actually be the mother of Jesus, or could she simply be just some other Mary?

In addition there is another Mary, who can be recognized in a more definitive manner. She is Mary, sister to Lazarus and Martha, who lived in Bethany — a matter of paces to the east of the city of Jerusalem at the top of the Mount of Olives. The most credible illumination of this Mary's life is found with the earliest recording in the Bible concerning her encounter with Jesus in the presence of her sister, Martha.

This engaging conversation is recorded in the Gospel of Luke 10:38-42 and becomes one of the most powerful incidents ever scripted in literary history, which seemingly never would be forgotten. In fact, within the circles of women today, there are groups who are named after these two sisters. Some call themselves Mary Circles and others become Martha Circles. There even are those who are branded Mary-Martha Circles. All of this remembrance and adulation simply adds to the seemingly immortal significance of this recorded incident.

Mary and Martha along with their highly valued brother named Lazarus were known as one of the most loved and respected companions of Jesus. Jesus was in their home as much, if not more, than anyone else. He was welcomed by them, deeply appreciated by them from every perspective and always felt comfortable being in their company. They loved Jesus dearly.

It was in this setting that Luke records a most provocative conversation with Jesus among these two magnificent women of totally differing personalities. Mary was sharing from the heart about spiritual matters that deeply concerned her. Jesus was relating insights to her in fathomed ways that apparently reached into the innermost self of Mary. This evidently upset Martha no end. At that, Jesus reportedly praised Mary in the presence of both sisters for taking the time to ruminate upon spiritual matters by stating: "Mary has chosen the good portion."

Other recorded incidents about this Mary are more questionable. For example, it is proclaimed in the Gospel of John 11:1-2, years after the Gospel of Luke was written, that she was the person, who anointed the Lord with perfume and wiped his feet with her hair. Later in John's 12:1-8, the details relating to this incident are expressed. This act reportedly occurred at the home of Lazarus. Mary took a pound of costly perfume made of pure nard, which was worth a year's wages to the ordinary laborer at that time. According to Jesus, it was for the apparent purpose of preparing him for his burial.

However, this same incident is recorded in Matthew 26:6-13 and Mark 14:3-7 in a totally different manner. It is with other personnel and, of course, scripted at a much earlier time. There, this event transpired in the house of Simon the leper, and the act evidently was performed by an anonymous person.

According to Luke 7:36-47, a similar incident of a woman from the street in a city is recorded. She also brought an alabaster jar of ointment before Jesus supposedly in the house of a Pharisee. Accordingly, she weepingly began to bathe the feet of Jesus with her tears and to dry them with her hair. Continuing to kiss his feet and anointing them with ointment, Jesus reportedly said that her sins, which are many, have been forgiven.

It is a question whether Mary, the sister of Martha and Lazarus, is the only person who performed this act. Was she one of many who did? Did she accomplish it for reasons dif-

251

ferent from the others, or was this act simply attributed to her because of her unique association with Jesus and because of her special place in the beloved family of Lazarus? Regardless of what actually did or did not take place, this Mary no doubt was an exceptionally gifted woman full of grace, charm and compassion.

Such an extraordinary manifestation of character is even furthered when Jesus arrived in Bethany after Lazarus had died and was laid in the tomb. Mary came to the place where Jesus was and immediately knelt down at his feet and said to him: "Lord, if you had been here, my brother would not have died," which deeply moved Jesus. It led him to tears and promoted others to say how much Jesus really loved Lazarus.

Martha, sister to Mary and Lazarus, exhibited a wholly different personality, as already implied, but she equally was loved by Jesus, her sister and brother. This character trait became evident in the first recorded incident with Jesus and her sister, Mary, at their home in Bethany according to Luke 10:38-42. Instead of sitting with Jesus and listening to him about spiritual matters, Martha after graciously welcoming Jesus to the home went about her many tasks.

Distracted about all of the things that needed to be accomplished and apparently troubled by the fact that Mary seemed to care less and was doing nothing to assist in what needed to be accomplished, Martha went to Jesus saying: "Lord, do you not care that my sister has left me to do all of the work by myself? Tell her to help me." At that, Jesus proclaimed to her: "Martha, Martha, you are worried and distracted by many things. You need only to choose the better part as exhibited in Mary's life, because that never can be taken away."

As recorded in John 11:17-45 at the death and burial of her brother, Lazarus, Martha does come into her own by assuming a leading role in what always is to be named by many as the greatest miracle of all time — the raising of Lazarus from the dead. When Martha heard that Jesus was coming to Bethany, she took the initiative and went out to meet him exclaiming: "Lord, if you had been here, my brother would not have died."

With great faith, Martha reportedly continued: "But even now, I know that God will give you whatever you ask of him." Jesus affirmatively responded to her: "Your brother will rise again." Martha replied to Jesus: "I know that he will rise again in the resurrection of the last day." Then, Jesus unhesitatingly announced to her: "I am the resurrection and the life. Those who believe in me, even though they die, will live. Everyone who lives and believes in me will never die. Do you believe this?" Without any apparent doubt in her mind, Martha proclaimed to Jesus: "Yes, Lord, I do believe that you are the Messiah, the Son of God, the one coming into the world."

Then, Martha went back and called her sister, Mary, to join her and Jesus at the tomb of Lazarus. When Jesus asked that the stone be rolled away from the tomb of Lazarus, Martha said to him: "Lord, already there is a stench because Lazarus has been dead for four days," which in Jewish terminology meant that the corpse was stone-cold beyond any possible hope of recovery.

At that point, Jesus stated to Martha: "Did I not tell you that if you believed, you would see the glory of God?" After the stone was rolled away and Jesus had offered a prayer, he exclaimed: "Lazarus, come out." Lazarus did come out proving to people that Jesus indeed was the giver of life.

Lazarus, brother to Martha and Mary, truly was the beloved one of his family, of Jesus and among many people throughout the area. His effectiveness did not really make a difference in the lives of others until after Lazarus had been raised from the dead — to live, eat, breathe and enjoy the company of people in a new and unique way.

When Jesus cried with a loud voice at the entrance of his tomb: "Lazarus, come out," the dead man did come out with his hands and feet bound with strips of cloth and his face wrapped in a cloth. Jesus proclaimed: "Unbind him, and let him go." As a result, many of the Jewish people, who had come with Mary and had seen what Jesus did, evidently believed in him.

Some of them went to the Pharisees and told them what Jesus had done. The chief priests and the Pharisees called a meeting of the council prior to the festival of the Passover and said: "What are we to do? This man is performing many signs. If we let him go on like this, everyone will believe in him, and the Romans will come to destroy both our holy place and our nation" (John 11:43-48).

Nevertheless, Caiaphas, who was high priest that year, stated: "It is better that one man die for the people than to have a whole nation destroyed" (John 11:50). From that day forward, they planned to put Jesus to death.

According to John 12:1-12, after Jesus had retreated into semi-hiding near the wilderness, he returned to Bethany at the home of Lazarus six days before the Passover. There, a dinner was prepared, but when a great crowd of Jewish people learned that Jesus was there, they not only came because of Jesus, but also to see Lazarus, whom Jesus had raised from the dead. The chief priests planned to put Lazarus to death as well, because it was on account of him that many Jewish people were deserting and believing in Jesus instead.

That fact became even more evident on the next day when a great crowd of people took branches of palm trees and went out to meet Jesus, shouting: "Hosanna! Blessed is the one who comes in the name of the Lord — the King of Israel" (John 12:13), but that did not last long. In a matter of days cheers turned into jeers, and people would cry:

Crucify the man named Jesus from Nazareth in the region of Galilee.

Salome is mentioned only in the Gospel of Mark along with Mary Magdalene and another Mary at the crucifixion of Jesus. They viewed his death from a distance. The mention of Salome's name there is of utmost significance, because she is listed as another one of Jesus' followers. In Mark 15:41, Salome is named as one who followed Jesus all the way from Galilee to Jerusalem and provided for him throughout her journey with him.

Simon of Cyrene was not a follower of Jesus per se, but by all indications in the Biblical record, his family did become some of Jesus' people later on. How do we know this to be true? It simply has to do with what is recorded in the Synoptic Gospels about this unique person named Simon of Cyrene.

What is asserted in these first three Gospel accounts is that this man was coming in from the country when he was compelled to carry the cross of Jesus for whatever reason. Beyond that point, only inferences are placed before any scriptural reader, but those thoughts seem solidly to be based and are most illuminating.

"Coming in from the country" more than likely meant that this Simon was on his way toward Jerusalem — probably for the festival of the Passover, while the execution squad was proceeding out of the city. The place called Cyrene was located on the north coast of Africa opposite from the island of Crete. It did contain a large Jewish population.

The names of Alexander and Rufus, who are cited as sons of this Simon, no doubt are noted here because they were well-known people among people in the early church. Simon of Cyrene, who was compelled to carry the cross for Jesus as he journeyed from elsewhere to Jerusalem, probably came to know Jesus and what he was all about quite well during that very short, intense, passionate, cruel time with him. As a result, he became transformed enough in the process to move his own sons and family in the direction of Jesus and his followers for many years to come.

Joseph of Arimathea seemed to be the key person in the burial of Jesus after his death upon the cross. All four Gospels of Matthew, Mark, Luke and John agree at this point, even though each one varies minimally from the others among some details. All in all, it is stated in the Biblical record that this Joseph was a very wealthy man (Matthew 27:57), a respected man of the council, or the Sanhedrin (Mark 15:42), a good and righteous person (Luke 23:50) and a disciple of Jesus, even though he may have been a secret one because of his fear of the Jews (John 19:38). He reportedly was a person who was from Arimathea, a Jewish village in the hill country just northwest of Jerusalem.

Even though Joseph of Arimathea was a member of the council, he apparently had not agreed to the plan and action that was taken against Jesus and was waiting expectantly for the kingdom of God (Luke 23:51). Evidently he heard about Jesus and had witnessed what was going on with him. This lay counter to what Joseph had thought to be true. So he decided to do something positive about this dreadful scenario. Out of great respect for Jesus, he wanted to accomplish at least the decent thing in properly caring for his maligned, battered and bleeding body when he drew his final breath and succumbed.

When that last act occurred, Joseph proceeded forthrightly to Pilate and boldly requested that he be given the body of Jesus for burial. At that point, Pilate was astounded that Jesus was dead in such a short period of time. Therefore, he asked a centurion to verify the death of Jesus, to which the centurion responded that Jesus had been dead for some time (Mark 15:44). At that, Pilate did grant the dead body of Jesus to Joseph of Arimathea.

Joseph proceeded to take down the corpse of Jesus from the cross. Afterward, along with the Roman soldiers and the centurion, and perhaps Nicodemus as well, he transported the bodily remains of Jesus to a new tomb belonging to Joseph himself. It was located in a garden place not too far away from the site of the crucifixion. There in his own new tomb, which Joseph had hewn in the rock and upon which no one ever had been laid (Luke 23:53), he took the deceased body, wrapped it in a clean linen cloth (Matthew 27:29-60), which he had purchased (Mark 15:46), and fulfilled it all in accordance with the custom of the Jewish people (John 19:40).

Afterward, a great stone was rolled against the door of the tomb, secured in the presence of Joseph of Arimathea, a guard of Roman soldiers, the centurion, Nicodemus, Mary Magdalene, another Mary, women from Galilee and in synchronization with the command of Pilate (Matthew 27:27-65).

CHAPTER 10

THE APOSTLES

The Apostles, as distinguished from the disciples, are witnesses to the appearances of Jesus of Nazareth in his resurrection. They encounter him face-to-face in his newly resurrected body. He walks and talks with them in wondrous, compelling, empowering, exceedingly dynamic and practical ways. How do we know that to be true? Again, by the results disclosed in these people's lives, as recorded in none other than the Bible!

First and foremost, they finally recognized and appreciated Jesus for who he really was — the one and only Messiah, the Christ, Son of the true, ever-living God. Beforehand, almost everyone thought of him otherwise. They distorted the true meaning of being that person to fit into their own mode of thinking or simply could not sustain their believing in him — especially when the going got really rough.

Now, however, they began to see Jesus in a totally different light — not that this change took place easily for them. It actually came about slowly and very hard, but it did transpire not only with those followers but among others. In fact, this transformation took place within individuals and among vast numbers of people, according to one of the most authentic documents in the Bible, as well as the earliest recording of the death and resurrection of Jesus (1 Corinthians 15:3-8). Therefore, when the reality of Jesus' resurrection finally did become accepted among the Apostles, followers of Jesus multiplied by leaps and bounds until it became evidenced that the whole world had been turned upside down (Acts 17:6). In fact, the whole Book of the Acts of the Apostles in the Bible verifies this truth line by line, page by page — to the very last word that is stated.

From the onset of people's newfound confrontation with the risen Jesus of Nazareth, however, there was utter shock, sharp disbelief, extraordinary fear and unbridled elation, as well as being completely dumbfounded. Gradually, problems with this extraordinary situation gave way to becoming the most important event in their lives, and the news of Jesus' new, ever-living presence among them spread like wildfire. Moreover, it did not go away, even though there were terrible forces against the whole scenario.

Disbelief was in evidence everywhere, but there was no way to disprove what had taken place. Nonetheless, that did not stop those who were against this seeming reality. From a human point of view, there was no doubt in anyone's mind that a risen person, even with the name of Jesus, could not in any way be possible. All people die, and there is nothing left thereafter except perhaps bodily remains and a memory. With the death of Jesus there seemed to be lost hopes and dreams of preponderant, tragic proportions.

According to Jesus' own reported words, "With God, all things are possible" (Luke 18:27). Definitely so — if indeed Jesus were God incarnate, whose purpose was to redeem humanity from the sins and errors of their ways, to heal them from all iniquities and to send them forth to further his mission in this world.

What finally brought them to the understanding that this encounter with the risen Jesus truly was real and that he was not some fake imposter or just another ghostly apparition? Several revelations surfaced immediately and could not be denied, which included: Jesus was the same person they had come to know, each in their own way, but he no longer was subject to the same functions. He ate food, but he did not need food to survive. He was recognizable in the same flesh, but he was not dependent upon bearing it any further.

He spoke to them as he always had, but now there seemed to be no doubt as to what he meant. The body of Jesus carried the same wounds that he possessed at his death, but now he appeared before people in a beautiful, perfected and glorified way. He truly became what he said was taking place: He was in the process of ascending to God the Father forever. At the same time, Jesus was still connected to human beings until that time when he would present his people faultless before the throne of grace, and they would be fully accepted into that glorious kingdom without end.

How did his followers come to realize the truth of Jesus as the risen, ever-living Lord, Savior and eternal Son of God? In many ways! Some recognized him for who he really was in the breaking of bread. It took others to actually see and touch his wounded side with their hands and to put a finger in the mark of the nails upon his hands. There were those who were blinded by his presence, struck to the ground by his voice and restored to new life by the anointing of others.

Some heard him through what appeared to be an ordinary person like a gardener. There were groups of followers who were confronted with the risen Jesus around a fire along the lakeside, and the risen Jesus inquired of them: "How much do you love me?" He sent them forth into the whole world to feed and tend people's needs, and to baptize them in the name of the Father, the Son and the Holy Spirit.

The most convincing and irrefutable evidence when people experienced the reality of Jesus as risen and exalted Lord is that they were willing to and did die the same terrible death as he did. No one would suffer what they did for the sake of a lie or even with a hint of not being true. They no longer would live and die selfishly for themselves, but for Jesus the Christ. Many examples of these people are named and included within the Biblical record.

Mary Magdalene clearly is the first Apostle or witness of the resurrected Jesus of Nazareth. Other women are listed right along with her, but she far and away is the most notable one of them all, according to the Bible. She is cited as the one who encountered the risen presence of Jesus ahead of everyone else and is described movingly in every account at the empty tomb of Jesus.

Others who were there and experienced the same awesome sight and message included: Joanna, Salome, at least one other Mary and maybe many of them, as well as other women — no doubt from Galilee (Matthew 28:1-9; Mark 16:1-6; Luke 24:1-11). In the Synoptic Gospels, varying accounts of what transpired at the tomb of the deceased Jesus at dawn on the first day of the week following the Sabbath are recorded, but in all three of these scripts, the day and time are the same, the stone was rolled away from the tomb and the tomb was empty.

According to the simplest, most straightforward, first written Gospel of Mark, it is stated:

> "When the Sabbath was over, Mary Magdalene, Mary the mother of James, and Salome bought spices so that they might go and anoint the deceased body of Jesus. Very early on the first day of the week, when the sun had risen, they went to the tomb.
>
> "They had been saying to one another, 'Who will roll away the stone for us from the entrance to the tomb?' When they looked up, they saw that the stone, which was very large, already had been rolled back.
>
> As they entered the tomb, they saw a young man dressed in a white robe sitting on the right side, and they were alarmed. But he said to them: "Do not be alarmed; you are looking for Jesus of Nazareth, who was crucified. He has been raised; he is not here. Look, there is the place they laid for him."

In the Gospel according to Matthew, this incident is described thusly:

> "After the Sabbath, as the first day of the week was dawning, Mary Magdalene and the other Mary went to see the tomb where Jesus had been laid. Suddenly, there was a great earthquake. An

262

angel of the Lord, descending from heaven, came and rolled back the stone and sat on it. His appearance was like lightning and his clothing white as snow. For fear of him, the guards of the tomb shook and became like dead men.

"But the angel said to the women: 'Do not be afraid. I know that you are looking for Jesus who was crucified. He is not here, for he has been raised from the dead, as he said. Come and see the place where he lay. Then, go quickly and tell his disciples.'

"So, they left the tomb quickly with fear and great joy, and ran to tell his disciples. Suddenly, Jesus met them and said: 'Greetings!' And they came to him, took hold of his feet and worshiped him."

With the Gospel of Luke, the event is put forth in this fashion:

"On the first day of the week, at early dawn, they came to the tomb where the dead body of Jesus had been laid — taking spices that they had prepared. They found the stone rolled away from the tomb, but when they went in, they did not find the body.

"While they were perplexed about this, suddenly two men in dazzling clothes stood beside them. The women were terrified and bowed their faces to the ground, but the men said to them, 'Why do you look for the living among the dead? He is not here, but has risen. Remember how he told you, while he was still in Galilee, that the Son of Man must be handed over to sinners, become crucified and on the third day rise again.' Then, they remembered his words.

"Returning from the tomb, they told all of this to the eleven and to all the rest. Now it was Mary Magdalene, Joanna, Mary the mother of James, and the other women with them who told this, but these words seemed an idle tale."

Finally, and perhaps best of all, this event is told in the Gospel of John 20:1, 11-18, featuring only one woman, Mary Magdalene. What reportedly transpired here between Mary Magdalene and the risen Jesus of Nazareth becomes the most powerful dynamic ever to be recorded among women throughout the entire history of humanity.

263

It is the turning point in the life of Mary Magdalene and among all people who in any way would be related to this person named Jesus. Where Mary reportedly turned, all humanity must turn to find new life. Here is that encounter straight from the Gospel of Saint John:

> "Early on the first day of the week, while it was still dark, Mary Magdalene came to the tomb and saw that the stone had been rolled away from the tomb. So, she ran to two of the remaining eleven disciples and said to them: 'They have taken the Lord out of the tomb, and we do not know where they had laid him! So, the two disciples went to the tomb, but Mary stood weeping outside the tomb.
>
> "As she wept, she bent over to look into the tomb, and she saw two angels in white sitting where Jesus had been lying, one at the head and another at the feet. They said to her: 'Woman, why are you weeping?' She said to them, 'They have taken away my Lord, and I do not know where they have laid him.'
>
> "When she had said this, Mary Magdalene turned around and saw Jesus standing there, but she did not know that it was him. Jesus said to her, 'Woman, why are you weeping? Who are you looking for?'
>
> "Supposing him to be the gardener, Mary said to him, 'Sir, if you have carried him away, tell me where you have laid him, and I will take him away.'
>
> "Jesus said to her, 'Mary!' She turned and said to him in Hebrew, 'Rabbouni!' which means Teacher. Then, Jesus proclaimed to Mary Magdalene: 'Do not hold on to me, because I have not yet ascended to the Father. Go to my brothers and say to them, 'I am ascending to my Father and to your Father, to my God and your God.'
>
> "Mary Magdalene went and announced to the disciples: 'I have seen the Lord!' Then she told them that he had said these things to her."

According to this portion of scripture, three things transpired with Mary here, by which all people must turn to find new life. First, Mary Magdalene turned away from the grave. Upon investigating the situation at hand, she turned her back on the tomb, did not look upon that dark, sinister, dismal scene anymore and had nothing to do with it ever again. In the resurrection of Jesus, death, defeat and evil had lost ultimate power and no longer held the last word. To believe that is to respond as Mary did.

Second, Mary Magdalene turned toward another person. Of course, she still was wrapped up in her own self with feelings of grief — by inquiring where the body had been taken, but the most important matter arose in that she did turn away from herself toward others. The natural human instinct always is to grab things unto the self merely for greedy consumption. Difficult as it may be, reaching beyond self toward other human beings is possible, as Mary Magdalene clearly demonstrated at this point.

Finally, according to this portion of the Bible, Mary Magdalene turned to recognize Christ. Unquestionably, this is the ultimate experience in human life. To see the risen and exalted Christ in the ordinary affairs of this existence is the essence of apostolic faith. Granted, people cannot see Jesus as Mary Magdalene did. Human beings comprehend the resurrected person of Jesus through the Holy Spirit today, and the Holy Spirit is the "Spirit of Jesus" (2 Corinthians 3:17-18; Philippians 1:19; Acts 1:2, 10:19, 13:2).

However, Jesus the Christ, who called Mary by name and directed her to a specific task, continues the same among people today. Responding positively to that calling is life and health and the peace that passes all human understanding. Moreover, when people do catch a vision of Christ's ever-living presence, the realization emerges into consciousness that he has been with them all along. Human beings just failed to recognize him.

With that unparalleled experience, people express from the hilltops to the stars, upon the streets of everyday life and throughout all time: "I have seen the Lord!" Nothing anywhere can move people into a higher plane of existence as well as that simple, personal, living encounter with the risen, exalted, ever-blessed Son of the eternal God.

As discovered by those first people at the empty tomb long ago: The Lord is risen! He reigns on high forever, but most important of all, he comes to quicken the spirit of human beings into a better way of life here and now.

Perhaps John Masefield in The Everlasting Mercy expresses it best:

O glory of the lighted mind,
How dead I'd been, how blind:
The station's brook to my new eyes
Was babbling out of paradise;
The waters rushing through the rain
Was singing — Christ has risen again.[1]

Peter, according to the Bible, was the first man to experience the resurrected Jesus, who quickly was followed by the other remaining disciples and many others thereafter. As with Mary Magdalene among women, Peter emerged as the strongest man among the other ones in the presence of the risen Jesus of Nazareth. He did not grow strong immediately or easily, but his transformation did occur and in an unparalleled way. Peter slowly but surely arose to become the unquestioned leader among Christ's people, which was in vast contrast to the person that he had been.

Prior to the resurrection of Jesus, Peter showed some signs of greatness, but that always seemed to be followed by exhibits of utter weakness. He was the first to proclaim that Jesus was the Messiah, the Christ, Son of the one and only, ever-living God. Immediately afterward when Jesus expressed that this would mean death by crucifixion, Peter insisted that such never would happen.

Then, Peter emphatically stated that even though others might fall away and desert Jesus, he never would do any such thing, but then he did deny Jesus three times in the presence of all kinds of people. Instead, he pronounced that he never knew Jesus or ever had anything to do with him.

Peter also started to walk on water toward Jesus with full faith and absolute confidence, only to fall into the rough waters of the sea with accompanying almost pathetic cries. He desperately wanted help, because Peter felt that he was perishing. These events occurred before the resurrection of Jesus. Afterward, Peter proved over and over again that he was a totally dedicated follower of Jesus until no one could doubt or deter him from that commitment anymore. There was absolutely no person who showed more faith in God through Jesus Christ than Peter from his encounter with the risen Jesus of Nazareth.

Why was the struggle to become invincible so slow, tedious, latent and seemingly took such a long time in coming for Peter? What was the big barrier? Perhaps it was because he had so far to come in reaching that point in his life. Maybe Peter was still reeling from his feelings of denial, failure and desertion. It could have been that he truly did believe that all was lost with the death of Jesus, and he really could not think otherwise or believe anything true about a resurrected person. Who knows?

Slowly but surely the phenomenal change of incredible, strengthened proportions in Peter, which only can be attributed to the real, true, actual presence of the risen, exalted, ever-living Jesus of Nazareth, was manifest in Peter's life. Nothing in Peter's own self ever could have made that happen, as all of the data about him already listed prior to this point suggests. It simply was not in him to be that kind of person consistently.

Specifically what did take place with Peter after the reported resurrection of Jesus? The immediate issue has to do with the question: Where was Peter on the third day after the death and burial of Jesus? Mary Magdalene and the other women were the first to discover the empty tomb and encounter the appearance of the risen Jesus of Nazareth, as already reported, but where was Peter?

The strong implication in the abrupt ending of Mark 16:7 was that Peter and the other ten disciples immediately fled to Galilee. Just as Peter and the other disciples among the circle of the twelve did not understand Jesus in the flesh, deserted him at his crucifixion and merely wished Jesus to fulfill their own preconceived notions, so did the same posture continue among the disciples after the reported death and resurrection of Jesus, according to the Gospel of Mark.

The exact opposite is recorded in Luke 24. Here, it is documented that any and all events related to the remaining eleven disciples occurred in and around Jerusalem, where all of them were lumped together in seeing and hearing from him. Furthermore, the only one mentioned by name here was Peter and that occurred only in passing. His first name, Simon, only was employed there (Luke 24:34) and that was among the two followers of Jesus on the road to Emmaus, who hurriedly returned to Jerusalem.

Perhaps the overall account of the events after the resurrection of Jesus is best stated in Matthew 28. Both Jerusalem and Galilee presumably are included in the recording of the encounter with the risen Jesus of Nazareth and the eleven disciples, even though Peter by name is not mentioned.

The most vivid and specific account of Peter's encounter with the resurrected person of Jesus from Nazareth is recorded in the Gospel of John 20:2-10, 19-23; 21:1-19, just as it was described in this portion of the Bible about Mary Magdalene. Not only Jerusalem and Galilee are mentioned, but Peter meticulously is portrayed in both places. It leaves no doubt in the mind of the reader that Peter becomes a totally transformed person in the process.

From that time forward, as stated in the Bible — especially with the Acts of the Apostles and throughout subsequent tradition, Peter no longer turns back or retreats into former ways but exemplifies only strength upon strength in mind, character and action. He truly is the rock upon which the whole church reportedly stands until the end of time. Here is the reported transformation that took place in Peter, according to the Gospel of John.

"So, Mary Magdalene ran and went to Simon Peter and another disciple, and said to them: "They have taken the Lord out of the tomb, and we do not know where they have laid him." Then, Peter and the other disciple set out toward the tomb. The other disciple out ran Peter and reached the tomb first. He bent down, looked in and saw the linen wrappings there, but he did not go any further. Then, Simon Peter came and went into the tomb.

"He saw the linen wrappings lying there, and the cloth that had been on Jesus' head, not lying with the linen wrappings but rolled up in a place by itself. Then, the other disciple, who reached the tomb first, also went in, and he saw and believed; for they did not understand the scripture, that he must rise from the dead. Then, the disciples returned to their homes.

"When it was evening on that day of the week, and the doors of the house where the disciples met were locked for fear of the Jews, Jesus came and stood among ten of them saying: 'Peace be with you.' After he had said this, he showed them his hands and his side. Then, the disciples rejoiced when they saw the Lord.

"Jesus said to them again, 'Peace be with you. As the Father has sent me, so I send you.' When he had spoken this, he breathed on them, and said to them: 'Receive the Holy Spirit. If you forgive the sins of any, they are forgiven them; if you retain the sins of any, they are retained.'

"After these things, Jesus showed himself again to the disciples by the Sea of Galilee in this way: Simon Peter said to six of the twelve disciples, 'I am going fishing.' The others said to him, 'We will go with you.' They all went out and got in the boat, but that night they caught nothing.

"Just after daybreak, Jesus stood on the beach, but the disciples did not know that it was Jesus. Jesus said to them, 'You have no fish, have you?' They answered: 'No.' He said to them, 'Cast the net on the right side of the boat, and you will find some.' So they cast it, and they were not able to haul the net in because there were so many fish.

"One disciple said to Peter, 'It is the Lord!' When Simon Peter heard that it was the Lord, he put on some clothes, having been naked, and jumped into the sea. However, the other disciples came in the boat dragging the net full of fish, because they were not far from the land.

"When they had gone ashore, they saw a charcoal fire there, with fish on it, and bread. Jesus said to them, 'Bring some of the fish that you have just caught. So, Simon Peter went aboard and hauled the net ashore full of large fish. Though there were so many, the net was not torn.

"Jesus said to them, 'Come and have breakfast,' and he took the bread – then the fish, and gave it to them. When they had finished breakfast, Jesus said to Simon Peter, 'Simon, son of John, do you love me?' Peter said to Jesus, 'Yes, Lord; you know that I love you.' Jesus said to him: 'Feed my lambs.'

"A second time, Jesus said to Peter, 'Simon, son of John, do you love me?' Peter said to Jesus, 'Yes, Lord; you know that I love you.' Jesus said to him, 'Tend my sheep.'

"Jesus said to Peter a third time [which had to be reminiscent of having denied Jesus earlier three times, and knowing that it took at least that many times for the message to sink deeply into Peter], 'Simon, son of John, do you love me?' Peter felt hurt because Jesus said to him the third time, 'Do you love me?' And Peter said to Jesus, 'Lord, you know everything; you know that I love you.' Jesus said to him, 'Feed my sheep.'

"Then, Jesus continued with Peter saying, 'Very truly, I tell you, when you were younger, you used to fasten your own belt and to go wherever you wished. But when you grow old, you will stretch out your hands, and someone else will fasten a belt around you and take you where you do not wish to go.' [He said this to indicate the kind of death by which Peter would glorify God.]

"After this, Jesus said to Peter: 'Follow me,' " and from that point onward, all further indications in the Biblical record reach the conclusion that Simon Peter really and truly was Peter the Rock among all of Jesus' people for all time.

First, Peter reportedly stood up among some 120 people who were acclaimed as "believers," and led them into replacing Judas Iscariot. That person would become one of the twelve disciples, now called Apostles (Acts 1:13-15).

On the day of Pentecost when the Holy Spirit was reported to have descended mightily on all of the people, there were those who were astonished and amazed, while others sneered and said: "These people are filled with new wine." In the midst of such seeming perplexity, Peter arose to speak strongly saying that this was the manifestation of the most Holy Spirit descending upon the people as was predicted by the prophet Joel (2:28-32).

Peter proclaimed to all of the sneering Israelites that Jesus of Nazareth, who had been crucified, was raised up by God and freed from death because it was impossible for him as God's Son to be held in its power. Peter continued by saying that we all are witnesses of this Jesus, whom God raised up, who received from the Father – the Holy Spirit and now has poured out the Holy Spirit on us here that you and the entire house of Israel can see, hear and know with certainty that God has made Jesus both Lord and Messiah.

When they heard this, they were cut to the heart. They said to Peter and the other apostles, "What shall we do?" Peter proclaimed to them: "Repent each and every one, and be baptized in the name of Jesus Christ so that your sins may be forgiven; and you will receive the gift of the Holy Spirit. This promise is for you, for your children and for all who are far away — everyone whom the Lord our God calls." At that, about 3,000 people welcomed this message, became baptized and were added to the number of Christ's people on this, the well-known birthday of the church (Acts 2:7-41).

After Pentecost, according to the Book of Acts 1-9, Peter led the way among the people of the now referred to Lord Jesus — by acts of healing, preaching in the temple area, being arrested for proclaiming that in Jesus there is resurrection of the dead, standing boldly before the representatives of the high priestly family to defend his position, being ordered not to teach or speak in the name of Jesus again, speaking against Ananias and Sapphira for withholding money with the sale of their property when all things were to be held in common, helping Philip in Samaria with another apostle by laying hands on new converts — who then received the Holy Spirit and healing a man named Aeneas in Lydda, as well as a woman named Tabitha, or Dorcas, in Joppa.

In chapter 10 in the Book of the Acts of the Apostles, Peter is reported as the key person in what has been heralded as the turning point in Biblical history. Moreover, Peter's response to the leading of the Holy Spirit through a divine vision that was coupled at the very same time with a Gentile named Cornelius, who was a centurion of the Italian Cohort in the Roman military, became a pivotal event in the earliest days of the Christian movement and catapulted Peter into dimensions of undeniable leadership far and above everyone else.

Furthermore, what transpired here was unquestionably the Lord's doing through the amazing power of the Holy Spirit. Peter now had become totally bonded with Jesus the Christ, who was one with the Father and the person of the Holy Spirit. Throughout the whole Bible, nothing can even begin to compare with this reported event, which brings a joy and peace even to the most indigent of people.

Peter's thinking, speaking and action here are superior to anyone else in the world, and the reported total response of the centurion named Cornelius equally is as phenomenal and significant for the future of people living anywhere on earth. The details, as provided for us in the Bible, are the needed, substantive proof for any and all people who ever live and is presented right from the Bible in Acts 10 as follows:

"In Caesarea, there was a man named Cornelius, a centurion of the Italian Cohort, who was a devout man who feared God with everyone of his household; he gave alms generously to the people and prayed constantly to God. One afternoon about three o'clock he had a vision in which he clearly saw an angel of God coming in and saying to him, 'Cornelius.'

272

"He stared at him in terror and said, 'What is it, Lord?' He answered, 'Your prayers and your alms have ascended as a memorial before God. Now send men to Joppa for a certain Simon who is called Peter; he is lodging with Simon, a tanner, whose house is by the seaside. When the angel who spoke to him left, he called two of his slaves and a devout soldier from the ranks of those who served him. After telling them everything, he sent them to Joppa.

"About noon that day, as they were on their journey and approaching the city, Peter went up on the roof to pray. Peter became hungry and wanted something to eat. While it was being prepared, he fell into a trance. He saw heaven opened and something like a large sheet coming down, being lowered to the ground by its four corners. In it were all kinds of four-footed creatures and reptiles and birds of the air.

"Then he heard a voice saying, 'Get up, Peter, kill and eat.' But Peter said, 'By no means, Lord; for I never have eaten anything that is profane or unclean.' The voice said to him again a second time, 'What God has made clean, you must not call profane.' This happened three times, and then suddenly the thing was taken up to heaven.'

"Now while Peter greatly was puzzled about what to make of the vision that he had seen, suddenly the men sent by Cornelius appeared. They were asking for Simon's house and were standing by the gate. They called out to ask whether Simon, who is called Peter, was staying there. While Peter still was thinking about the vision, the Spirit said to him, 'Look, three men are searching for you. Now get up, go down, and go with them without hesitation; for I have sent them.'

"So Peter went down to the men and said, 'I am the one you are looking for; what is the reason for your coming?' They answered, 'Cornelius, a centurion, well spoken of by the whole Jewish nation, was directed by a holy angel to send for you to come to his house and to hear what you have to say.' So Peter invited them in and gave them lodging.

"The next day he got up and went with them, and some of the believers from Joppa accompanied him. The following day they came to Caesarea. Cornelius was expecting them and had called together his relatives and close friends. On Peter's arrival Cornelius met him, and falling at his feet, worshiped him. But Peter made him get up, saying, 'Stand up; I am only a mortal.'

"And as Peter talked with Cornelius, he went in and found that many had assembled; and he said to them, 'You yourselves know that it is unlawful for a Jew to associate or visit a Gentile; but God has shown me that I should not call anyone profane or unclean. So when I was sent for, I came without objection. Now, may I ask why you sent for me?'

"Cornelius explained how an angel of the Lord had come and told him to get Peter and bring him here. Then he said to Peter: 'All of us are here in the presence of God to listen to all that the Lord has commanded you to say.'

"Then, Peter began speaking to them: 'I truly understand that God shows no partiality, but in every nation anyone who fears and does what is right is acceptable to God. You know the message that God sent to the people of Israel, preaching peace by Jesus Christ — he is Lord of all. That message spread throughout Judea, beginning in Galilee after the baptism that John announced; how God anointed Jesus of Nazareth with the Holy Spirit and with power; how he went about doing good and healing all who were oppressed by the devil, for God was with him.

"'We are witnesses to all that he did both in Judea and in Jerusalem. They put him to death by hanging him on a tree; but God raised him on the third day and allowed him to appear, not to all people, but to us who were chosen by God as witnesses and who ate and drank with him after he rose from the dead. He commanded us to preach to the people and to testify that he is the one ordained by God as judge of the living and the dead. All the prophets testify about him that everyone who believes in him receives forgiveness of sins through his name.'

"While Peter still was speaking, the Holy Spirit fell upon all who heard the word. The circumcised believers who had come with Peter were astounded that the gift of the Holy Spirit had been poured out even on the Gentiles, for they heard them speaking and extolling God. Then Peter said, 'Can anyone withhold water for baptizing these people who have received the Holy Spirit just as we have?' So he ordered them to be baptized in the name of Jesus Christ.

According to chapter 11 in the Book of Acts, the apostles and the believers, who were in Judea, heard that the Gentiles also had accepted the word of God. So when Peter went up to Jerusalem, the circumcised believers criticized him, saying:

> "Why did you go to uncircumcised men and eat with them?"
>
> Peter began to explain it all to them step by step concluding as follows: "And as I began to speak to them, the Holy Spirit fell upon them just as it had upon us at the beginning. And I remembered the word of the Lord, how he had said, 'John baptized with water, but you will be baptized with the Holy Spirit.' If then God gave them the same gift that he gave us when we believed in the Lord Jesus Christ, who was I that I could hinder God?' "

When they heard this, they were silenced. And they praised God, saying, "Then God has given even to the Gentiles the repentance that leads to life." All that can be added at this point seems to be one word expletives such as: Astounding! Incredible! Miraculous! Phenomenal! Wow!

About that time, according to Acts 12, King Herod Agrippa I laid violent hands upon some of them who belonged to the church. In the process Peter was arrested during the Festival of the Unleavened Bread. When Herod had seized Peter, this king put Peter in prison with four squads of soldiers to guard him with the supposed intent of bringing Peter out to the Jewish people after Passover. They seemed to be pleased with Herod's violent actions against the church.

While Peter was kept in prison, the church prayed fervently to God on behalf of Peter. On the very night before Herod was going to bring Peter out — bound with two chains and sleeping between two soldiers, while guards in front of the door were keeping watch over the prison — suddenly an angel of the Lord is said to have appeared. He tapped Peter on the side and woke him saying: "Fasten your belt and put on your sandals."

Peter reportedly did as he was told. Then, the angelic person said to him, "Wrap your cloak around you and follow me." Peter did what he was told, but in the process Peter did not realize what was happening to him or whether the angel's help was real. Peter just thought that he merely was seeing some sort of a vision.

After passing the first and second guard, they came before the iron-gate that led into the city of Jerusalem. It just seemed to open for them of its own accord, and they proceeded outside walking along a lane. Suddenly the angel left Peter. At that point, Peter became aware of what was happening to him and said: "I know now that the Lord has sent his angel to rescue me from the hands of Herod and from all that the Jewish people were expecting."

As soon as Peter realized this, he proceeded to the house of Mary, the mother of John called Mark, where many had gathered and were praying. When Peter knocked at the gate, a maid named Rhoda came to the entrance. Upon recognizing Peter's voice, she was so overjoyed that instead of opening the gate she ran back inside and announced that Peter was standing at the gate. They all said to her, "You are out of your mind," but Rhoda insisted that it was true. They all said, "It has to be his angel."

Meanwhile, Peter continued knocking. When they finally did open the gate, they saw Peter and were amazed. Upon motioning for them to be silent, he described how the Lord had brought him out of prison. Then he left and went to another place. When morning came, however, there seemingly was no small commotion among the soldiers over what had become of Peter.

When Herod had searched for Peter and could not find him, he examined the guards and ordered them put to death. Nonetheless, soon thereafter when Herod was addressing people himself and egotistically accepting the acclaim of the people as being a god and not a mortal, he was struck down by what was said to be an angel of the Lord. It resulted in Herod being eaten alive until dead, which of course is unver-

276

ifiable. Nevertheless, the death seemed appropriate to people who experienced nothing from Herod but terror as well as inappropriate thoughts and actions during his lifetime.

The crowning achievement of Peter in Judea occurred at the Church Council in Jerusalem as described in chapter 15 in the Book of Acts. Accordingly, there were Jewish Christians in the area who were teaching that unless people of the faith, especially new ones, are circumcised according to the custom of Moses, they could not be saved, and there was no small dissension in the whole church over this matter.

There were those who believed that such a procedure was needed, while others — especially among Gentile Christians and those sympathetic toward them, were convinced that circumcision in no way was necessary for Christ's people. Thus, the lines were firmly drawn, and the debate raged furiously. In the midst of that most heated discussion, Peter — having just come off of the experience with Cornelius and his people — arose to lead the council in turning the tide toward a more open stance over this volatile issue.

Peter proclaimed:

> "My brothers, you know that God made a choice among us that I should be the one through whom the Gentiles would hear the message of the good news and become believers. And God, who knows the human heart, testified unto them by giving Gentiles the Holy Spirit. Therefore, in cleansing their hearts by faith, God has made no distinction between them and us.
>
> "Now, therefore, there is no need in putting God to the test any further by placing on the neck of the disciples a yoke that neither our ancestors nor we have been able to bear. On the contrary, we wholeheartedly believe that we will be saved through the grace of the Lord Jesus, just as they will!"

As a result of these powerful words along with such expressions from others, it seemed good to the Holy Spirit and via the consent of the whole church — not to trouble the

277

Gentiles who turn to God anymore, nor to impose any further burden upon them over this matter again.

Following that formidable action, there appears to be no other material about Peter from a biographical standpoint in the Biblical record. However, Peter's name does appear in letters of Paul and, of course, is associated with the letters of First and Second Peter. Nonetheless, tradition is extremely powerful that Peter's influence spread throughout the Mediterranean region, as strongly suggested in 1 Corinthians 1:12, which is a far cry from his roots around the Sea of Galilee. Most importantly, Peter is said to have been crucified on an upside-down cross in Rome at the hand of Emperor Nero in 64 AD, because Peter did not feel worthy to be executed as Jesus had been.

<u>Cleopas</u> and another follower of Jesus on the reported same day of the appearance of the risen Jesus to women at the empty tomb near dawn, which was the third day after his crucifixion, were on the road from Jerusalem to Emmaus. At that point, they were joined by a third traveler, according to Mark 16:12-13 and Luke 24:33-53, which turned out to be the experience of a lifetime.

Nothing quite like it has been recorded in the annals of history, and this encounter has become another powerful and dramatic incident in the transformation of ordinary people whose lives never will be the same again. Furthermore, the impact of this event has ramifications upon enormous amounts of people in hearing the word of God from the Bible and in celebrating the Eucharist, or the Sacrament of Holy Communion, for generations upon generations to come.

First, who are these people on the road to Emmaus with what is referred today as Easter Sunday? Traditionally, it has been assumed that they are two men, one of whom is named Cleopas, as already stated, but there is Biblical data that may suggest otherwise. In the Gospel according to John 19:25, it clearly is pronounced that standing near the cross

278

of Jesus during his crucifixion were the mother of Jesus and his mother's sister, Mary, the wife of Clopas, in addition to Mary Magdalene.

Therefore, could it be that the other follower of Jesus on the walk from Jerusalem to Emmaus was indeed — Mary, the sister of Jesus' mother and the wife of Cleopas even though Cleopas is spelled differently in the Gospel of John? Moreover, could she even be the "other Mary" already cited in Matthew 27:61 and 28:1 of the Bible? That possibility adds another important dimension to the appearances of the resurrected Jesus of Nazareth among people close to him.

There are reported appearances of the risen Jesus among women, individually and corporately, as well as among men, singly and together. Also, the resurrected Jesus of Nazareth was found to be among many people at one time. Even the statistic of 500 human beings has been suggested in the Bible but not unto a husband and wife as could be true of the two people walking on the road to Emmaus three days after Jesus died by crucifixion and put in a reportedly well-sealed tomb.

This author believes the appearance of the resurrected Jesus to a supposed solidly married couple would be an enormous blessing and superlative joy to any couple who are loyal to the life of the church week after week, year after year! Regularly and devotedly they attend upon hearing the word of God and receiving the blessed sacraments instituted by Christ. It would be marvelous, if it were true at this point, as well as among any individuals who continually are so inclined.

Nevertheless, as important as this thought may be, it is far from being the highlight here. The Biblical accounting of the event itself is what really shines above all else and is recorded in the Gospel of Luke as follows:

"On that same day," when the risen Jesus of Nazareth appeared to the women at the empty tomb where he had been buried fol-

lowing his death by crucifixion, "two of his followers were going to a village called Emmaus about seven miles from Jerusalem. They were talking with each other about the things that
had happened. While they were talking and discussing, Jesus
himself came near and went with them, but their eyes were kept
from recognizing him.

"And Jesus said to them, 'What are you discussing with
each other while you walk along?' They stood still, looking sad.
Then, one named Cleopas answered him, 'Are you the only
stranger in Jerusalem who does not know the things that have
taken place there in these days?'

"He asked them, 'What things?' They replied, 'The things
about Jesus of Nazareth, who was a prophet mighty in deed and
word before God and all the people, and how our chief priests
and leaders handed him over to be condemned to death and
crucified him. But we had hoped that he was the one to redeem
Israel. Yes, and besides all this, it is now the third day since
these things took place.

"'Moreover, some women of our group astounded us. They
were at the tomb early this morning, and when they did not find
the body there, they came back and told us that they indeed had
seen a vision of the angels who said that he was alive. Some of
those, who were with us, went to the tomb and found it just as
the women had said, but they did not see him.'

"Then, Jesus said to them, 'Oh, how foolish you are, and
how slow of heart to believe all that the prophets have declared!
Was it not necessary that the Messiah should suffer these things
and then enter into his glory?' Then, beginning with Moses and
all the prophets, he interpreted to them about himself in all the
scriptures.

"As they came near the village to which they were going,
Jesus walked ahead as if he were going on. But they urged him
strongly, saying: 'Stay with us, because it is almost evening,
and the day is now nearly over.' So, he went in with them.

"When Jesus was at the table with them, he took bread,
blessed and broke it, and gave it to them. Then, their eyes were
opened, and they recognized him, and Jesus vanished from their
sight. They said to each other, 'Were not our hearts burning
within us while he was talking to us on the road - while he was
opening the scriptures to us?'

"That same hour, they got up and returned to Jerusalem, and
they found the eleven and their companions gathered together.

They were saying, 'The Lord has risen indeed, and he has appeared to Simon!' Then, the two of them told what had happened on the road, and how Jesus had been made known to them in the breaking of bread."

Thomas reportedly was not with the other ten disciples when Jesus appeared to them behind closed doors and showed them his hands and his side (Luke 24:36-40; John 20:20). According to John 20:24-29, the other disciples told him, "We have seen the Lord!" But Thomas said to them, "Unless I see the mark of the nails in his hands, and put my finger in the mark of the nails and my hand in his side, I will not believe."

A week later his disciples again were in the house, and Thomas was with them. Although the doors were shut, Jesus came and stood among them and said, "Peace be with you." Then, he said to Thomas, "Put your finger here and see my hands. Reach out your hand and put it in my side. Do not doubt but believe." Thomas answered him, "My Lord and my God!"

Jesus said to Thomas, "Have you believed because you have seen me? Blessed are those who have not seen and yet have come to believe."

Thus, Thomas evolved into a true apostle of the Lord Jesus Christ and joined with Peter and five others afterward at the Sea of Galilee (John 21:1-14). Also, he is listed as one among many, who devoted themselves constantly to prayer after the reported ascension of Jesus and prior to Pentecost (Acts 1:13-14).

According to tradition, Thomas was led on an unrelenting course as missionary of the Gospel of Jesus, his now Lord and Savior. He traveled all the way to India to establish a church that seemed to be small in number but still is recognizable in that country some twenty centuries later.

James, son of Zebedee, also is named with six other of the twelve disciples in that encounter with the risen Jesus at the Sea of Galilee (John 21:1-14) and is listed as one of many who devoted themselves constantly to prayer later on (Acts 1:13-14). His life was cut relatively short, however, when King Herod Agrippa I laid violent hands upon some who belonged to the church (Acts 12:1).

In the process, Herod had this James put to death with the sword around 44 AD, which evidently pleased some of the Jewish people. Because of his faithfulness through that unwanted and unwarranted ordeal, James indelibly has been etched in the minds and hearts of people ever afterward.

John, the younger brother of James and son of Zebedee, evidently lived much longer than others and some say beyond anyone else of the twelve disciples. He is noted as an Apostle in John 21:1-14 and also as one who linked with others in constant prayer according to Acts 1:13-14. Then, John reportedly joined Peter in healing a man at the Beautiful Gate of the temple in Jerusalem (Acts 8:14-25), as well as laying hands on Samaritans, which resulted in the Samaritans receiving the gift of the Holy Spirit (Acts 8:14-17).

Tradition further attributes John as responsible for the Gospel according to John, the three letters of John and the Revelation of John, which are recorded in the Bible, and as spending his latter days in exile on the island of Patmos with Mary, the mother of Jesus.

Nathaniel is the final disciple who is listed by name with the reported appearance of Jesus at the Sea of Galilee (John 21:1-14) and as later being in constant prayer with others, according to Acts 1:13-14, but two others are said to have been at this scene as well. Those two people may have included Philip; James, the Son of Alphaeus; Judas, the son of James, or otherwise named Thaddeus; or even Simon the Zealot. No one really knows who these two men may have been.

All eleven remaining disciples reportedly were witnesses to the appearance of the risen Jesus of Nazareth as stated in Matthew 28:16-17; Mark 16:14-16; Luke 24:33-53; 1 Corinthians 15:5. This leaves very little or no doubt in the Biblical record that they were Apostles of the Lord Jesus too, even though as such — they are not mentioned specifically any further.

Philip, though not mentioned specifically in the Bible as a witness to the appearance of the resurrected Jesus of Nazareth, but truly he was one of them. Without question he was one of the strongest, leading people after Jesus' reported resurrection. The spiritual power of the resurrected Jesus in Philip especially is noted following the martyrdom of a man named Stephen, when followers of the risen Lord Jesus reportedly were scattered and went about from place to place proclaiming the word (Acts 8:4).

At that time, Philip proceeded to the city of Samaria and proclaimed to them that "Jesus is the Messiah." Apparently, the crowds listened eagerly to what was said by Philip, as well as to hear and see the signs that he did. Moreover, unclean spirits crying with loud voices came out of many who were possessed, and many people, who were lame or paralyzed, evidently were cured (Acts 8:4-7). When people were said to have believed the proclamation of Philip about the Kingdom of God and the name of Jesus Christ, they were baptized (Acts 8:12).

According to Acts 8:26-40, an angelic messenger of the Lord proclaimed to Philip: "Get up and go south to the 'wilderness' road that leads from Jerusalem to Gaza." There an Ethiopian eunuch, who was a court official with the queen of the Ethiopians, was returning home in his chariot from worshiping in Jerusalem and reading from the prophet Isaiah 53:7-8.

When Philip heard him reading, he asked the eunuch if he understood what was being read. In answering negatively and inquiring about its meaning, Philip started with these two verses from Isaiah in proclaiming the good news about Jesus as being the one described in that portion of scripture.

283

At that, the eunuch commanded the chariot to stop beside a water place and reportedly was baptized by Philip before going on his way rejoicing. From that point onward, Philip evidently continued his missionary work on behalf of the Lord Jesus through the region of Azotus. He further proclaimed the good news to all of the towns in which he came into contact. As a result, more people were added to the community of Christ's people.

Whether Mary, mother of Jesus, is herself a witness to the risen Jesus, her Son, is not recorded in the Bible per se, unless she is the other Mary, or the one referred to as the mother of James and Joses. Jesus' mother Mary specifically is listed after Jesus' crucifixion only in Acts 1:13-14 along with those in constant prayer, but Mary's son named James, who also was the brother of Jesus, definitely is listed as one to whom the risen Jesus appeared (1 Corinthians 15:7). Thus, even though Mary, the mother of Jesus, is not specifically recorded in the Biblical record as a witness to the appearance of her resurrected Son, it is hard to fathom that her son James was an Apostle and she was not. According to the Bible, Mary's great significance to her Son, Jesus, is related to his birth, life and death.

James, the brother of Jesus and leader of the early church in Jerusalem, not only is recorded as a witness to the resurrected Jesus but also became a significant force in the very early beginnings of the Christian movement, according to the Biblical record. Probably his best reported moment occurred in his speech at the Church Council that is recorded in Acts 15. He spoke on behalf of the conservative Jewish Christian party, which he headed. That faction of the church wanted Gentiles, who had become believers in Jesus as the Messiah, the Christ, Son of the living God and were baptized in his name, also to become circumcised according to the custom of Moses before being fully accepted into the Christian community.

On this monumental day in the early history of the church, James, the brother of Jesus and leader of the church, stood up after everyone else had spoken, proclaiming: "Simon Peter has related how God first looked favorably upon the Gentiles, to take from among them a people for his name" (Acts 15:14). "Therefore, I have reached the decision that we should not trouble these Gentiles, who have turned to God, but we just should write to them and ask that they abstain from things that have been polluted by idols" and such (Acts 15:19-20).

What a marvelous statement! Evidently, these were the final, convincing words that the whole assembly needed to hear for unanimous approval at that point and put to rest forever the necessity of circumcision among all new people who had come to believe and live as Christ's people. After that, this James is mentioned elsewhere in the Bible only by name as the leader of the church in Jerusalem, is assumed to be the author of the Letter of James in the Bible and is said to have died there around 66 AD.

Paul, who originally was named Saul of Tarsus, was considered by his highly regarded and most reliable source of any of his recorded words — to be the last of the Apostles. In his first letter to the Corinthians 15:8-10, Paul clearly states: "Last of all, as to one untimely born, Jesus appeared unto me. For I am the least of all the apostles, unfit even to be called one, because I persecuted the church of God. But by the grace of God, I am what I am," as his Apostle, which has not been in vain because of what has been accomplished with me by the grace of God.

How did that come to be? Miraculously, it might be stated! Also, it is somewhat similar to the other apostles in that he too did not believe in Jesus. In fact, as already mentioned, he radically was opposed to him and his followers. Whether Paul knew Jesus before he died is beside the point, even though he was born in 4 BC as Saul of Tarsus, a town near the seacoast off the northeastern part of the Mediterranean Sea around the same time that Jesus reportedly was born in Bethlehem of Judea.

Also, Saul of Tarsus, later named Paul, was in Jerusalem studying under the superb tutelage of Gamaliel, the finest and most notable Jewish, Pharisaic teacher of the era around 8 AD. Furthermore, it is near the same time that Jesus at twelve years of age lingered among the teachers in the temple area — listening to them and asking questions during the festival of the Passover. It may be remembered that all who heard Jesus at the time said that they were amazed at Jesus' understanding and his answers (Luke 2:41-42, 46-47), which parallels Paul's expertise concerning his relationship with Judaism.

Furthermore, Paul may have heard about the crucifixion of Jesus or possibly even witnessed that horrific event. There seems to be no way of knowing, but it is known by all reports that Paul radically opposed Jesus. He violently persecuted the followers of Jesus over an extended period of time after the reported death and resurrection of Jesus, because Paul was a Pharisaic Jew under the strictest adherence to the Law of Moses. That in and of itself made Jesus and his followers the enemy of everyone, including God, according to this man named Saul of Tarsus.

The first evidence that Paul was this vicious kind of person, who would defend to the utmost what he believed to be true, is noted in the Book of Acts 7:58 and 8:1-8 at the stoning and burial of Stephen. Stephen was one of seven men who was full of the Holy Spirit, of faith and of wisdom. He had been anointed with the laying on of hands in order to help the Apostles by serving other followers of Jesus.

In that portion of the Bible, it is stated that in dragging Stephen out of the city of Jerusalem and in beginning to stone him, the witnesses laid their coats at the feet of this young man named Saul of Tarsus. Saul is said to have fully approved of this murderous act. When devout men buried Stephen and made lamentation over him, Saul reportedly continued to ravage the church by entering house after house, dragging off men and women and having them committed to prison.

In Paul's own words later in his letter to the Galatians 1:13-14, he stated: "I was violently persecuting the church of God and was trying to destroy it. I advanced in Judaism beyond many among my own people of the same age, for I was far more zealous for the traditions of my ancestors than anyone else."

Around 33 AD, according to chapter 9 in the Book of Acts, Saul still breathing threats and murder against the followers of Jesus — evidently went to the high priest and asked him for letters to the synagogues at Damascus. If he found any who belonged to the Way, or the Christian faith, men or women, he would bring them bound to Jerusalem.

Then an overwhelming event, recorded several places in the Bible, occurred to such an extent that Paul absolutely and completely turned around 180 degrees! Here is the description of what transpired in the life of Paul, according to the Biblical record in Acts 9:1-9; 22:3-11; 26:2-28 and Galatians 1:13-16:

"I [Paul] was on my way traveling to Damascus with authority received from the chief priests, when at midday along the road in approaching Damascus I saw a light from heaven, brighter than the sun, shining around me. I fell to the ground and heard a voice saying to me, 'Saul, Saul, why are you persecuting me? It hurts you to kick against the goads.'

"I asked, 'Who are you Lord?' The Lord answered, 'I am Jesus of Nazareth, whom you are persecuting.' I further asked: 'What am I to do, Lord?' The Lord said to me, 'Get up and stand on your feet, for I have appeared to you for this purpose, to appoint you to serve and testify to the things that you have seen and to those in which I will appear to you.

" 'I will rescue you from your people and from the Gentiles, to whom I am sending you to open their eyes — that they may turn from darkness to light and from the power of Satan to God, in order that they may receive forgiveness of sins and a place among those who are sanctified by faith in me.'

"Then, since I could not see because of the brightness of that light, those, who were with me and saw the light but did not hear the voice of the one speaking to me, took me by the hand and led me to Damascus, where I stayed for three days without sight, neither eating or drinking."

Now there was a disciple in Damascus named Ananias, and the Lord said to him in a vision, "Ananias." He answered, "Here I am Lord." The Lord reportedly said to him "Get up and go to the street called Straight, and at the house of Judas, look for a man of Tarsus named Saul. At this very moment, he is praying, and he has seen a vision of a man named Ananias come in and lay hands on him so that he might regain his sight."

Ananias answered, "Lord, I have heard from many about this man, how much evil he has done to your saints in Jerusalem. Here in Damascus, he has authority from the chief priests to bind all who invoke your name." The Lord said to Ananias, "Go, for he is an instrument whom I have chosen to bring my name before Gentiles and kings, and before the people of Israel. I myself will show him how much he must suffer for the sake of my name."

Ananias went to the house, entered and laid his hands on Saul, saying: "Brother Saul, the Lord Jesus, who appeared to you on your way here, has sent me so that you may regain your sight and be filled with the Holy Spirit." Immediately, something like scales fell from Paul's eyes and his sight was restored. He got up and was baptized. After taking some food Paul did regain his strength.

In his own written words, Paul later summed up this whole episode by stating in his letter to the Galatians 1:15-

16, "When God set me apart and called me through his grace, God was pleased to reveal his Son to me, so that I might proclaim him among the Gentiles."

According to Acts 9:19-28, Paul was with the disciples in Damascus. Immediately he began to proclaim Jesus in the synagogues saying: "He is the Son of God." All who heard Paul were amazed and said, "Is this not the man who made havoc in Jerusalem among those who invoked the name of Jesus? And has he not come here for the purpose of bringing Jesus' followers bound before the chief priests in Jerusalem?"

Paul, however, became increasingly more powerful and brilliantly confounded the Jewish people, who lived in Damascus. He proved with his superior intellect that Jesus was indeed the Messiah. After some time had passed, Jewish people there plotted to dispose of Paul. They watched the gates day and night in order that they might kill him, but disciples took him by night and let him down through an opening in the wall — lowering him in a basket.

When Paul came to Jerusalem, he attempted to join the disciples, but they were afraid of him because they did not believe that Paul was a disciple. His companion, Barnabas, took Paul, brought him to the Apostles, described how Paul on the road to Damascus had seen the Lord, who had spoken to him, and how in Damascus Paul had spoken boldly in the name of Jesus.

As a result of this beneficent man's initiative, Paul was able to go in and out among the people of Jerusalem and speak boldly in the name of the Lord Jesus. However, when Paul spoke and argued with the Hellenists, they attempted to kill him. When believers learned of it, they brought Paul to Caesarea and sent him off to Tarsus.

Sometime afterward, Barnabas was sent to Antioch where he witnessed a great many people turning to the Lord. Barnabas went to Tarsus and brought Paul to Antioch. Together they met with those in the church, who for the first time were called Christians. Paul taught many people there for an entire year (Acts 11:25-16). When a group of prophets and teachers one day were worshiping the Lord among the Christians in Antioch, the Holy Spirit said: "Set apart Barnabas and Paul for a mission, to which I have called them."

After fasting and praying, hands were laid upon the two of them. Around 47 AD they were sent off on their first missionary journey along with a fellow named John Mark, who was to assist them (Acts 13:1-5). The three of them went to Cyprus, Perga (where John Mark deserted the other two of them), the province of Galatia, Antioch in Pisidia, Iconium, Lystra, Attalia, Selucia and finally back to Antioch in Syria.

Paul and Barnabas traveled from Antioch to the Church Council in Jerusalem, where together they led the way in opening the Christian faith to the Gentiles without the necessity of additionally requiring them to do the rite of circumcision according to the custom of Moses. When back in Antioch Paul asked Barnabas to go on a second missionary journey in 50-52 AD. Barnabas wanted again to take John Mark with them, but Paul refused because John Mark had deserted them the last time.

The two of them parted company. Paul instead chose Silas, or Silvanus, and gathered the young Timothy along with them to tread into regions yet untouched by any other missionary endeavor on behalf of the Lord Jesus Christ. In the process, they covered the towns and regions of Cilicia, Derbe, Lystra, Iconium, Mysia, Troas in the Roman province of Asia and crossed over to Macedonia, Greece and Europe.

Paul, Silas and Timothy were joined by Luke. The four of them journeyed to Neapolis and Philippi. In Philippi, the magistrates ordered Paul and Silas to be stripped of their clothing, to be beaten with rods, flogged and thrown into prison until ultimately freed. At that point, Luke stayed in Philippi while the other three continued upon the Egnation

Way, which was the main transportation artery that connected the eastern provinces with Italy and onto Amphipolis and
Thessalonica.

When trouble arose in Thessalonica, they proceeded to
Beroea. When enemies from Thessalonica pursued, Paul set
out by sea to Athens, leaving Silas and Timothy to encourage believers in Beroea. Paul left Athens and traveled west
to Corinth and remained there for eighteen months, where he
stayed longer than any place — other than Ephesus.

Paul's first and second letters to the Thessalonians most
likely were written in Corinth between 51 and 52 AD. Paul
left Corinth and went by ship to Ephesus where he probably
wrote his letter to the Galatians. Afterward, Paul proceeded
by ship to Caesarea and on to Jerusalem to report on his trip
before returning to Antioch in Syria.

Paul left Antioch in Syria on a third missionary journey
that transpired between 53 and 56 AD. This probably was
caused hurriedly by the opponents of Paul in the churches
that he had planted. Such places included Derbe, Lystra, Iconium, Antioch in the province of Pisidia, Laodicea, and then
on a direct route to Ephesus.

Paul wrote his first letter to the Corinthians in Ephesus during the spring of 55 AD. No writing in the Bible has
proved to be more authentic than this one because none other has better external testimony. Verification later by such
notable people as Clement, Justin Martyr, Athenagoras and
Tertullian validate its historicity.

Furthermore, these supposedly two huge scrolls miraculously were carried and delivered to new Christians in
Corinth by ordinary people such as Timothy and the delega-
tion that returned to Corinth with him after coming to Paul
for advice during his several year stay in Ephesus. That these
writings lasted through the centuries is more proof in and of
itself that a factual gem, such as this and other similar writings, exist before the whole world — even today.

It is recorded in the Acts of the Apostles of the Bible that a riot in Ephesus at that time sent Paul to Troas, over to Macedonia through the Roman province of Achaia or Greece. Paul stayed in Corinth for three months and wrote his letter to the Romans. He planned to sail from Corinth straight to Antioch in Syria, but a plot against his life was discovered. Paul retraced his steps back through Macedonia to Troas. From Troas, Paul proceeded to Assos, Mitylene, Samos and Miletus where he said his last farewell to the elders of the church from Ephesus.

There, he proclaimed that the Holy Spirit testified to him that imprisonments and persecutions are waiting for him in every city. Paul declared that he has endured all of the trials that came to him, kept his integrity in tact by doing no wrong to deserve any evil placed upon him. Moreover, he continually testified to both the Jewish people and the Greeks about repentance toward God and faith toward our Lord Jesus Christ (Acts 20:19-23).

From Miletus, Paul proceeded by ship to Cos, Rhodes, Patara, Phoenicia, Tyre, Ptolemais, Caesarea and then by land to Jerusalem where he brought news of his third missionary journey to the elders there. When a plot to murder Paul was uncovered, Paul was taken by night to Antipatris and then to the provincial prison in Caesarea where the governor, Felix, was to hear the Jewish case against Paul.

This whole saga is magnificently portrayed in chapters 21-28 with the Acts of the Apostles. Those who love historical drama and how the risen and exalted Lord through the amazing power of the Holy Spirit is evidenced in the lives of ordinary human beings, will not want to miss reading this powerful and dynamic portion of scripture. Do pick up the Bible now and read Acts 21-28. It just may be the best thing that has been done for awhile and even could transform a whole perception on life in the midst of very difficult moments, as it did with Paul, his companions and many others through the years!

After appealing his case to Caesar while in prison at Caesarea, Paul was sent on a 2,000 mile trip to Rome. Under house arrest in Rome, Paul perhaps wrote letters to the Ephesians, Philippians, Colossians, and to the person named Philemon. According to tradition, Paul was executed by beheading outside the walls of Rome via decree from Roman Emperor Nero in 64 AD, because Paul was a Roman citizen.

---

1. John Masefield, *The Everlasting Mercy* (Portland, Maine: Smith and Sale, 1911).

CHAPTER 11

EARLY CHRISTIAN PEOPLE

Early Christian people were known as believers in Jesus the Messiah, the Christ, Son of the ever-living God and as followers after his Way. Unless they were among crowds of other Christians, however, they did not experience the risen Jesus — face-to-face and person to person as the Apostles evidently did. However, they were aware of his ever-living presence among them through the amazing power of the Holy Spirit, whom they knew without a doubt as the Spirit of Jesus.

Furthermore, they looked to the Apostles, who had been with the risen Jesus personally for teaching, leadership, guidance and motivation in matters of faith, hope and love. For the most part, these early Christian people were solid people of the church in contributing to the needs of others, worshiping the Lord, participating in the sacraments on a regular basis, being mission-minded in all aspects of their life together, enduring suffering and even joyfully willing to die for the Lord, whom they loved.

Of course, there were some people, who reneged on their faith and did not act with honesty and integrity as followers of the Lord, such as a husband and wife named Ananias and Sapphira according to Acts 5:1-6. They were dishonest, stingy and lied before the Apostles, who were led by Peter and the Holy Spirit. As a result, this couple in front of everyone else — lost everything.

There was a person named Simon the sorcerer who performed magical tricks of greatness and amazed the people of Samaria. However, when Philip proclaimed the good news about the Kingdom of God and extolled the name of Jesus before the people, many of them were converted and baptized on the spot. Even Simon himself believed, was baptized and stayed close to Philip thereafter.

This Simon also was amazed with the signs and miracles that subsequently were taking place in Samaria. When the Apostles at Jerusalem heard that Samaria had accepted the Lord, they sent Peter and John there. The two of them proceeded to Samaria and prayed for them that they might receive the Holy Spirit too. When Peter and John laid their hands upon these Samaritans, they received the Holy Spirit.

However, when Simon the sorcerer saw that the Spirit had been given through the laying on of the Apostles' hands, he reportedly offered them money, saying:

> "Give me this power so that anyone on whom I lay my hands also may receive the Holy Spirit." Peter, however, said to that Simon: "May your silver perish with you, because you thought that you could obtain God's gift with money! Your heart is not right before God. Therefore, repent of this wickedness, and pray to the Lord that the intent of your heart may be forgiven." Simon evidently responded: "Pray for me to the Lord that I may be released from this gall of bitterness and chains of wickedness," which hopefully did transpire. — Acts 8:9-24

Again, there was a person named Apollos, who was a native of Alexandria. He was an eloquent man, versed in the scriptures, well instructed in the Way of the Lord, spoke with burning enthusiasm, taught accurately the things concerning Jesus, greatly helped the people by the grace of the Lord and powerfully refuted those of Jewish persuasion by showing through the scriptures that the Messiah is Jesus!

A problem arose within the Christian community with Apollos, however, in that he knew only the baptism of John the Baptist, which, as already stated previously, meant repentance of sin in the hope that the Kingdom of God might come from God some day. John the Baptist really did not believe that the Kingdom of God already was being inaugurated in

Jesus of Nazareth and among his followers as well — by the amazing power of the Holy Spirit.

While Apollos was in Corinth, Paul reportedly passed through the interior regions and came to Ephesus, where Paul found some people, who by the grace of God, Apollos had helped to become believers in the Lord Jesus Christ. When Paul asked these Ephesians if they had received the Holy Spirit when they became believers, they replied: "No! We have not even heard that there was a Holy Spirit."

Paul inquired: "Into what then were you baptized?" They replied: "Into John's baptism!" Paul proclaimed: "John baptized with the baptism of repentance, telling people to believe in the one who was to come after him, that is — Jesus." Upon hearing these words, they were baptized in the name of the Lord Jesus, and when Paul reportedly laid his hands upon some twelve in number, the Holy Spirit came upon them (Acts 18:24-19:8).

This scenario meant that followers of John the Baptist existed long after his death. Believers in John the Baptist paralleled those who believed in Jesus. In this instance and perhaps others like it, the perception of believing in John the Baptist was corrected and overcome by a clear understanding of what believing in Jesus as Messiah, the Christ and Son of the ever-living God really meant.

People who failed to grasp the real importance of Jesus, however, were the vast exception rather than the rule. Most everyone believed and adhered to what was asked and required of them as true Christians. As a result, more people joined with them, and people of the Christian faith multiplied by leaps and bounds. Even the worst of supposed tragedies turned out to become a positive beyond all imagination beginning with the very first martyr of the Christian faith.

Stephen emerged in the early Christian community as a man full of grace, power, faith and the Holy Spirit according to Acts 6:1-9. When it became apparent that more than

Apostles were needed to care for widows and people who were neglected because of increasing numbers of followers, Stephen surfaced as the first on the list of seven men chosen and consecrated for this high honor of serving among the people by the apostolic laying on of hands.

In the midst of the great wonders and signs that Stephen did among the people, however, people from elsewhere stood up and argued with Stephen. At that point, they could not withstand the wisdom and the Spirit with which Stephen spoke. As a result, these men instigated others to spread the word among people, as well as among the elders and the scribes, that Stephen was speaking blasphemous words against Moses and God.

Suddenly, they accosted Stephen, seized him and brought him before the council or the Sanhedrin. By reportedly setting up false witnesses, Stephen was accused of saying things against the holy place of the temple and the law — by insisting that this Jesus of Nazareth will destroy this place and change the customs that Moses handed on to us. Apparently all of the council in that moment focused intently upon Stephen and saw his face shining like that of an angel.

According to chapter 7 in the Book of Acts, the high priest confronted Stephen directly: "Are these things so?" Stephen replied by reciting a lengthy history of the Jewish people. It concluded with exceedingly caustic words before the whole assembly: "You stiff-necked people, uncircumcised in heart and ears; you forever are opposing the Holy Spirit, just as your ancestors did. Which of the prophets did your forbearers not persecute? They killed those who foretold the coming of the Righteous One, and now you have become his betrayers and murderers. You are the ones that received the law as ordained by angels, and yet have not kept it!"

When they heard these things, they became enraged and ground their teeth at Stephen, but filled with the Holy Spirit, he gazed into heaven and was said to have seen the glory of

God and Jesus standing at the right hand of God. Then, Stephen reportedly proclaimed: "Look, I see the heavens opened and the Son of Man standing at the right hand of God!"

They covered their ears, and with a loud shout all of them rushed together against Stephen. They dragged him out of the city and began to stone him. While they were stoning Stephen to death, Stephen prayed: "Lord Jesus, receive my spirit, and do not hold this sin against them." When he had said this, Stephen died. Devout men then buried Stephen and made great lamentation over him.

That was not the end of Stephen. His influence, even in his death, mightily continued. Philip's strong evangelical mission resulted immediately thereafter, according to Acts 8:4-40. Even Paul, who at that point was Saul of Tarsus, consented and approved of this dastardly act. Moreover, he continued his murderous ways against Jesus and his people immediately thereafter. Nevertheless, the shining example of Stephen's death in the Lord Jesus actually became the catalytic agent in Paul's conversion. This was the radical turn around in his life and mission — and ultimately Paul's own death, all of which was reported in a previous chapter.

Even Peter's missionary thrust reportedly was affected by this man named Stephen (Acts 9:32-11:18). Finally, the church in Antioch of Syria was founded as a result of Christians being widespread after the martyrdom of Stephen (Acts 11:19 ff). So, the commitment, message and mission of the church did not end or even slow down with the death of Stephen. The now Lord Jesus and his people only multiplied and became stronger because of Stephen and the way that he died.

Barnabas, who hailed from Cyprus, was a Levite named Joseph. When he became a part of Jesus' people, he reportedly sold a field that belonged to him, brought that money to the Christian community and laid it at the Apostles' feet.

At that, the Apostles gave him the name of Barnabas, which means "son of encouragement" (Acts 4:36-37).

When Paul came from Damascus to Jerusalem after his conversion and was not accepted among the Christian community because they did not believe him to be a follower of Jesus, it was Barnabas who confidently took Paul before the Apostles. He described how Paul had seen the Lord on the road to Damascus, and how in Damascus he had spoken boldly in the name of the Lord Jesus. That brought acceptance of Paul among Christians and allowed him to speak freely in their behalf from that point onward (Acts 9:26-28).

When Barnabas was sent to Antioch in Syria and saw the grace of God being manifest among the great number of believers who had turned to the Lord there, it again was Barnabas who forthrightly proceeded to get Paul and bring him to Antioch where the two of them taught among the people of the church for an entire year. At the end of that time, prophets and teachers in Antioch sent Barnabas and Paul first on a journey to Jerusalem with staples of relief during that time of famine (Acts 11:21-30). Then they were sent on a first missionary journey to points west and north of Antioch (Acts 13-14).

Afterward, according to chapter 15 in the Book of Acts, it was Barnabas and Paul who at the Church Council meeting in Jerusalem led the way in insisting upon opening up the boundaries of the church to include the Gentiles, as already reported in a previous chapter of this book. It also has been stated that Barnabas and Paul separated over the issue of John Mark's desertion on the first missionary journey together. Barnabas gladly did take John Mark with him and sailed to Cyprus this time. This is the last word recorded about Barnabas in the Book of Acts.

However, Paul mentions Barnabas in some of his letters by stating that Barnabas worked for a living like Paul did and also assumedly was celibate as was Paul (1 Corinthians 9:5-6; Galatians 2:1-6). Even though disagreements may have surfaced upon occasion with Barnabas, he remained a faithful follower of the Lord Jesus. He forever was joyfully loyal to the Christian community as his Christian name, "son of encouragement," suggests.

John Mark, as could be imagined, has many mixed messages associated with his name. The first time that John Mark is mentioned in the Book of Acts is in association with Peter when he left prison and proceeded to the house of Mary, who is referred to as the mother of John Mark (Acts 12:12).

There is the statement in Acts 12:24 and 13:5 that John Mark was recruited in Jerusalem by Barnabas and Paul to assist them on that first missionary journey west and north of Antioch in Syria, but John Mark apparently deserted them at Perga and returned to Jerusalem. That led to a split between Paul and Barnabas. So, John Mark accompanied Barnabas to Cyprus.

However, questions continue to persist with John Mark. Is the house in Jerusalem of Mary, whose son is listed as John Mark, the place where Jesus celebrated what today is known as his Last Supper? Again, what are the reasons why John Mark reportedly deserted Paul and Barnabas and returned to Jerusalem?

Then, in Paul's letter to the Colossians 4:10, additional greetings are sent from Mark, the cousin of Barnabas, to the church in Colossus. Further words then follow: "If he comes to you, welcome him." Also, according to 2 Timothy 4:11, since only one other person is with Paul at that point, his apparent expression presumably to Timothy is: "Get Mark and bring him with you, for he is useful in my ministry." In both of these Biblical statements, is this the same John Mark, or another person named Mark?

Again, with the writing in the Bible listed as the Gospel according to Mark, is this the same John Mark mentioned in the Book of Acts or someone else? According to many Biblical scholars, the Gospel of Mark has been identified with

John Mark on the basis that a gospel could not be attributed to such a person unless he actually was the author. A careful study of the Gospel of Mark makes it somewhat difficult to believe that John Mark of Jerusalem was the Mark who wrote this gospel in Rome in 65 AD after the first persecution of Christians including the apparent murder of Peter and Paul by the dictate of Emperor Nero in 64 AD.

The author of the Gospel of Mark seems to treat Palestine and Palestinian Judaism as being an outsider. It presents much of his information from a Gentile Christian point-of-view, which did not come from the memory of the Apostles at all. In fact, Gentile Christianity placed heavy reliance upon learning about Jesus from what often is referred to as the Old Testament scriptures, which was believed to be about Jesus rather than from the witnesses of Jesus himself.

Furthermore, Jesus in the Gospel of Mark is not merely the Jewish Messiah, but the strong Son of God who is able to deliver people from the powers of evil that are in evidence everywhere. Mark's Gospel among the four gospels listed in the Bible is the most chronological one, which is representative of Gentile Christianity in Rome and not of Jewish Christianity in Jerusalem. Therefore, questions about John Mark persist to this very day and leave even the most devoted person of faith always to wonder about this fellow named John Mark.

Silas, also known as Silvanus, is pictured in a totally different light in the Bible beginning with chapter 15 in the Book of Acts. The first mention of Silas comes following the Church Council in Jerusalem when Silas, along with another leader of the brothers, was sent with Paul and Barnabas to take the letter to the church in Antioch of Syria, which wholeheartedly had been approved by the council.

In that letter, according to Acts 15:25-28, it was stated: "We unanimously have decided to choose representatives from us and send them to you along with our beloved Barn-

302

abas and Paul. Therefore, we have sent Silas and another brother to tell you in person the same things that are in the letter, because it seemed good to the Holy Spirit and us."

When the four of them journeyed to Antioch, they gathered the congregation together and delivered that letter. When the members of the church reportedly read it, they rejoiced at the exhortation, while Silas and the other chosen one, both of whom also were prophets, said much to encourage and strengthen the believers there.

After the two of them as delegates from the Council in Jerusalem had been in Antioch for some time, they were sent off in peace by the believers there, but it seemed good to Silas to remain in Antioch. Obviously, that set the stage for Paul to choose Silas on his second missionary journey when Barnabas selected John Mark to accompany him.

On that second missionary journey, according to chapter 16 in the Book of Acts, it was Silas who was dragged through the marketplace in Philippi with Paul. Appearing before the authorities there, they were beaten with rods, flogged, thrown into prison and finally released. In the process, however, the jailer became a believer in the Lord Jesus and was baptized along with his whole household.

Then in Thessalonica, after arguing at the synagogue and evidently proving from the scriptures that it was necessary for the Messiah to suffer and rise from the dead, and that Jesus is the Messiah, some of them were persuaded and joined Paul and Silas. Many devout Greeks and leading women did also (Acts 17:1-4).

After others in Thessalonica accused these believers, who were led by Paul and Silas, of acting contrary to the decrees of the Roman Emperor and proclaiming another king named Jesus instead, those believers sent Paul and Silas off to Beroea. When they arrived in Beroea, the two of them went to the synagogue, and the Jewish people there were more receptive to them than those in Thessalonica. They welcomed the message eagerly and examined the scriptures every day to see whether these things were so.

As a result, many of them came to believe in the Lord Jesus. That included quite a few Greek women and men of high standing. However, when Jewish people in Thessalonica learned that Paul proclaimed the word of God in Beroea also, they went there to stir up and incite the crowds. So, the believers immediately sent Paul away, but Silas and another one remained in Beroea. Ultimately, Silas rejoined Paul in Corinth, which becomes the last mention of his name in the Book of Acts.

However, Paul refers to Silas in some of his letters primarily as a greeting to places like Thessalonica where they had been (1 Thessalonians 1:1; 2 Thessalonians 1:1). Then, in 2 Corinthians 1:17-22, Paul makes specific statements referring to Silas, which convey some powerful images relative to the Christian faith.

Paul asks the question:

> "Do I make my plans according to ordinary human standards, ready to say 'Yes, yes' and 'No, no' at the same time?" In answer, Paul states: "As surely as God is faithful, our word to you has not been 'Yes and No,' for the Son of God, Jesus Christ, whom Silas and I proclaimed among you, was not 'Yes and No,' but in him it always is 'Yes.' In him, every one of God's promises is a 'Yes.'
>
> "For this reason, it is through Jesus Christ that we say the 'Amen,' to the glory of God. It is God who establishes us with you in Christ and has anointed us, by putting his seal upon us and giving us his Spirit in our hearts."

It would be hard to improve upon a statement such as that, because it seems to ring true from every vantage point. Furthermore, it would seem that nothing better could be said about Silas among the people of Corinth or to anyone when this thought registers deeply within the heart of the human personality.

Timothy, or Timotheous, who accompanied Paul and Silas, is known in the Bible as a beloved, faithful, young brother, child and follower of the Lord (1 Corinthians 4:17). No one seemingly receives accolades in the Christian community like Timothy and rightfully so, according to the Bible.

Born and raised as the son of a Jewish woman, who was a believer, while his father hailed as a Greek, Timothy as a disciple of the Lord Jesus himself was gathered by Paul and Silas at Lystra to accompany them on that second missionary journey. However, in order to placate the Jewish people in those places along the way, Timothy was circumcised, because people evidently knew that his father was Greek.

That seemed to work as a blessing for all people because Timothy was received well by almost everyone, even though upon occasion it was not without warnings from Paul for people to do so. For example, near the end of Paul's letter to the Corinthians, which Timothy may have helped in delivering from Ephesus to the people in Corinth, Paul sharply states: "If Timothy comes, see that he has nothing to fear among you, for just as I am — he is doing the work of the Lord. "Therefore, let no one despise Timothy. Send him on his way in peace, so that he may come to me, for I am expecting him with the brothers" (1 Corinthians 16:10-11). That warning may or may not have been heeded, because Paul then states in 2 Corinthians 2:1, "I have made up my mind not to make another painful visit to you."

According to that statement, Paul hurriedly may have made a visit to Corinth from Ephesus, because of turmoil in the Corinthian church, which did not fare well for Paul at all. Even though it is only conjecture that this quick and painful visit to Corinth actually did occur, many think that such a statement from Paul, in what is called his second letter to the Corinthians, seems strongly to imply that it did take place.

In any event, Timothy may have been caught in not the best of circumstances at Corinth, but by all reports he still remained the beloved, faithful follower of the Lord Jesus Christ.

Lydia appears in the Bible as most likely a wealthy business woman from the city of Thyatira in Asia Minor, because she was a dealer in purple cloth. Being most valuable and very expensive, purple cloth often was worn as a sign of nobility or royalty, but that is not what stands out about this person named Lydia, according to Acts 16:14-15. She just simply glows as a worshiper of the one, true, ever-living God.

While Lydia was at a place of prayer with other women by the river outside the gate of Philippi, which was the leading city in Macedonia and a Roman colony, Paul and the others with him sat down and talked to these women. They appeared to them as lovely, devotionally minded people. Lydia especially is said to have listened eagerly to what Paul had to say. Then, her heart opened beautifully to the Lord.

As a result, Lydia and her whole household were baptized. Afterward, she urged Paul and his companions that if she were judged faithful to the Lord, "come and stay at my home." When accordingly she prevailed upon them in this marvelous way, they did accept her special invitation.

After Paul and Silas were released from prison in Philippi, Lydia again hosted them in her home. They were seen and encouraged by the brothers and sisters there until they moved on to other places south and west from that point (Acts 16:40). Thus, Lydia not only found compelling truth in the words of Paul and his companions, but more importantly, she humbly and joyfully displayed genuine Christian hospitality, which is the basis of all human activity and the most everlasting quality among all people (Romans 12:13; 1 Corinthians 13:13).

Luke specifically is noted by name in several of Paul's letters. According to Colossians 4:14, Luke is reported as the "beloved physician." In Paul's second letter, which is addressed to Timothy 4:11, it is stated: "Only Luke is with me." In Paul's letter to Philemon in verse 24, Luke is referred to as one of Paul's "fellow workers." According to all of this Biblical evidence, Luke no doubt is a companion of Paul.

The question of when and where Luke traveled with Paul only can be surmised indirectly but that does seem highly likely to be true. Both the Gospel of Luke and the Acts of the Apostles from the onset of each script are addressed to the same person named Theophilus (Luke 1:3; Acts 1:1). For that reason, these two writings traditionally — not only have been joined together as Luke-Acts, but also it has been assumed for a long time that Luke is the author of both Biblical writings.

Furthermore, the change in nouns from "they" in Acts 16:6-8 to "we" and "us' in Acts 16:9 onward in the Book of Acts has been interpreted by many people as the point where Luke was the one saying: "Come over and help us" in Europe. The further use of the words "we" and "us" in the Book of Acts almost certainly means that Luke joined Paul, Silas and Timothy thereafter. Whatever decision may be reached about this person named Luke in the Bible, it is certain that the world would be much poorer without him and what he had to say.

Crispus and Sosthenes are listed in the same parts of the Bible — as officials in the synagogue at Corinth. Crispus reportedly became a believer in the Lord together with everyone of his household. All of them were baptized in addition to many others (Acts 18:17-18).

When Gallio was proconsul in the Roman province called Achaia, and therefore ruled over the city of Corinth, its capital, Jewish people in the vicinity made a united attack against Paul and brought him before the Roman tribunal in Corinth. They proclaimed concerning Paul, "This man is persuading people to worship God in ways that are contrary to the law."

Just as Paul was about to speak, Gallio said to the Jewish people gathered there: "If it were a matter of crime, or serious villainy, I would be justified in accepting your complaint, but since it is a matter of questions about words, names and your own law, see to it yourselves. I do not wish to be judge of these matters."

Afterward when Gallio had dismissed them from the tribunal, all of the accusers seized the official of the synagogue named Sosthenes and beat him in front of the tribunal, while Gallio is said to have paid no attention to any of these things (Acts 18:12-18). That, however, is not the end of any word about Sosthenes in the Bible.

In Paul's first letter to the Corinthians, it is proclaimed to the church of God in Corinth that not only Paul is an Apostle of Christ Jesus, but also Sosthenes is "our brother." This must mean that Sosthenes was one who became part of the church at Corinth also. So, people in the life of the church continued to multiply from everywhere at the initiative of the Apostle Paul and his companions.

Aquila and Priscilla, also named Prisca, probably shine as the most prominent and wondrous Christian couple in the early life of the church. They exemplify everything that is excellent in the lives of people committed to Lord Jesus and to the ongoing life of his people in every conceivable situation and circumstance. Moreover, they are one of the closest companions and allies of Paul along with those who traveled with him.

Paul met this husband and wife initially upon his arrival for the very first time in Corinth from Athens. Priscilla and Aquila evidently were Jewish people who recently had come to Corinth from Italy because the Emperor Claudius ordered all Jewish people to leave Rome.

When Paul arrived in Corinth, he went to see Priscilla and Aquila, because they were of the same tentmaker trade as he. This couple became Christians when they listened attentively to Paul's sermons and absorbed everything that they heard. As a result, they helpfully were able to minister and teach others about what they so succinctly had gained in the faith.

Most notably, this gift was evidenced with Apollos. After staying in Corinth for a considerable time, Paul accompanied by Aquila and Priscilla said farewell to the believers there and sailed for Syria. When they reached Ephesus, Paul left the two of them at that point, but when Priscilla and Aquila heard Apollos speaking with burning enthusiasm about the things concerning Jesus while knowing only the baptism of John the Baptist, they took him aside.

They explained the Way of God carefully and more accurately to Apollos. As a result, Apollos afterward through grace helped others greatly by showing them that the Messiah, the Christ truly is Jesus (Acts 18:18-26).

After Paul returned to Ephesus from Syria, he wrote to the believers in Corinth saying: "The churches of Asia send greetings. Aquila and Priscilla, together with the church in their house, greet you warmly in the Lord" (1 Corinthians 16:19).

When Paul later arrived at Corinth, he wrote his letter to the Romans proclaiming: "Greet Priscilla and Aquila. They have worked with me in Christ Jesus and have risked their necks for my very life. I give thanks not only to them, but also to all the churches of the Gentiles. Greet also the church in the house of Priscilla and Aquila" (Romans 16:3-5).

Those statements seem to sum up everything about this devoted couple named Aquila and Priscilla. They accurately taught what was learned about Jesus from Paul, traveled closely with him, defended him to the hilt, established churches in their own home at each place in which they lived and always encouraged others to join in faith with them at every point along the way. What more could be asked of anyone?

Titus is mentioned in the Bible solely with Paul's letters. What can be gleaned from these writings is very scant indeed. What can be found in evidence about this fellow, however, is that he was thoroughly Greek and yet a strong, young believer in the Lord Jesus, somewhat like Timothy. Taught and nurtured by Paul, Titus reportedly stood before leaders of the church in Jerusalem as a living example of what was being accomplished by the Lord Jesus among the Gentiles (Galatians 2:1-3).

Titus became one of Paul's trusted traveling companions and closest friends. Later, Titus became Paul's special ambassador (2 Corinthians 7:5-16) and eventually an overseer of the churches on Crete, according to the reported letter to Titus 1:5. Slowly and carefully, Titus developed into a mature Christian and a responsible leader. The letter that was addressed to Titus tells how to organize and lead churches. As a result, Titus became another very important link in the spread of the Christian faith throughout the Mediterranean region — especially among the Gentiles.

Very little, if any thoughts are conveyed about people from this point forward in the Bible, but each one who is listed becomes known as important to the Lord and to the community of the faithful people who are lovingly devoted to the Lord and his mission. One person who is mentioned twice in the Book of Acts close to the beginning and then near the end, definitely needs to be highlighted, because of what was accomplished during the latter days of Paul's ministry and is documented in the Bible.

Philip the Evangelist, according to Acts 6:5, was chosen as one of the seven honored people along with Stephen, who became set apart for serving Jesus' people. He really is noted in chapter 21 of Acts as the one in Caesarea, who housed Paul's entourage on the way to Jerusalem for the last time.

The four unmarried daughters of Philip the Evangelist possessed the gift of prophecy. When another prophet named

310

Agabus came and predicted that the Jewish people in Jerusalem would bind up Paul and hand him over to the Gentiles, everyone wept. They urged Paul not to go there.

Paul proclaimed: "What are you doing weeping and breaking my heart? I am ready not only to be bound, but even to die in Jerusalem for the name of the Lord Jesus." Since Paul could not be persuaded otherwise, all of them including Philip the Evangelist remained silent excepting to say, "The Lord's will be done."

Biography in the Bible ends with the same words that excruciatingly, prayerfully and powerfully were expressed by Jesus in the Garden of Gethsemane as he faced his last hours. Although many of his people in the early Christian community came to the same gruesome end as Jesus did, they accomplished it gloriously for Jesus' sake and never looked back.

It may have taken 300 years of being constantly belittled and tortured, but Christians continued being faithful to their Lord Jesus day after day, year in and year out. Ultimately, they peacefully took over the known Mediterranean world at that time by the decree of Emperor Constantine. He declared the whole Roman Empire in the fourth century onward to be Christian.

As a result, Jesus of Nazareth, who became known among his followers as Messiah, Lord, Christ and Son of the ever-living God, ultimately in fact conquered the whole Roman Empire that previously had put him to death upon a cross.

CHAPTER 12

EPILOGUE

Where do we go from here with the Bible and all that is espoused therein? Is biography as shared in those pages valid anymore, and does any of it make any difference for us today? That is the crucial issue before us now. Furthermore, who even cares?

It is true that much has changed since those times when people in the Biblical era lived and penned what is enclosed within those pages, which at this point is called Holy Writ. For example, more names for deity, even for the one, true God of the Bible, have been added to the nomenclature among human beings.

Instead of Yahweh, Adonai, Elohim, Father, Son and Holy Spirit, Allah and a host of other expressions from such people known as Buddhists, Shintoists, Taoists, Hindus, Confusionists, Native Americans and the like also have entered human vocabulary and activity.

Who is to be believed? Who holds the truth? Who is to be followed? Perhaps Vachel Lindsay sums it up best for us:

> "What is the final ending?
> The issue, who can know?
> Will Christ outlive Mohammed?
> Will Kali's altars go?
>
> This is our faith tremendous —
> Our wild hope, who can scorn —
> That in the name of Jesus
> The world shall be reborn!"[1]

How? By the love of Christ! Why? Because as expressed in song, people need the Lord![2] At the end of broken dreams, he is the open door (John 10:9 NKJV)!

1. Gerald Kennedy, editor, *A Second Reader's Notebook* (New York: Harper & Brothers, 1959), p. 456.

2. Greg Nelson and Phill McHugh, *Steve Green Songbook* (Chatsworth, California: Sparrow. Birdwing Music/Cherry Lane Music Publishing Company, Inc., 1984), p. 51.

CPSIA information can be obtained at www.ICGtesting.com
Printed in the USA
LVOW131136200412

278360LV00003B/2/P

9 781449 746179